conservation and development
in historic towns and cities

conservation and development

in historic towns and cities

Edited by
PAMELA WARD

Oriel Press Limited

© Oriel Press Limited 1968
First published 1968

SBN (68UK)85362 046 6
L.C. 68–55979

Published by
ORIEL PRESS LIMITED
at 27 Ridley Place, Newcastle upon Tyne, NEI 8LH, England.
Printed by
The University Printing Service, Newcastle upon Tyne.

There are a number of people here whose minds must be going back eighteen months when, as in my case, I found myself in my office facing three diffidently determined undergraduates — Michael Burbidge, Michael Harris and Pamela Ward. They proposed to stage a conference on historic towns, they wanted help, and they were not prepared to take 'No' for an answer. It was impossible not to admire their enthusiasm, nor could I fail to note the extraordinary phenomenon of three young people developing a passionate interest in historic towns, with so deep an understanding of the meaning and importance of conservation. It boded well for the future. Out of the efforts of these undergraduates has sprung this whole conference. I would like to take this opportunity to pay my tribute to them.

Colin Buchanan
at the Historic Towns and Cities Conference, York
April, 1968

ACKNOWLEDGEMENT

This book is a symposium of some of the many stimulating contributions to the Historic Towns and Cities Conference held in association with the Institute of Advanced Architectural Studies at the University of York in April, 1968. We should like to thank the very many people who contributed to the Conference, either individually, or on behalf of official bodies, throughout the two years of research and organization; during the period of the Conference and subsequently.

CONTENTS

INTRODUCTION

"Good planning is only good management" - Donald Insall
"A city without old buildings is like a man without a memory" - Konrad Smigielski

In Spring 1965 Donald Insall and Konrad Smigielski were among a group of speakers at public meetings in York organized by a group of the city's students. The others were Arthur Ling and Patrick Nuttgens. The feasibility of a national conference on conservation in historic towns and cities was suggested by the success of these lectures, measured in good attendances, and in enthusiastic support for a subsequent Brains Trust to discuss the planning problems in a historic city such as York.

The impression grew that Britain was behind other countries in the preservation of historic areas, and in safeguarding environment of particular architectural, archaeological or historic interest, but also that successful work in this field in different parts of Great Britain was not necessarily known by other local authorities with similar problems, nor to all the various organizations concerned.

The Historic Towns and Cities Project began early in 1966 and aimed to study, define and analyze the problems of reconciling present and future development, and traffic requirements, with the long-term conservation and improvement of the character and environment of British historic towns and cities. The problem is present in all towns, whether historic or not, but it was felt that the particular problem in towns and cities where an important part of the fabric is of historic value or significance should be dealt with urgently and possibly separately. The Civic Amenities Act shows that the problem is now recognized as ubiquitous.

Information was collected on the policies, views, functions and methods of organizations and individuals concerned with the field of conservation in Britain and overseas, together with details of relevant legislation and administrative procedure. In the long term it was hoped to use the results of this study to draw up a detailed structure for a national conference to be held in York in association with the Institute of Advanced Architectural Studies. The conference was to consist chiefly of the men who ultimately guide the future of Britain's historic towns and cities, the members of planning committees and other councillors. Other members of the planning and architectural professions were to be included.

The Historic Towns and Cities Conference took place in York, under the active presidency of Lord Harewood, in April 1968, with Patrick Nuttgens of the Institute taking the chair in turn with him. Its purpose was to clarify the concept of conservation as the reconciliation of change and preservation in a historic area, within a planning context, and on an economically viable basis, and to demonstrate the possibilities of environmental improvement, preferably instigated by local authorities in these areas, which takes account of economic, cultural and aesthetic factors.

It was the first opportunity for an exchange of information and ideas concerning this question between all those involved - whether in local or central government, the professions, specialist groups, amenity societies, etc. - on equal terms, to feature their combined efforts and to compare the British situation with that of selected countries overseas.

This book is the result of the conference. During the editing of the vast quantity of material which supplemented the main reports and papers it has become clear that it would be impossible to include everything which was contributed. Inevitably many speakers covered similar ground from different points of view and our aim has been concision, and a practical presentation, rather than the repetition and recognition of every contribution made.

The need to produce a volume of lasting value has made it seem appropriate to exclude many matters of technical detail which are subject to constant change, and likewise to relegate the changing state of British legislation to a separate publication which will give the opportunity to include, at the same time, other technical aspects in some detail, particularly procedural check-lists and current costings. The bibliography of the whole subject is so extensive that we have reluctantly concluded that it could not be included in a single volume publication.

economics

A. J. Youngson

BRITAIN'S HISTORIC TOWNS

I have to begin with a confession. I am neither an architect nor a town-planner, but merely an economist with an amateur interest in cities old and new. I can therefore offer no expert appraisal of the problems involved in conservation, far less suggest solutions. I can only raise some of the general issues; try to delineate the wood without having very much knowledge of the trees - never an entirely satisfactory proceeding. I can only offer a long-range view, a report on the general situation by a non-architect and non-town-planner, primarily addressed to any similarly handicapped persons.

There are three big questions - one of them a purely preliminary question - which I should like to discuss in turn. First, why should we conserve? Second, what are the forces against conservation? Third, what is the price of conservation?   * * * * * * *

Why should we conserve? The answer, I believe, is two-fold. First, many historic buildings, streets, skylines, even whole areas of a town, are beautiful. One might describe the city as a machine for living in, but even if we accept that, it remains true that the city is a machine which we find very difficult to make beautiful. Motor cars, aircraft, bridges - these we seem to know how to design. They are not only made to be very useful, there is a certain fitness, an elegance even, in their shape and construction which gives them a kind of beauty. Some civilizations make wonderful glass and wonderful ceramics; we make wonderful cars and wonderful bridges; but we have not yet built a wonderful town - unless you think New York is wonderful, as in some ways it undoubtedly is. To me, it is the modern town *par excellence.* It is wonderfully grand, wonderfully exciting, wonderfully intimidating. But no-one would suggest that it is charming, relaxing, inviting to live in. In some ways, it is really a wonder that anyone lives in it at all. It is impressive - one is astonished that it is there. It is, I think, the most extraordinary human construction that I have ever seen. But it is certainly not a *beautiful* town - wonderful in that sense - like Bath or Paris or Isfahan. And in a world in which there are so few beautiful town-areas left (perhaps not a single town which is not now to some extent in ruins aesthetically) it is increasingly important to preserve the beautiful places which we have.

Secondly, and closely connected with that, the streets or buildings which we should conserve are significant also as a part of history, a reminder of the style and ideals of another age. We are not the fifth act of the human drama; we are only one of the scenes. Earlier generations have sometimes brought to a higher degree of perfection than we can some attitude to life, and have expressed it in their buildings: the neighbourliness, the sense of an intense community life which you get in the closes of Edinburgh or the medieval streets in York; the feeling of energy and self-confidence and yet repose which you find in, say, St. James's

Square or Bath; the gaiety of Regency Brighton. Our ability to criticize our aims and achievements depends a good deal on our capacity to escape from the assumptions of our own civilization and to understand the aims and achievements of other ages. Keeping in touch with the past, which is so powerful a means of renewing the present, becomes more and more difficult as the material evidence of the past disappears. And no material evidence is more persuasive, more convincing of the possibility of a different way of life, than the living-places of people. No-one knows this better than the Americans, who, albeit intermittently, are keen preservers of their past. I was surprised in New England a couple of years ago to find how many very attractive eighteenth century wooden buildings remain, how well they are looked after, and how much the Americans know about them. Of course the classic case of restoration - not merely conservation - is Williamsburg, the capital of Virginia in colonial days, and there you have not only the buildings restored but the inhabitants restored as well, down to the shoemaker and the candlemaker and the wig-maker, in appropriate eighteenth century costume making eighteenth century wigs in his little eighteenth century shop. You may think that this is going a little far, but it is very effective. And it fills a real need. Preservation (or restoration) is not a whim, a luxury we cannot really afford. People *need* to feel some anchors in the past. The American tourists who pour across to Europe every summer do not come just for the novelty. They come for the history. They come because they feel - correctly - that they cannot properly understand themselves until they know something about places which in a sense made them what they are - Athens and Rome, Paris and London. We take it for granted. But it would be a tragedy if through negligence we come to the state the Americans and Australians are in now, of looking for scraps of the past to hang on to, when we have still a rich heritage of buildings and small towns and parts of larger towns.

* * * * * * * *

Secondly, what are the forces against conservation? If there are beautiful buildings to be saved, if we can only lose by losing touch with the past, why - apart from simple philistinism, simple ignorance of values - is there any difficulty?

There are three forces opposed to conservation, very fundamental forces: growth of population and rising standards of living; technological change; and changing social aims. As society grows richer - and let us not forget that our standard of living, as the economist measures it, is getting on for a level twice as high as it was in 1938 - as society grows richer, its views of what constitutes tolerable housing change almost as radically as anything else. In poor societies, people live where they can: a hundred years ago one-third of the entire population of the state of Victoria "lived under canvas, rag, bark, or the open sky", while those who lived in houses lived, on the average, two to each room. The situation in some of our own cities was not much better in the 1860s. Now we insist on sanitation, light, air. Old houses become what we call sub-standard, and we compel people to move into hygienic living conditions, although their new environment may be ugly, lonely, or even downright inconvenient. It is your lungs and stomach that are looked after in the modern world, along with your teeth: your soul can look after itself. Other kinds of housing become hard to use for other reasons. How much architecture, for example, was founded on the domestic servant, that indispensable adjunct of both the classical and the gothic revivals? William Morris could try to recreate the middle ages because he was living in a society which was, contrary to his belief, still somewhat medieval; that is to say, it was full of domestic servants. In his time, domestic service was, after agriculture, the commonest of all occupations; there was something like one domestic servant for every twenty-five of the population. Today, almost no domestic servants remain: a few thousand, working in boarding houses and Oxford and Cambridge colleges and lunatic asylums and similar institutions. But without servants, many houses - fine, even splendid houses from the strictly architectural point of view - become unworkable. They are relics of another age, and we don't want to recreate the social conditions that once made them desirable homes.

Linked with this, modern technology makes different demands on space. Office space is needed, shopping space, and, above all, traffic and parking space. As we all know, towns have grown enormously in area and population even in the past forty years. Forty years ago there were fifty-four towns in Britain with more than 100,000 inhabitants each; now there are seventy. And it is not only the big towns that are growing; interestingly enough, the fastest-growing towns in Britain in the 1950s were those with a population between 10,000 and 15,000, and between 30,000 and 75,000: and that group of towns includes one quarter of those listed by the report on economic and social aspects of conservation as being of historic quality.

This urban expansion is a product of technological and economic change. There is the increasing complexity and inter-relatedness of the processes of production and consumption; and there are apparently still unexhausted economies of scale; that is to say, economies which can be realised only by having more and more people working in or in connection with fewer and fewer centres of work. Thus pressure on urban space increases, urban land becomes more valuable, and the motive to destroy old buildings is strenthened.

The development of transport works in the same direction. Transport and communications are in many ways the foundation of the social and spatial changes in modern life. A great economist wrote, some seventy or eighty years ago, "Improvements in transport make it worthwhile to do a great many things which it was not worthwhile to do before." That has always struck me as a profound observation. Transport, carrying the business which raises our standard of living, helps to produce the great conurbations and then helps to make them so unlovely and so difficult to enjoy. Our age is distinguished from all preceding ages by the extreme mobility of people and of goods. Old buildings and old streets often stand in the way of using new transport or new technology generally, or the pursuit of new social aims.

And so the question arises: can we adapt these buildings, preserve something of our old environment, at a reasonable cost? - not allow the past to obstruct the raising of business efficiency; and hence the standard of living, and yet not find that a higher standard of living means a steady deterioration in the appearance of the built environment? In short, what is preservation worth? How big a bill should we pay, and where are we to find the money?

* * * * * * * *

5

Williamsburg, meticulously preserved.

Greenfield Place, Newcastle upon Tyne, threatened with demolition.

In some circumstances it is possible that conservation will directly pay for itself. As people grow richer and old buildings grow scarcer, the desire to visit historic buildings or towns spreads. People increasingly have the money and the inclination to interest themselves in the past, and they show a strong tendency to interest themselves in architectural history. It is not for nothing that Professor Pevsner has published thirty-three volumes of his splendid *The Buildings of England*. That has been an outstanding cultural but also a notable commercial success - I have the publisher's word for it. Correspondingly, towns with a visibly distinguished history, like Lavenham or Winchester or Richmond, have the means to attract trade and perhaps new residents as well as just attention. It is a big selling point for a town in the modern world that it has interest, character. If it exploits its historical advantages properly, it may be able to build up a profitable tourist trade. This may create as many problems as it solves. Tourism provides income, but it tends to be low-wage income, and may merely divert resources from other uses. Tourism also generates traffic, and this may threaten the character of the town, or prove expensive to deal with.

But it is probably worth looking into all this, because there is the further argument that the advantages which bring people into a town also help its general economic development. And this rather vague argument, that amenity attracts population and in the long run helps along general economic development is, I think, very important *in the long run*. This is especially true of historical amenity; we seem to find it as hard to build good modern amenities as to build attractive modern buildings. It is also by no means a new argument. It was used in 1752 by those who proposed to build the New Town of Edinburgh. They extolled "situation, conveniency and beauty", declaring that a city where these concur "should naturally become the centre of trade and commerce, of learning and the arts, of politeness, and of refinement of every kind". Business follows beauty. Does it sound a little far-fetched? I am not at all sure. I am not at all convinced that trade and commerce are one thing and learning and the arts are another and that the two shall never meet. It is fundamentally a question of economic location, of the location of industries and of businesses in general, and that is something of a puzzle to the modern economist. We used to say that businesses should be located near their raw materials, or near their markets, or in some inter-mediate situation depending on transport costs. That does not seem to be generally true any more, partly because transport costs have become a less important element in total costs. Nowadays we sometimes argue that business location is chiefly determined by the availability of suitable labour, and that has force. But it is becoming rather clear that employees, especially better-paid employees, are much more easily attracted to or kept in areas which have what might be called incidental amenities - nearness to clean countryside, good schools, good shops, places of interest, a sense of character. We find this in the University of Edinburgh. Over the past few years it has been very difficult to recruit well-qualified young men to university departments. Demand has exceeded supply. But our difficult-ies in Edinburgh have certainly been less than in most places, and this has certainly been due in part to the fact that people feel that Edinburgh has the important advantage of offering an interesting and attractive environment. Of course wages are still tremendously important, as is housing; but in the long run, especially as the standard of living continues to rise, the town with something distinctive, something cultural to offer, is going to be at a progressive advantage. And you may well get a bigger return on your money, a more satisfactory response to your not quite disinterested efforts to promote the higher values, by preserving that old guildhall, or that old row of almshouses, than by trying to build a new palace of culture on the site of the disused canal.

So in the long run and to some extent - a not inconsiderable extent, I think - amenity, not least historical amenity, will pay. But it will not pay directly and completely. So we still have to face the questions: (i) what is the true cost? (ii) who is to bear this cost?

At this point economics can be of some help. Take a very simple case. Suppose that we would like to preserve a historic building which stands on a site wanted for commercial development. What is the social cost of preventing that development? The answer, in principle, is perfectly clear. We must calculate the financial return on the proposed development on that site - say, 10,000 square feet of office space - and compare it with the return which would be secured by building comparable accommodation on the next best site. The difference in return, suitably capitalized, is the cost of retaining the historic building in question. The cost of conservation is not simply the loss of development on site A, because if development does not take place on that site it will, in all normal cases, take place somewhere else. The true cost of doing anything is measured by the return which would be got through the best alternative use of the resources in question. This is an extremely important economic principle.

Take a more complicated case. Suppose that there is a choice between widening an existing road through a town, knocking down some historic buildings in the process, and building a by-pass. What has to be done, once again, is to try to identify and measure the benefits and costs of development with the original buildings retained (i.e. with the by-pass) as against the benefits and costs with the original buildings demolished. This is certainly very difficult, because the development proposed is a major one, and I am not going to argue that economics can produce "the answer", that there is some technical means of economic analysis whereby you can determine the optimal expenditure on conservation. Economics is not so much a science for solving problems of choice as for clarifying problems of choice. "Mr. Pitt," George III is reported to have said to his great Minister, "you must take a wife." "Yes sire," Pitt replied; "whose wife shall I take?" Economics is a little like that: it does not absolve you from the responsibility of choosing what situations you want to achieve. But it can make possible better informed choices.

Cost-benefit analysis is a modern technique which was originally devised in the U.S. to deal with the problem of water-resource development. In that problem the costs of building dams, channel-works, associated roads, generating stations, distribution systems, etc., can be extremely high, easily exceeding £30 million or £40 million. The consequences for farming, flood control, the availability of power (perhaps throughout the country) for many years ahead, are very great; these beneficial consequences affect thousands, possibly tens of thousands, of people; are difficult to identify and difficult to measure.

Nevertheless, cost-benefit analysis is a great deal better than guessing. And I would plead that this kind of analysis should be more widely used, not least where the re-planning of cities is complicated by the presence of buildings of aesthetic and cultural value. Thus in the case of the road through the town *versus* the by-pass the construction costs are known in each case, and these have to be discounted at a suitable rate in order to obtain an annual cost; the maintenance costs have to be determined; and this gives the capital cost plus the public operating costs. The next step is to estimate the volume and nature of traffic likely to flow along each route, remembering that road improvements will (a) attract traffic from other alternative routes, and will (b) generate additional traffic which did not find it economical to use the previous facilities. These traffic volumes are the benefits of the investment. But they have to be weighted by

  (i) the time taken for the journey multiplied by the cost of man-hours involved in driving that distance;

 (ii) the saving in vehicle-hours resulting from more rapid movement;

(iii) the saving in goods in transit resulting from more rapid movement;

(iv) the reduction in private operating costs in the way of fuel, wear and tear of vehicles, and so on.

Only when all this has been taken into account can one arrive at an annual cost and benefit for each route. And the difference between the net benefits of the two is the cost of preserving the buildings which would have to be demolished if the road were built through the town.

This is a very summary statement which ignores many of the difficulties. But cost-benefit analysis is a technique which has been used in connection with a great many large investment projects, especially in the U.S. - indeed, they would quite often hesitate to start on large capital works without an investigation of the kind I have outlined. So it is eminently practical. It does not yield a unique solution for various reasons and of course it does not tell you, in the case I have outlined, whether you should do project A or project B. But it does tell you, approximately, what conservation is going to cost - not, please notice, what conservation is worth.

Given this figure - let us suppose it is going to cost £1 million more to build the by-pass and preserve the buildings than to build through the town - the question is, who should bear this burden? It seems to me that this ought to be divided between local (or regional) and central government. I should have thought that the local authority should pay a share on the ground that it is the local people who have the benefit of living in a town thus kept interesting and beautiful, and it is they who will gain from trade arising from the character of the town. But I emphasize that one has to say local *or regional* authority because the benefits of conservation may accrue not to the town itself but to near-by towns in the same region; that is to say, businesses may locate in Middlesbrough because of the attractions of smaller towns all the way south to Scarborough; and it would not be fair that smaller towns should pay to maintain amenities which benefit nearby larger ones. But in addition to that, a historic town is part of the national heritage. People who do not live in it value it. It is a national possession, in a sense; and for that reason central government ought to pay its share, just as it does in buying pictures for the National Gallery in Trafalgar Square or maintaining the Royal Opera for the benefit of the nation. The Royal Opera is heavily subsidized, and no-one supposes that the subsidies are paid by those who live in the immediate vicinity of Covent Garden.

Similar considerations apply to other aspects of the economics of conservation. If a local authority prevents development for conservation reasons, it foregoes an increase in rateable value; that is to say, an increase in its income; and I am told that it may even lay itself open to claims for compensation. Thus the cost of conservation falls almost entirely on local authorities, whose income, as is well known, is obtained almost wholly from a tax on property values, the yield of which is inflexible without making obvious and unpopular changes in the rate poundage. Alternatively, the cost falls on private owners. In either case, there is a strong argument for subsidy from national funds.

* * * * * * *

Finally, I have been speaking about conservation. That is a reasonable word to use, and yet not a word of which I am particularly fond. It suggests to some the mere prevention of change, the careful husbanding of limited resources. We do mean that, but I hope we mean more than that. Successful conservation regards preservation as an essential element - but only an element - in the building or re-building of more beautiful cities. The way to preserve old customs, said Walter Bagehot, is to enjoy old customs. And the way to preserve old buildings is to make them a living, useful, enjoyable part of the cities in which we live. I am impressed, looking back on the history of cities, with the scale of the efforts which were sometimes made to build a fine and handsome setting for urban life. Today, when we are so much richer than our ancestors, we are certainly capable, in terms of command over resources, of far greater efforts, and yet our building is often so much poorer than theirs. To some extent this may be the fault of our architects, but I doubt if much blame attaches to them. I think it is true that we do not put enough money into building, especially we do not put enough money into public amenities of all kinds; and there is, I think, a persuasive historical reason for that which, however, I do not wish to go into just now. But even if we gave our architects a great deal more money and told them to go ahead and build us some fine new cities, I am not sure that the result might not be rather disappointing - if they will excuse my saying so. And the reason is that I have a depressing vision of a rich Britain with many new or extensively renewed cities - not just small satellite towns, but major cities - and I have a fear that the new order thus produced would be one of what I would call undifferentiated cities. They would be all in one style, all in one material, all to one scale, monotonous, one looking just like another. Our universities are approaching this sort of condition, I think. It is becoming true that you are not very sure now whether you are in the University of York, or the University of East Anglia, or the University of Edinburgh, or the University of Exeter. All are built to the U.G.C. standard specification and built in much the same style, and you really do not know which is which. I have a fear that we might make our towns like that too and you would not know whether you were in Aberdeen or Plymouth. The real safeguard against this is preserving, conserving the best of the old, keeping the character, keeping the history, keeping the individuality. And we have to do it boldly. Preserving a stray building here and there is merely going to look odd. We must not lose sight of the desirability of conserving wide areas, at least in a few instances. These must not be museum areas; in our concept of conservation, what is preserved must fit in to the active life of the ever-evolving city. Moreover, conservation of old areas entails, in an expanding economy, the building of new areas. I shall be told that would cost a great deal of money. So it would. But look at it quantitatively. Total capital expenditure by public authorities today is in the neighbourhood of £2,500 million per annum. Even if expenditure arising through conservation policies were to be increased by only one half of one per cent of public authority capital expenditure, that would be about £12·5 million. Total expenditure on libraries, museums and the arts is about £50 million, so £12·5 million would be one quarter of what is spent on libraries, museums and the arts. I imagine that such an expenditure would make a very considerable difference in the next ten years. So let us not give up too easily. Successful conservation must be part of the enormous operation, which must occupy us increasingly to the end of the century, of fashioning finer and more beautiful settings for our intensely urban life. Do not let us be persuaded that we cannot afford something without which we and our children and our children's children will be seriously and irretrievably poorer.

Venice, formerly the capital of a commercial empire. The environment has remained; the function of the city has changed.

1. THE CHANGING FUNCTION OF TOWNS

1.1

The very fact that a town is of historic interest suggests that its economic raison d'etre may no longer be valid because of the dynamic nature of the economic system. If economic forces were given unrestricted play a great many historic towns would either be submerged by new pressures or be left to decline into backwaters; in the same way many individual buildings would be pulled down for profitable redevelopment or left to decay through neglect or lack of use. Clearly this cannot be allowed to happen, but if the best use of scarce national resources is to be made in maintaining and enhancing the quality of our historic buildings, an understanding of the way in which economic forces can be harnessed as an ally instead of being treated as an enemy is essential.

The aim of this report is to provide a general approach to this problem. It can be no more than general because historic towns are not an homogeneous group. Each has its own individual problems and solutions. Nor does this report attempt to be comprehensive; instead it concentrates on a few of the vital problems such as the changing functions of historic towns, the question of industrial and commercial investment and the respective roles of public and private enterprise in redevelopment and conservation.

1.2

The Questions to be asked

To consider the position of those towns for which conservation policies may be appropriate from the point of view of their changing functions we need to know and understand :-

(a) the different functions of each town and how they are changing;
(b) the position of each town in its region setting;
(c) the effect of unrestricted economic forces both within the town and within the area of which it forms a part;
(d) the effect of statutory and administrative controls upon free market forces; and,
(e) the results of the implementation of existing planning policies.

The question can then be asked "To what extent can these economic and social forces best be guided and controlled to encourage realization of the historic conservation considered necessary?"

1.3

The Size of the Problem

This question can be considered first by looking at the total problem of which there exists two measures. The first is the work of the Council for British Archaeology. They list 264 towns of historic quality, of which 51 are "so splendid and so precious that the ultimate responsibility should be a national responsibility". The second is the result of an enquiry of planning authorities initiated by the Historic Towns and Cities Conference Secretariat to which most but not all authorities have replied. A comparison of the two lists (excluding Scotland) shows a total of 365 towns, of which 154 are common to both lists.

A total of 365 towns is not in itself a problem. If looked at on a population size scale it is even less so.

Town size population	No. of historic towns
Villages - population not known	74
0 - 2,500	36
2,501 - 5,000	48
5,001 - 7,500	41
7,501 - 10,000	23
10,001 - 15,000	41
15,001 - 20,000	25
20,001 - 25,000	11
25,001 - 50,000	31
50,001 - 75,000	19
75,001 - 100,000	7
Over 100,000	9
	365

These figures show that 61% of all the towns listed have a population of less than 10,000 and 82% less than 25,000 persons.

In terms of the functional position of each town, and taking the Council for British Archaeology's list as being based perhaps on a more uniform standard for the country, the towns may be roughly classified as follows:

	No.	%
Static or with little or no external functions	125	47
County Market Towns	88	33
Sub-Regional Centres	27	11
Regional Centres	24	9
	264	100

It does not necessarily follow that the special quality which led to the inclusion of a town on the list is one that is likely to be affected seriously by a change in size or functions. Accepting as a minimum the 51 most important towns suggested by the Council for British Archaeology, a general examination of all the other towns listed suggests that another 100, making 150 in all, need considering from the point of view of "functional control". The identification of these towns would follow from the more detailed measurements referred to earlier, but a group of about this size requiring special economic and planning controls should be acceptable within the national context.

1.4

Assessing Function and Change

The measurement of the functional position of each listed town and of the likelihood of a threat to its historical heritage should not be either a long or difficult process. For over half the towns, because of their size or the clarity of their historic interest there should be no problems. Most of the others will already have been the subject of detailed study for normal planning purposes. What is required is a generally accepted basis so that comparability between towns may be secured.

Although the measurement of likely change may not be difficult, the point at which the changes become dangerous is incapable of precise definition. Here the relationship between the physical heritage and the level of functional activity which forms its present setting will call for a high degree of interpretation. For example, if a building, or group of buildings, of historic interest stands well apart from areas within which economic growth is likely to be concentrated, then this growth may be allowed to continue. If, however, the area of growth coincides with or is very near to that of historic interest, then it will be necessary to determine the 'ceiling' level, above which that activity will begin to impinge on the proper enjoyment of the historic interests. The skill will lie in determining the level and reducing the rate of growth before that level is reached.

1.5   *Control of Change*

It has been said that "the built environment is a living record of a country's social development. It makes sense only as a part of a continuous process. Within that process conservation is the control of the rate of change". If this definition is accepted, then we must accept not only that the measurement is a continuing process, but also that the basis of control may have to be varied. This is not to beg the question which requires that a decision must be taken, even though it may later be modified.

Returning to the original question, it becomes clear that economic viability in addition to good intentions is essential to conservation. The problem is therefore to be able to generate activity as well as to control it. The appropriate level of that activity is as mentioned above, a matter of decision, and as such, it will be the key decision in a policy of conservation.

That it is possible to harness both economic and social forces to such a policy has been and is continuing to be demonstrated. It is shown most strongly in the Government's efforts to secure a wider distribution of industry and population. The basic requirement is a decision of Government, expressed through all the departments concerned, confirming the purpose of the necessary controls and making them binding on all, whether normally subject to planning control or not.

1.6   *Old Towns and New Development*

The Expanded Towns programme and even some of the New Towns themselves have made possible conservation of a high order. In the former case this has been achieved by restoring active life to historic towns which were once centres of greater social and economic activity. In the latter case it has been achieved by separating the 'historic' and new development so that they can live happily together. Hemel Hempstead and Stevenage are good examples. Some of the listed towns are now the subject of overspill arrangements; many others would appear to be good subjects for consideration.

The Expanded and New Town policies are supported by special powers, but it is practicable to apply similar principles to other towns. Cambridge is an example. After the last war there was a growing realisation that the historic University City was in danger of being overcome by industrial expansion. That danger was met by a clear policy decision, supported by successive governments, that the primary function of the City should remain that of a University town. The implementation of that policy saw

Above: Cambridge — the calm of Peterhouse Quad and the busy street beyond the arcade.

Below: Wisbech (see 1.6)

the dispersal of population and industry over a wider area with the City, of about 100,000, its growth rate slowed down by these policies, lying at the centre of a closely integrated region. Whether the right economic balance between the different parts has yet been struck remains to be seen.

The policy has already restored with new employment and population the fortunes of one other "listed" town, namely Linton, and it is hoped that Wisbech - also listed - will soon begin to benefit.

1.7 *Summary*

Put shortly, our growing knowledge of the forces causing change and of the degree to which they can be guided, makes possible the implementation of a policy of conservation, whether such a policy requires restriction or an expansion of growth.

2. *PRESERVATION THROUGH ECONOMIC VIABILITY - INDUSTRIAL AND COMMERCIAL INVESTMENT*

2.1 *Conversions and New Uses*

Whatever the overall policy for the town the aim with individual historic buildings, especially in central areas, must be to make them economically viable. With some old buildings, such as churches and some private houses, this is virtually impossible; though there are rare exceptions, such as at Oxford where a church was converted to a college library and at Cambridge where one was converted to public meeting rooms.

A great many old buildings do, however, lend themselves to commercial conversion because of their location. The historic building in a commercial centre, if it can be made a commercial proposition, will fit more easily into its environment than if left to stand alone. Unfortunately, building, planning and other regulations have often thwarted conversions of this sort. Where a building or group of buildings is worthy of preservation, there is a strong case for relaxing or not enforcing these regulations.

It is not always necessary for the whole of a building to be preserved. For example, the rear and interior parts of the Nash Terrace in Regents Park are being rebuilt to suit modern requirements, with only the front elevation being preserved. While this expedient is, as a general rule, more expensive than a completely new building of similar accommodation it often represents a reasonable compromise which is economically viable and an attraction to prospective owners and tenants.

2.2 *The Case for Redevelopment*

One limitation on the conversion of old buildings which must be faced is that it may be impossible to adapt them, usually because they are too small to meet the requirements of certain large retail space users. Such users often find it difficult to persuade the local planning authority to let them redevelop because it is felt that any new building will not fit in with the historic character of a street. In such circumstances it may be better to admit that redevelopment is preferable. It is possible to design new buildings which harmonise with the historic buildings around them; and it is sometimes possible to save the historic building, the site of which is being redeveloped, by moving it to another site, as was recently done with a medieval timber framed house in Hereford.

2.3   *Change of Use?*

Another limitation on conversion to commercial use is that industry and commerce should, generally speaking, be kept out of residential areas. There are, however, cases where the introduction of commerce in particular, can help to preserve areas and buildings which would otherwise decay. These areas are usually ones with houses which are too large and expensive to run as private houses. They can be converted to useful office accommodation for the professional and smaller commercial firms. Such use is greatly to be preferred to the alternative of decaying empty buildings or multiple occupancy slums. It also has the advantage of tapping private sources of finance, though it must be coupled with intelligent restriction of development foreign to the new character.

A practical example of this is the Park Circus area of Glasgow. Although the original attractions of lower property values and easier car parking have disappeared, the demand for accommodation in this area is still great and the intrinsic merits of the buildings and layout of the area are still attractive. The local authority had to play a part in stimulating and co-ordinating the conservation and improvement, although much use was made of private architects who produced plans for small parts of the area which were subsequently co-ordinated. The Scottish Civic Trust also took an active part. Where the economic pressures are in the right direction, action such as this is likely to produce a far more practical result than any amount of assistance from public funds.

Conversely to the introduction of commercial development into residential areas, it may be possible to develop residential accommodation in predominantly commercial central areas. There is undoubtedly a great deal of upper floor accommodation in central areas which would lend itself to residential use. It should be borne in mind that upper floor conversions from commercial to residential use can seldom be justified on economic grounds alone. With the increase of smokeless zones such accommodation will become more attractive and its introduction would certainly enhance the environment to be preserved. The price of central accommodation either new or converted, is, however, high because of the acquisition costs of land usually devoted to non-conforming industrial or commercial uses. One solution would be a revision of the present housing subsidy arrangements to make possible more intensive uses of central area properties.

3.   THE ROLE OF PRIVATE ENTERPRISE

3.1   *The Law*

By and large, the record of private ownership in the conservation of individual buildings and areas that have historic or architectural value has been mixed. From the Ancient Monuments Act, 1913, to the Civic Amenities Act, 1967, statutory controls have sought to oblige owners to undertake their responsibilities more seriously.

The most common failing has been sheer neglect, where economic or functional obsolescence has made it financially unattractive to keep buildings in a reasonable state of repair. Often the stage is reached where demolition is the only course of action open. More rarely the neglect is wanton, when the forces of decay are encouraged to do their worst.

Until the passing of the Civic Amenities Act, 1967, the penalties for altering or demolishing a listed building without consent were restricted. It often paid an owner, therefore, to break the law and take the consequences. A blatant example was the demolition of the Malt House at Kingston-upon-Thames where the clearance of this building added many thousand pounds to the value of an adjoining development site and where the fine on conviction was limited to £100.

The Civic Amenities Act itself has caused casualties. In August, 1967, Nelmes Manor, a seventeenth century house at Hornchurch, Essex, was demolished by its owner because he feared that its status as a building of historic interest would bring heavy responsibilities once the new Act came into force.

3.2   *The Private Owner's Problem*

The problem for private owners is economic. Although many take pride in the status of their buildings, there is a limit to how far they can go in accepting heavy outgoings or losing the chance of profitable redevelopment. Many individual owners have shown great ingenuity in preserving the economic life of their buildings. Where a number of owners are involved in a conservation area, however, the problem is complicated. The pattern tends to be set by the least responsible and, once decay has begun, Gresham's Law applies with the bad driving out the good.

Perhaps the greatest skill has been shown in adaptations and conversions. Windmills, lighthouses, oasthouses and the like have been converted into houses; large mansions have been broken down into flats or converted to institutional use; groups of Georgian terraced houses in central areas have been transformed into hotels or offices. Less happily, corn exchanges have become cinemas, although there is a remarkable example in Salisbury of a medieval Staple Hall serving admirably as a cinema foyer. In Godalming an interesting old dissenter's chapel has made the conversion to a cinema and now back to a church for another sect. Not all adaptions are happy, but, where the choice is between conversion or demolition, half a loaf is usually better than none.

Occasionally, the need for removing a listed building is overwhelming and it is possible to transfer it completely to a new site. This was done in respect of the Old Temple Bar many years ago and more recently at Hereford as mentioned in paragraph 2:2. Such opportunities are rare. Dismantlement and rebuilding is expensive, while intact removal can only be undertaken where a frame building is involved.

As far as conservation areas are concerned, the greatest factor in preserving the character of the eighteenth and nineteenth urban scene has been the existence of the aristocratic estates, especially in London. The Bedford, Grosvenor, Portman, Eyre, Smith's Charity, Portland, Cadogan, Calthorpe estates and many others have been responsible for preserving the quality of our best urban areas. With such estates the traditions of maintaining the prestige and standards of their houses have counted for more than economic gain over periods which in some cases extend back nearly 300 years. The Leasehold Reform Act raises serious problems for these estates, so that the community will be unable to rely on them in the future, as in the past, as protectors of conservation areas.

The record of private owners has, in fact, been encouraging having regard to the economic pressures on them to make the best use of their property assets. Frequently, they have set an example which many local authorities, often beset by similar economic problems, would do well to follow.

Now that the responsibilities placed on private owners by the Civic Amenities Act, 1967, are much heavier than in the past, it is even more important than ever to recognize the problems and needs of such owners. The success of conservation in urban areas depends upon their goodwill and enthusiasm. But if private enterprise is to play a greater part in conservation in the future, it must be recognized that with the exception of some altruistic or public minded owners the private sector will only play its part if there is adequate financial inducement or no more attractive alternatives.

At present, such inducement is lacking. The effect of the present system of Preservation Orders is to leave the burden on the owner of the building. The powers of local authorities to assist owners are limited to their powers to make grants or loans under the Local Authorities (Historic Buildings) Act, 1962, unless they are prepared to meet the whole of the deficiency in value by acquiring and maintaining the building. The interest of the national exchequer in such expenditure is only indirect in so far as it is reflected in the rate support grant or in its contribution to redevelopment areas which may include some conservation. Expenditure on conservation is not generally attractive to rate payers or members of local authorities.

It is not, therefore, surprising that many private owners have in the past chosen the softer options of redevelopment or doing nothing. The Civic Amenities Act has already given local authorities power to carry out repairs to unoccupied listed buildings, and the Town and Country Planning Bill, by providing for listed buildings to be compulsorily acquired at a penal price in cases where they have been deliberately neglected with a view to redevelopment, provides a deterrent against the unscrupulous owner. But negative control in itself will be quite ineffective. There should be a more positive policy which recognises that conservation implies reversing, promoting or deflecting trends and not freezing a status quo. The problem is to generate dynamism and make the market aware that changes are occurring.

There are three main reasons why the private sector finds conservation economically unattractive to each of which the public sector could provide a solution. First, funds may be lacking for the particular type of work needed; secondly, there may be no incentive for the first investor to take the plunge; and thirdly, the proposals for conservation may either in part or in toto be financially unattractive.

3.3   *Possible Solutions*

To deal with the first problem there are several possible solutions. Local authority mortgages could be provided at low rates and over generous periods or local authorities could offer purchase and leaseback arrangements, the purchase price providing either the capital necessary to carry out improvements or alterations, or the local authority could carry out the work itself and reimburse itself by increased rentals. Another possi-

Grey Street, Newcastle upon Tyne – one of the first conservation areas to be designated.

bility would be some form of investment grant machinery to parallel the system in Development Areas.

The best way to tackle the second problem would be for the local authority to make the first move by, for example, purchasing selected properties to demonstrate the potentialities of what could be done. Local authorities can help overcome the third problem by occupying the conserved area at rents which show some return to immediate investment with an eye to the eventual involvement of the private sector.

If conservation is to be successful it is essential that there should be no alternatives which are economically more attractive. The redevelopment of the actual conservation area, or building within it should either be prohibited, or be less attractive economically. Furthermore, opportunities for duplication of the functions performed by these areas and buildings within the same location should be prevented if this would mean the economic obsolescence of the conservation area. Some siphoning-off of pressure may, however, be justified, but in any event critical survey and analysis should be undertaken to these ends.

Private sector investment in conservation can be encouraged by the formulation of authoritative, forward-looking plans, not only for the conservation area, but for surrounding areas also, where the economic justifications for conservation may be nullified as easily and effectively as within the conservation area.

3.4   *The Local Authority's Role*

Essentially, conservation must be seen to be part of the local authority's positive planning duties. The return on effective conservation accruing to the local authority will be felt over a wider area than that of the conservation area. It would be wrong therefore for the private sector to be called upon to act as if the contrary were true in its case.

3.5   *Local Authorities Recouping Cost*

The discussion on the role of private enterprise would not be complete without some mention of the possibility of local authorities recouping some of the cost of conservation. It may be argued that if a local authority is to assist private owners in increasing the value of their property by the offering of special terms, then it is only reasonable that they should themselves recoup some of the benefit.

This, however, raises two questions, the first being whether it is practicable as the law is at present. Recoupment is not possible if no part of the particular property is "touched". When quinquennial revaluations for rating take place, individuals whose property is enhanced by improvements financed by local authorities have their rate burden adjusted. This reflects an insignificant part of the increase in capital value and is not a satisfactory solution.

The only other practical way of achieving recoupment would be for the local authority to acquire property, by compulsion if necessary, before carrying out improvements and to dispose of it afterwards. This raises two difficulties: first, the question of governmental control on local authority spending and, secondly, the disinclination of local authorities to part with freeholds once acquired. Here, to safeguard the wishes of owners, a freehold pre-emption clause could be specified by the Minister in any C.P.O. he might approve. By this means it might be possible to obviate the necessity of a conveyance to and from the local authority but merely to agree the difference between the 'before' and 'after' values. Following the principle of betterment levy at forty per cent there might be some merit in the owner paying a proportion of the difference. Any compensation could far outweigh recoupment in other directions. The second question is whether local authorities, if they recoup for benefits, should not also compensate when property is adversely affected. Not only will owners of historic buildings suffer loss by having to bear the cost of preservation orders and by restrictions on redevelopment, but other owners may also suffer a depreciation in the value of their property brought about by conservation proposals.

3.6 *Summary*

Summing up this part of the report, it would be fair to say that there is considerable willingness on the part of private owners to help with conservation as shown by the record of the past. However, to play their part fully they need financial inducement as well as restriction. This can be provided in a number of ways. Since it is doubtful if recoupment of this extra financial outlay by central and local government is possible, it would also be wise to stress that public funds are limited and that it will, therefore, be impossible to conserve all that we would like. A high degree of selection will be necessary.

4. *COST-BENEFIT ANALYSIS*

In discussing criteria for conservation it may be asked whether the traditional skills of the valuer and the economist are sufficient or whether any newer methods of assessment are needed. One which has received a good deal of publicity is cost-benefit analysis.

This method may be used to assist decision-making, particularly investment decisions in the public sector where market prices give little guide. It is unquestionably right when faced with a large number of relevant variable factors to analyse, collate and summarize the effect of each. This is an exercise which any prudent man would undertake before forming an opinion; there is, however, a difference between the way this may be done where the factors are measurable as against the case where they are intangible. The study of conservation gives rise to a number of considerations of the intangible, of architectural merit, aesthetic quality and historic importance are examples.

This new technique is relatively untried at the present time - especially in the field of conservation - and it is thus not surprising that there is a difference of professional opinion as to its usefulness. Professional Institutions are indeed undertaking a study of this subject.

5. *ECONOMIC CRITERIA FOR A SUCCESSFUL CONSERVATION POLICY*

5.1 *Priorities*

The unknown quantity at present is the amount of capital necessary to conserve what is worthy of preservation in our historic cities. Before this can be assessed it is vital that priorities should be established. What one town regards as important may not be so in the context of public investment in the country as a whole.

A useful first step in measuring the size of the problem would be for Central Government to seek information from each local authority on the lines of Circular 50/66 (42/66 Welsh Office). From the results of this questionnaire, Central Government could decide how much public capital can be provided for a given period to specific towns. Returns could be made periodically so that a rolling programme could be established.

So that the amount of public capital can be matched against the "invisible export" of tourist spending it is important for an immediate study to be made of foreign tourist spending in various towns.

5.2

Local Authorities' Use of Capital

Local authorities to whom public capital is allocated should use it in a number of ways: firstly, in the conservation of buildings in their owner-ship and for environmental improvements: secondly, by mortgage facilities at low interest rates or by direct grant to private owners of up to a given percentage of estimated cost, probably 50% as in house improvements under the Housing Acts: thirdly, for the acquisition and improvement of privately owned buildings which are incapable of economic preservation even with grant aid: fourthly, the acquisition of buildings which will improve in value as the result of public expenditure but with rights of pre-emption at the en-hanced value in favour of existing owners: fifthly, in providing an advisory service to the public on ways and economic results of conserving old property.

5.3

The Necessary Staff – for Local Authorities

It is likely that many local authorities will not have the staff experienced in these specialist matters and this raises the whole issue as to the best body to initiate and carry through conservation policies. Some town councils may be indifferent to its historic "assets". Others may be passionately devoted but without funds. Some others may inflate their demands on Central Government in order to secure a disproportionate share of the global allocation. For any realistic financial policy to be made by Central Government there must be a common basis of measurement. A revision of local authority boundaries could well affect the interest in and policies for conservation already in being. In the event of a local authority failing to initiate or implement a policy of conservation, there should be powers enabling Central Government to do the work on behalf of that local authority. The appropriate Ministry should have a panel of experts in architecture, landscape, valuation and administration in order to provide a local authority with the specialist skills it could not reasonably be expected to have on its own staff.

5.4

The Necessary Staff – to assist Private Owners

In the private sector much can be achieved by example of economic success in preserving historic buildings. But such examples are rare because of the hard fact that conservation is not profitable and the risk of loss very real. The sheer cost of building work is unknown because of the lack of people with sufficient skill both in the professions and the building industry. The introduction of a firm government policy on conservation should induce professional bodies to provide (by examination or post-qualification diploma) the necessary specialists. Government training schemes could well bring into being the necessary number of specialist firms in the building industry.

5.5 *Possible Inducements*

The Civic Amenities Act provides some degree of compulsion, but what is needed is some inducement for private investment in conservation. One way might be by tax relief on net cost subject to a reduction of such relief in relation to any increase in value that might result. It must be remembered that conservation does not require a single capital sum, but, in most (if not all) cases, a higher than average annual maintenance cost which would have to be reflected in any scheme for tax relief.

5.6 *Summary*

The vital point to remember is that to try and preserve too much will result in preserving too little. The first step must be the selection of priorities in order that the feasibility of exploiting all or part of the range of available resources as set out in this paper and including area development policy decisions, private investment and grant aid monies may be explored and used to best effect.

Leazes Terrace, Newcastle upon Tyne. 19th century property converted into university residence.

W. F. J. Fussell

CONSERVATION – COST AND PROFITABILITY

1.
Profitability

Given the right circumstances conservation of existing structures on a large or small scale can be financially profitable, providing proper professional advice is sought at all stages of the operation. Profitability depends to a great extent on the selection of the correct procedures and, in the case of the larger projects, these are normally suggested by the quantity surveyor.

"The Englishman's home is his castle", and the status-symbol of historic connection is a financial asset. Old properties (however dilapidated) capable of being converted into homes will continue to be in demand and there are people who are prepared to spend sometimes up to four times the purchase price on conversion.

Domestic conservation has been given encouragement by the substantial increase in grants of one sort or another, as detailed in the 1968 M.H. L.G. White Paper "Old Houses into New Homes". These additional grants enable many domestic properties to be converted and improved to the financial benefit of their owners.

Local Authority housing problems can sometimes be profitably solved by conserving existing buildings. The Guardian article (26th August, 1967) "All mod cons in a converted rum warehouse" had this to say about comparative costs :
"Comparing costs in nine rehabilitation projects and six new housing schemes, the G.L.C. has found that rehabilitation costs 63% of building new. This figure is computed for an occupancy of 2·7 people in both new and rehabilitated homes. A new home costs £5,200, or £1,904 per person occupying it; a reconditioned home costs £3,307, or £1,158 per occupant. These figures do not include provision of ancillary services like garages or children's playgrounds, but they do include all professional fees."

The G.L.C. are not alone in carrying out a successful conservation programme – other Local Authorities have success stories. Recent government pronouncements indicate that large-scale rehabilitation of twilight and rural areas is just around the corner. The government have at long last realized that in certain circumstances *conservation can pay*.

2.
Cost Limits

Often the question is asked: "When does it become uneconomic to conserve an existing structure – if the consideration is purely financial?" Nearly all government projects are subject to some sort of cost control: normally there is a rigid cost limit which not be exceeded. Likewise the private building owner is subjected to cost control by his bank manager or his desire to keep within specified cost limits.

A "rule of thumb" method of establishing a cost limit for conversion and improvement of an existing building follows. This method has been used successfully by at least one government department.

Step 1: Decide the function of the building, e.g. offices, domestic, shops, etc.

Step 2: Decide the cost per square foot that this type of accommodation would cost if built as new.

Step 3: Decide the total floor area required if this accommodation were built as new.

Step 4: Calculate the total cost of the new equivalent building from steps 2 and 3 above, and allow about 10% for external and ancillary works.

Step 5: Take two-thirds of the total arrived at in step 4 and this will be the cost limit for conservation in most circumstances.

This "rule of thumb" must obviously be used with considerable discretion as it ignores all sociological, historic, sentimental and other considerations that must, of necessity, form part of the conservation thought processes.

3. *Cost Plan*

The cost limit having been established, the next logical step is to allocate this sum to the various sections of the work as contemplated at the sketch plan stage. A cost plan can be drawn up which would allocate the available cash to the following major elements:

(a) New work in extensions, etc.

(b) Conversions and improvements.

The estimated cost of the new work can be sub-divided into the following elements :

  (i) Sub-structure,

  (ii) Structural envelope,

  (iii) Finishings (internal and external),

  (iv) Fittings, and

  (v) Heating, plumbing and electrical installation.

These elements can be further sub-divided if required. The estimated cost of conservation and improvement work can be calculated on a room-by-room basis, plus a separate section for external repairs and work to ancillary buildings. Professional fees are normally excluded from the cost plan.

At the cost planning stage it should also be possible for the quantity surveyor to consider and produce comparative costs of alternative schemes for consideration by the building owner. At the design and estimating stage the aspect of recurring maintenance cost should also be considered (not forgetting that there will be comparable costs in the case of new building!).

4. *Tendering Procedures and Contractual Arrangements*

The cost of a project is influenced by the chosen contractual arrangement. It is generally accepted that "cost-plus" is more expensive than competitive tendering.

For minor building works (say under £7,500) the new 1968 Joint Contracts Tribunal's *Agreement for Minor Building Works* (published by the R.I.B.A.) is recommended. The heading to this Form reads : "This Form of Agreement and Conditions is designed for use where minor building works or maintenance work, for which a specification

and drawings have been prepared, are to be carried out for an agreed lump sum and where an Architect/Supervising Officer has been appointed on behalf of the Employer. The Form is not appropriate for works for which bills of quantities have been prepared or for which a schedule of rates is required for valuing variations."
Using these arrangements the tender-documents would consist of detailed drawings, specifications and form of tender.

If a schedule of rates for valuing variations is required, or if the work is of such a specialist nature that it is not possible to prepare bills of quantities, then the R.I.B.A. Form of Contract (without quantities) is recommended.

When it is possible to prepare either full or approximate bills of quantities then it is recommended that the R.I.B.A. Form of Contract (with quantities) is used — this form giving maximum flexibility to the building owner, architect, quantity surveyor and contractor. The tender-documents would consist of bills of quantities, outline drawings and form of tender, and it is suggested that the rules laid down in the N.J.C.C. *A Code of Procedure for selective tendering* should be followed.

In some instances it may be desirable to use the 1967 — R.I.B.A. *Fixed fee form of prime cost contract*; for example, when the project is so complex that it is impossible to draw and specify, or when a rapid start is required by the building owner which precludes traditional pre-contract planning by the architect. This form of contract establishes a fixed fee payable to the contractor for management and provides for the payment of the prime cost of labour, materials and plant. As with all prime cost contracts there is no facility to prevent waste in the use of labour, material and plant.

5.   *Contractor Selection*
Irrespective of the building owner's selection of an architect, or the architect's selection of the appropriate contract arrangement, little progress will be made unless great care is taken in the selection of the contractors who are to be invited to tender for the work.

From an initial list of about ten firms it is suggested that a final short list of about four firms be drawn up. Firms will generally be eliminated when, on investigation, they are found to possess neither the necessary technical and financial resources nor the previous experience to tackle the project. These facts can be ascertained by proper interview which, although time-consuming, pays dividends in the long run.

6.   *Bills of Quantities*
Section 3 describes the cost plan and its layout which will assist the architect while his detailed plans are developed. These detailed plans are cost-checked by the quantity surveyor before he starts measuring for the bill of quantities. It is suggested that the bill of quantities should be laid out in much the same sections as the cost plan so that comparison at tender stage is possible. The preliminaries to the bill of quantities should be more comprehensive than for "non-conservation" work and cover such items as ownership of things removed, access, storage, shoring, programme, etc.

7. *Large Scale Estimating Techniques*

Due to the complexity of estimating (with any degree of accuracy) the cost of conservation of whole cities and towns, methods have evolved that permit a "cost sample" (for a particular study area) to be calculated. This cost sample can be used as a mean for similar areas within the city or town's boundaries.

Buildings other than those covered by the general cost sample normally fall into one of the following categories:

(a) Those of national or historic interest,

(b) Those of civic or local interest, and

(c) Those possessing townscape interest.

Generally it is possible to estimate the cost of conservation of buildings in those categories quite accurately by measurement and pricing of approximate quantities, or by comparison with cost information accumulated for previously completed projects.

Likewise the cost of new building and civil engineering works such as pedestrian precincts, play-spaces, parking areas, roads, bridges, etc. can all be estimated. The degree of accuracy of these estimates depends on the amount of information available to the quantity surveyor from the various consultants.

It is possible in certain circumstances to prepare a C.B.A. (Cost Benefit Analysis) so that alternative proposals, both of design and degree of conservation and new work, can be properly compared. Experience has shown that alternatives have to be considered in great detail if the quantity surveyor is to be provided with sufficient well defined information to permit the preparation of a proper and realistic C.B.A.

8. *Possible Future Aims*

(i) Because of the lack of detailed cost information relating to conservation the Royal Institution of Chartered Surveyors could be asked to expand their Building Cost Information Service to include broad cost information on completed conservation projects.

(ii) In order to give cost guidance to Local Authorities contemplating conservation projects it would be of benefit to these Authorities if cost advice could be obtained from the Ministry of Housing and Local Government.

(iii) Approximately £2,500 million was spent on local authority projects last year, of which a minute proportion was in respect of conservation. It would not seem unreasonable if 2% of this vast sum was allocated for pure conservation work.

* * * * * * * *

A comment

There is a tendency to draw attention to costs and forget about profits in conservation.

Losses should be set against gains through conservation. The true cost of a conservation scheme to a local authority or developer is the loss on the losers less the profit on the winners. Expressed as a formula this is :

$$Ll - Pw = RC$$

where Ll is loss on the losing elements in the scheme, Pw is the profit on the winning elements and RC is the real cost.

"Norwich has been concerned to make restoration pay and still be beautiful."
Eleven existing Tudor cottages were converted and planned as six cottages in 1956/7 at a total cost of £10,637.
"Before" and "after" photographs by City Architect's Department.

"Restored buildings let as offices pay their way."
10,12 and 14 Princes Street Norwich: medieval buildings with Georgian and later modern reconstruction of No. 14 (badly carried out), replanned and reconstructed as offices in 1964/5 at a total cost of £16,712.
"Before" and "after" photographs by City Architect's Department.

N. R. Stocks

A FURTHER NOTE ON COST BENEFIT ANALYSIS

1.

Different Methods

Cost Benefit Analysis (C.B.A.) has tended to become associated in many planners' minds with one particular method – the Balance Sheet method. There are however very many other methods; most C.B.As in other fields than planning are custom-built for the particular job. It may therefore be important to stress that in referring to C.B.A. you are not necessarily implying the " Balance Sheet" method, the latest examples of which are so complicated that they tend to put people off.

No form of C.B.A. achieves the impossible, i.e. quantifies genuine intangibles. Many people think it does and then become indignant when the decision is still left in doubt. What a good C.B.A. does is to juxtapose the tangibles and the intangibles in such a way that the decision-taker can clearly see what level he must ascribe to them if he is to come down on one side or the other. C.B.A. is least successful where it is comparing investment or planning decision of dissimilar kind, or where intangibles loom large on both sides of the decision. *Conservation is a subject loaded with intangibles.*

2.

What is it proposed to use C.B.A. for? Presumably to determine whether a particular building or group of buildings should be conserved, or whether a particular town should receive conservation funds. From this information it would presumably be hoped to claim an appropriate budget from the National and Local Government purse.

It is far more likely that the budget to be devoted to conservation will be fixed at a higher level than will be concerned with the details of local C.B.As, and will rather be the residue after meeting other competing claims. In this event the exercize becomes one of allocating a fixed budget of public resources, in some "optimal", i.e. most cost-effective way.

If several alternative programmes of conservation, say in a county, were then drawn up and costed, net of any returns that may accrue from letting or selling a conserved building, the costs of each of the programmes could be added up and expanded or contracted (probably contracted!) until their costs matched the available budget. If the total cost of the alternative programmes were to be contracted, the individual programmes to be dropped out should be those that consumed a large amount of budget in relation to their benefits (intuitively assessed). Greater favour, for a given cost, would, for example, be given to those proposals where conservation was a positive part of some wider planning objective, or, more obviously, where the buildings were of finer quality.

Admittedly you would still be landed with the problem of assessing benefits, but it would be done against a known cost yardstick. Furthermore, it would focus the issue. It would be waste of time, for example, arguing about proposals which would be marginal to a £2m budget if the actual available budget were £100,000. Budgeting is a potential ally to planning which most planners, and unfortunately most Treasurers, do not seem to recognize.

If, as seems likely in our present undernourished state of relating economic to physical planning, no useful information on the probable budget can be obtained, it would be useful to discount the net costs (i.e. costs net of any financial returns) at a given rate % according to the year in which programmed payments would have to be made, and then concentrate resources as they become available on those schemes which showed the highest Net Present Value (in this kind of exercize highest N.P.V., probably means the "smallest negative figure", since costs would exceed financial returns), in relation to benefits.

In these paragraphs I am talking about costs and returns to *Central and Local Government* and not, as in a C.B.A, about all social costs and benefits. In this kind of problem I believe in doing what can reasonably and meaningfully be done, even though it yields only a partial solution, rather than for ever labouring at some pseudo-scientific analysis which pretends to be a solution to the whole problem.

traffic

REPORT OF THE STUDY GROUP
CONVENED BY THE INSTITUTION OF
MUNICIPAL ENGINEERS

Chairman: Colin Buchanan CBE
Secretary: Mrs. B. Y. Fairweather

Group Members

J. F. A. Baker CB CEng MICE MIMunE MInstHE
Automobile Association
R. E. G. Brown
Traders' Road Transport Association
A. H. F. Jiggens CEng AMICE MIMunE
City Engineer, Chester
J. V. Leigh MBE BSc(Eng) CEng MICE MIMunE
County Surveyor, Hertfordshire
L. M. Perkis CEng AMICE ARICS AMIMunE
City Engineer, Winchester
H. M. Watson MTPI CEng AMICE AMIMunE
County Planning Officer, Worcestershire
J. A. E. H. White ARICS
Marks and Spencer Limited
A. A. Wood DipArch DipTP ARIBA AMTPI
City Planning Officer, Norwich

Assessors

N. S. Despicht
Assistant Secretary, Ministry of Transport,
assisted by D. F. Howard
E. L. Gillett
Assistant Secretary, Scottish Development
Department
P. J. Hosegood
Assistant Secretary, Welsh Office

PEDESTRIANIZATION IN ALNWICK

J. D. Nicholl DipTP AMTPI
Assistant County Planning Officer,
Northumberland County Council

FOOT STREETS IN NORWICH

A. A. Wood DipArch DipTP ARIBA MTPI
City Planning Officer, Norwich

LEGAL AND FINANCIAL MATTERS
CONCERNING TRAFFIC IN HISTORIC
TOWNS

Ministry of Transport

1. *THE PROBLEM*

We defined our terms of reference as follows: to consider the impact of motor traffic on the character and environment of historic towns, and to suggest short and long term policies for enhancing the environment while permitting the necessary use of motor transport.

In one sense, the problems caused by traffic in historic towns are no different from those which are arising in most other towns. These problems may be classified in two groups. In the first place there is the sheer difficulty of extracting the maximum benefit from the motor vehicle. The great advantage of the motor vehicle – the quality which places it in a class of its own in relation to all other methods of mechanical transport – is that it can provide in a very literal sense a door-to-door movement service for people and goods. But so many vehicles are now being used in urban areas that they are tending to become self-defeating. They are literally getting in each other's way. The result of all this is congestion and delays which in total are costing urban communities a great deal of money.

The second group of difficulties concern the adverse effects of motor traffic on the environment for living. There are accidents resulting in death and injury and damage to vehicles, all of which cost the community very large sums of money annually. Three-quarters of all accidents take place in urban areas. The noise of motor traffic has been identified as the predominant source of nuisance in urban areas, and a serious nuisance into the bargain. Fumes from motor vehicles are coming to be regarded as a serious nuisance, with the sinister suggestion that they may be associated with lung cancer. In certain cases, where buildings in which delicate scientific work is being undertaken lie alongside traffic routes, the problem of vibration may be serious. In addition to these practical matters ranging from accidents to vibration, there is also the more subjective problem resulting from the intrusion of the motor vehicle, moving or stationary, into the visual scene.

These difficulties have appeared in towns for three main reasons. In the first place there has been a great increase in the number of vehicles in use – car ownership has been building up steadily over the years, and more and more use is being made of commercial vehicles for a great variety of purposes. In the second place the physical fabric of towns has proved unsuitable for the use of large numbers of vehicles – streets are too narrow, there are too many intersections each one of which tends to be the scene of confusion, and there is a dearth of places where vehicles can park or stop for the purpose of delivering goods to premises. Thirdly, and this applies especially to town centres, the amount of usage has tended to increase as shops, offices etc. have been called upon to cater for more and more people. Many towns have grown enormously in their outer areas with the addition of housing estates, but the central areas, hemmed in on all sides by older development, have been unable to expand in proportion, yet they have remained the centre of attraction for steadily growing populations.

The two main problems — the frustration of the utility of the motor vehicle, and the harmful environmental effects of motor traffic — will be found in every historic town as much as in any ordinary town. But the very fact that the town is historic exacerbates the problem in a number of ways. The mere presence of the traffic prevents the full study and enjoyment of the town by reason of the confusion and the danger resulting from the traffic. In many cases the people who might occupy historic buildings for resident-ial or business purposes, and who could be expected to cherish them, are driven out either by the sheer nuisance of the traffic or the fact that park-ing and other facilities are restricted, and this in turn tends to lead to build-ings being neglected and then to physical decay. As for the intrusion of motor vehicles into the visual scene, this may be a matter of opinion in the case of ordinary towns, but few people would disagree that in historic towns the degree of intrusion now prevailing detracts in a most serious way from the appearance of places which by common consent are a valuable legacy from the past. Finally, there is the peculiar danger in historic towns that the difficulties of traffic circulation may produce a pressure for conventional road improvement schemes (such as widenings, cutting of corners, erection of multi-storey car parks and even comprehensive development) which in themselves could be devastatingly destructive of architectural and historic character.

2. THE NATURE OF TOWN TRAFFIC

2.1

Long Term Importance of the Motor Vehicle
It would be unwise to imagine that the traffic problems now arising in towns — historic or otherwise — are likely to be resolved in the foreseeable future by the invention of some new form of transport which will supersede the motor vehicle. The motor vehicle is, essentially, a very simple device — it is a mechanized cart, and the advantages of carts for many urban transport purposes have long been recognized, and they give every appearance of continuing to be valued for a long period ahead. It is possible to visualize a town of a kind altogether different from the towns we know, in which the movement system does not rely on motor vehicles at all, but as long as towns remain an assemblage of buildings more or less in the traditional form — and the essence of conservation, of course, is to maintain this form in the case of historic towns — then the advantages of a fairly small land-based mechanically propelled vehicle roughly in the form of a motor vehicle are bound to be very great. There is great scope for improving the motor vehicle — it is hoped that it will become much quieter and will not emit fumes and will be able to move sideways. In the course of such development the source of motive power may change so that, strictly speaking, it is no longer a motor vehicle but even so it will continue to present many of the characteristics of the motor vehicle.

2.2

Traffic and Buildings
Accepting, therefore, that the motor vehicle, or something very like it, is likely to be with us for a long time, it is necessary to take it seriously. An important preliminary to understanding how it can be catered for positively is to understand the manner and purposes for which it is used in urban areas, and the nature of the traffic which results.

As mentioned already, the outstanding characteristic of the motor vehicle is its ability to provide a door-to-door service. It can in fact provide more than this — provided that buildings are appropriately designed, the motor vehicle can penetrate *inside* buildings to various floor levels, with the result (to give an example) that goods can be transported almost literally from the factory bench to sales counter. Similarly, a person can get into a car literally in his own house and get out inside his office building many miles away, having passed the intervening journey in reasonable warmth, comfort and privacy. It is easy to see from this that (with one important exception which is discussed later) the vehicles moving in the streets of any urban area are, in fact, making journeys between buildings of various kinds, though for present purposes the term "building" needs to be extended to include parking places, goods yard, depots and so on. Some vehicles will be moving between buildings situated within the urban area; others will be entering the area, having come from buildings right outside it; while others will be leaving buildings within the area for other buildings outside.

2.3

Purpose & Characteristics of Journeys

The *purposes* of these journeys are multifarious. *People* move about for a great variety of social and business purposes; and *goods* in enormous quantities and variety have to be distributed to buildings in order to maintain the life of the town. The *pattern* of these journeys is, of course, dependent upon the disposition of the buildings. Since there are a vast number of buildings arranged in intricate and sometimes chaotic ways, it follows that the pattern of the journeys which result is extremely intricate and sometimes chaotic.

One characteristic of urban journeys is worth mentioning. Almost any journey between two buildings tends to consist of three sections. There is a zig-zag movement out from the building of origin; this followed by what might be called the "main run"; then there is a zig-zag movement towards the building of destination. Transportation studies the world over have thrown a great deal of light on the "main run" movements, but less is known about the shorter zig-zag movements. The relevance of the zig-zag movements is that they represent the stage when vehicles are casting closely around buildings seeking a way out or a way in. This is the stage when buildings and vehicles become closely involved, and when it is desirable for buildings and local circulation arrangements to be designed as part of the same process. Much of the urban traffic problem is connected with the zig-zag movements, and it is during these movements that some of the worst frustrations and delays are experienced, and when traffic interferes most severely with other aspects of urban life including the freedom of movement of pedestrians.

2.4

Through Traffic

Mention was made above of the fact that there is one important exception to the rule that the vehicles moving in the streets of an urban area are all connected ultimately with the buildings of the area. The exception concerns the phenomenon of "through traffic". The connection with buildings is still true, but the buildings are not the buildings of the area concerned. For an explanation it is necessary to recall the settlement pattern which we have inherited in this country. Broadly speaking it consists of towns and villages at a distance apart roughly equivalent to a day's journey by horse. The linking roads run from the *centre* of one settlement to the *centre* of the next. This arrangement worked well enough for centuries, but it started to give trouble when the motor vehicle arrived with its ability to make journeys of several hundred miles in a single day. The trouble being that the old pattern forced all vehicles bound on longer journeys to pass through the centres of settlements en route, whether they had business there or not. Thus has arisen the phenomenon of "through traffic" – the towns are an obstruction to the passage of the through traffic, and the through traffic is a nuisance to the town.

It is not always accepted that through traffic is a nuisance. Many shop-keepers, for example, have maintained that through traffic is essential to prosperity, and there is truth in this when the shop is really dependent on passing traffic, as a petrol filling station or a café might be. But with the rapid growth of traffic in recent years it is now becoming more and more widely accepted that the disadvantages of heavy volumes of through traffic in a town outweigh any incidental trading advantages there might be.

Much misunderstanding exists, however, as to the part which through traffic plays in congesting an urban area. Many people seem to think it is the whole cause of congestion, and that a by-pass would solve all problems. The answer is that in the case of a small town astride a busy main road, the through traffic is a large proportion of the whole traffic in the town. In this case a by-pass would bring much relief. But in the case of a large town, which generates a great deal of traffic by virtue of its own activities, the through traffic is generally a much lower proportion of the total traffic in the town. In this case, a by-pass would be far less effective in reducing congestion within the town, though this is not to say that the by-pass might not be fully justified for the sake of easing the passage of the through traffic.

Most small and medium sized towns which are located astride class-ified roads present a theoretical case for by-passing, but for various reasons it may not be possible or even sensible to provide by-passes. The fact is that to by-pass every town in every direction (which, virtually, is the theoretical requirement) poses such a vast task with so much loss and severance of land that it appears impractical. Some towns will doubtless be provided with by-passes, others may have to rely on more strategic re-routings of through traffic on the regional road system, whilst a few will have to reconcile themselves to the accommodation of through traffic on their own road systems.

However, the main point to be understood about through traffic is that its removal (by whatever means) from all but the fairly small town will bring about only a temporary alleviation of traffic problems. As vehicle ownership increases in the future, it is the town's own traffic that tends to build up into a sizeable problem of its own.

2.5   *Town Traffic – Types of Movement*
Returning to the question of the nature of *town traffic*, whilst it is generally true that the great mass of movements are associated with the buildings which constitute the town, it is possible to discern a number of fairly sharply-defined types of movement. There is, of course, the main classification between the movement of people in cars, buses and coaches, and the movement of goods in a variety of trucks. People

move for the purpose of getting to work, to go shopping, to go to school, for recreation and entertainment, and for a great variety of social and business errands. Goods movements are enormously varied — supplies have to be delivered to shops, money to banks, goods to and from warehouses, raw materials to factories and so on. It is an immensely complicated story, but it is analyzable and demonstrable, at any rate as to the main characteristics for any town.

Many people, when putting forward "solutions" for urban traffic problems, fail to understand the complex nature of traffic, and thus are led into making erroneous generalizations. There is, for example, a great tendency for people to assume that traffic consists only of private cars — the important commercial, business and industrial traffic (including the use of many cars), which is the life-blood of towns, is overlooked.

2.6
Town Traffic — Directions of Movement
The main *directions* of traffic movement are also identifiable. A town with a "strong" central shopping business area will cause movements to take place in a radial direction — from residential area into the centre for example, or from outside the town to the centre. Industrial areas, wherever they are situated, will give rise to clearly discernable movements, as will goods yards, depots, docks and recreational centres such as football grounds. In many towns, especially the smaller ones, it is the radial movements that are still dominant in the overall pattern; but in larger towns where industries and new shopping areas have developed in peripheral locations, a highly complex pattern of circumferential movements may exist. These movements may be rendered difficult by reason of the lack of adequate circumferential roads.

2.7
Traffic Analysis
Although urban traffic movements are very numerous and vastly complicated, they are nevertheless quantified and analyzable as to kinds, quantities and directions. Moreover, given knowledge of present movements, it is perfectly possible to forecast future movements for several decades ahead. This includes movements resulting from development which does not yet exist, or from vehicle ownership rates which have not yet been achieved. The importance of this lies in the fact that some of the measures required to accommodate traffic are very expensive capital constructions, and it is important that these should either have sufficient in-built capacity to deal with the growth of traffic or should be readily adaptable at a future date. It is important also that the sites of future constructions, such as roads, should be reserved.

2.8
Future Growth of Traffic
As for the growth of traffic, there are two factors that are relevant. The first is that more and more people are becoming able to afford cars; and as businesses expand and diversify, so there is a tendency for more commercial vehicles to be used. The second factor is that the population is itself increasing fairly rapidly, so there will be still more people and businesses seeking the use of motor vehicles. Taking these two factors together, there is a fair certainty that the present number of vehicles will be trebled before the end of the century, with private cars accounting for the greater part of the increase. By about the end of the century, a condition of "saturation" of vehicle ownership should have been reached — that is to say, everyone who wants a vehicle will have

the means to buy one — so further increases after that date will depend on the growth of population rather than on the meeting of unsatisfied demands.

It is only necessary to contemplate the present problems of traffic, especially in towns, and to consider what they may become under the pressure of three times as many vehicles, to realise that very serious problems lie ahead. The most careful planning and control of development will be needed if a situation of chaos is to be avoided.

2.9 *Summary*

Perhaps the most important point to be remembered about the nature of town traffic is that it is a matter of comparatively small vehicles being used for a vast variety of intricate movements for which it is very difficult to visualize any effective substitute for the motor vehicle. Trains can be used for certain mass movements, but when it comes to delivering money to banks, or beer to public houses, or prisoners to law courts, or old ladies to their solicitors, then the motor has well-tried advantages. Urban traffic is made up of many thousands of such movements.

3. DEALING WITH TOWN TRAFFIC

3.1 *The Principle*

If the motor vehicle is accepted as the mainstay of urban transport systems then it is plain enough that some kind of physical modification of the structure of existing towns is needed in order to exploit it.

Given the twin objectives of improving accessibility and maintaining or enhancing environmental conditions, the principle of this physical modification is not difficult to see. It is bound to be an application of the same principle which is applied to the design of large buildings to deal with circulation problems, namely the canalization of longer movements from locality to locality onto a corridor system which has the effect of leaving the rooms of the building to deal only with the internal traffic that belongs to them. The rooms, free from all extraneous traffic, then have some chance of maintaining reasonable environmental conditions. When this concept is applied to a town the corridor system becomes the highway network of the town, and the rooms become areas of more-or-less homogeneous development (e.g. shopping areas, residential areas, educational areas) where there is a prima-facie case for insulating them from all but their own traffic.

3.2 *The Network*

Several interesting results emerge when this principle is applied to a town. The pattern of the network, for example, is derived from a combination of two factors. It depends primarily on the *location* of the main activities which take place in the city, but it must then be bent and adjusted to take account of the "environmental areas" into which the development of the city must be divided. The pattern of the network declares itself when these two aspects are analyzed there is no need to rely on rules of thumb regarding the pattern, such as the popular notion that every town needs and must have an inner ring road. Then again, the size or capacity of the links of the network depend on the amount of traffic which has to be carried, but this in turn depends on the kind and intensity of the activities which take place in the environmental areas. Once again these are matters which are proving to be analyzable and capable of considerable quantification for both present and future conditions.

Alnwick, "............ intrusion of motor vehicles into the visual scene ...."

Notion of Limited Capacity

However the most interesting result which emerges when the concept of the network and environmental areas is applied to a city concerns the "capacity for traffic" of the environmental areas themselves. This is best explained by taking the case of an ordinary street, say in a residential area. It can be seen that such a street will have a certain sheer capacity for traffic depending on its width and the frequency of the intersections. It will not be possible for more than this amount of traffic to pass along the street. This may be termed the "crude capacity". Such a volume of traffic would be very likely, however, to be a great nuisance to the residents in the street in the sense that there would be danger, noise, fumes, vibration, and intrusion. If the environment of the residents is to be preserved, then it can be seen that a much lower volume of traffic must be specified. This can be termed the "environmental capacity" of the street. In other words, if the environment is to be secured, then the street has a *strictly limited capacity for traffic considerably lower than its sheer capacity to pass vehicles.*

If this is accepted as being true for a single street, then it is but a short step to appreciate that it must be true for an environmental area as a whole, whether it be a residential area, or a shopping centre, or a university, or any other kind of unit. This notion of *limited capacity* is of the greatest importance in the consideration of contemporary traffic problems. It is after all no different in principle to the fact that a dwelling has a certain capacity for residents; there is some flexibility but if more people are packed into the dwelling than it can reasonably contain then it becomes a slum.

When an environmental area has been defined in an existing town, it is found that its "capacity for traffic" depends to a large extent on the way in which it is laid out or designed. If, for example, it consisted of narrow streets, without sidewalks, and with the doors of the dwellings opening straight onto the carriageway, then obviously the capacity would be very low. But if it consisted of a sophisticated design, perhaps with the dwellings elevated above the traffic altogether, then the capacity would be much higher. From this it can be concluded, in respect of any existing environmental area, that its future capacity for traffic will depend on the extent to which it will be possible to alter it physically, and this in turn will depend on the amount of money which the community is prepared to spend upon such alterations and upon the extent to which a "new look" will be acceptable. From this it follows again, that if the community decides that a new look is unacceptable — the area may, for example, be one of outstanding historical character where no physical changes are acceptable — then there is no alternative for the community but to accept the prospect of a permanently reduced capacity for traffic.

This really brings one to the heart of the urban traffic problem. By way of summary, it can be said, in respect of any urban area, that if it is desired to have certain environmental standards, then the amount of traffic which the area can accommodate is strictly limited, but the amount may be increased in proportion to the amount of money which the community is prepared to spend on physical alterations and the extent to which a new look is acceptable. From this rough and ready "law" there seems to be no escape. It will be found to be applicable in all circumstances, even if its consequences may be very difficult to accept. But there is one major qualification to be added to it. When the possibilities of physical alterations to urban areas are studied in a theoretical way, it is found, even if complete reconstruction in the most radical manner is postulated, that there is still a limit to the amount of traffic that can be accommodated. In other words there is an absolute limit dictated by the design problems of space and circulation, irrespective of questions of cost. Moreover, when the problems are brought down to the reality of a town, then it is found that a number of practical considerations intervene which limit traffic volumes still further.

3.4   *Difficulties of Contriving the Network*
Perhaps the most important of these considerations is the sheer difficulty of contriving the network. It has to be admitted that to create an efficient full-scale network in an existing city, whether by carving out new roads or adapting existing ones, is an extremely difficult and costly operation. There is bound to be considerable displacement of property (which may have to be re-located elsewhere) involving hardship for many people. The roads themselves, if they are built on the surface, tend to disrupt the urban area by reason of their great width. If built sub-surface, which is probably the best design, they are extremely expensive on account of the services — drains, sewers, cables etc. — which have to be altered. If built as elevated roads, which does allow local life to flow underneath them, they tend to be overshadowing of the surrounding areas. In no case do wide roads make very comfortable neighbours for other purposes of urban life. The worst difficulties attach to the interchanges, which can absorb very large areas of valuable land presenting formidable problems of severance and displacement of property.

None of these difficulties destroy the concept of the network, but they do mean that according to circumstances it may not be possible to provide a very "powerful" network. In such cases it is likely that the capacity of the network will be the controlling factor of the amount of traffic that can be catered for in the urban area, rather than the capacity of the environmental areas to receive traffic. But whichever is the controlling factor the balance must still be preserved between the two.

3.5   *Consequences of Traffic Limitation*
Thus it can be said that in addition to the fact that there is an absolute limit to the amount of traffic an urban area can accommodate, there are almost certain to be practical considerations which, in the case of sizeable densely-developed areas, will restrict the volume to lower levels. All the indications are that these levels are likely to be *below the potential demands for the use of motor vehicles as they will develop in the future.* This conclusion has far-reaching implications. If a town is really faced with the prospect of not being able to accommodate all the use of vehicles that people are likely to desire, then two courses are open; either to accept the position and to set up a control system which will keep the number of vehicles in check, or to disperse the activities in order to reduce the movement loads and to provide more space for accommodating those that remain.

If the first of these two possible courses of action is adopted then it has to be asked where the restraint on vehicle numbers is to fall and how it is to be exercised. It is not difficult to see *in principle* where the restraint should be exercised — obviously there should be some preference given to the use of motor vehicles for the essential purposes of maintaining the commercial business and industrial life of the city as against other uses which are much more a matter of personal choice and convenience. The latter group are primarily exemplified in the use of private cars for the journey-to-work — this is a category of vehicle movement which is not absolutely essential to the functioning of urban areas, and which can, if necessary, be discharged more economically in terms of space by bulk methods of transport. In between these two groups (which may usefully be described as the "essential" and the "optional") lie a whole range of intermediate uses of motor vehicles — semi-business uses, social uses, shopping journeys, school journeys etc. — the degree of satisfaction of which will depend upon local circumstances. It can be said, categorically, however, that in virtually all sizeable urban centres there is no prospect of being able to accommodate all the future desires for the use of cars for the journey to work. This conclusion is reached not out of spite, but is dictated by the facts of the situation.

3.6   *Control of Traffic Volumes*
As to the *method* by which control over vehicle numbers should be exercised, this question poses severe political and administrative problems. The control of parking is obviously very important in this respect, and a strong case can be argued that the public authority should retain control of the whole parking situation - *where* parking is provided, *how much parking* is provided and *what charges* are levied — and should be prepared to exercise this control very firmly in the pursuit of wider objectives. But there are other methods — systems of permits and licences for entry to specified zones, for example, and the more sophisticated ideas now being studied for pricing the use of road space by electronic means ('black boxes') — which may prove useful in suitable cases.

3.7   *Importance of Public Transport*
The supremely important point which emerges from this discussion, however, is that a limitation on the use of private cars in crowded centres seems quite inevitable. This is not the same as saying that private cars should be banned at all times — such a course would run any politician or administrator into acute trouble — but some control must be exercised to restrain numbers in the interests of the community. This conclusion has extremely important implications for the development of bulk transport systems for the movement of people. These systems (buses, trains and any sophisticated derivatives thereof, or any other system which research may produce) are essential to the functioning of concentrated urban areas.

3.8   *Urban Dispersal*
The second main alternative course of action to deal with the situation in existing towns would be a policy of dispersal in order to reduce the movement loads and to provide more space for the movements that remain. This is a valid theoretical approach to traffic problems — there are possibilities of re-dispersal of activities within the envelope of the existing town or of dispersal in the form of "overspill" to places outside the town altogether — but it is an approach which requires some caution in application. The point is that when it comes to the large-scale re-

arrangement of urban areas, then many matters other than transport and traffic are involved. The whole purpose and functioning of towns comes into question. However, it is probably fair to say that most of our older towns present more or less extensive problems of redevelopment arising from sheer obsoleteness of the fabric, and that upon redevelopment the need to improve spatial standards for many purposes results in an "overspill" of population which has to be accommodated elsewhere. Thus a process of dispersal is at work, and advantage can be taken of it to improve the conditions for movement.

3.9

The Problem of the Street

The fundamental difficulty which the motor vehicle presents in urban areas is that it has rendered *the street* out-of-date as a form of urban layout. This is obviously a serious matter, because streets have been the backbone of urban areas ever since they began, and all cities are laid out on the basis of streets. Obviously all this cannot be changed overnight, but there can be no doubt that if people seek to use large numbers of vehicles in urban areas then new methods of arranging buildings are needed. When this question is explored a new design concept seems to emerge — it comprises the design of buildings, parking areas, and circulation routes as one comprehensive process. Thus, to give an example, the traditional shopping street, with its separate individual shops, gives way to the comprehensively designed shopping centre with its pedestrian areas and shared parking arrangements. The larger the area that can be dealt with in this way the greater are the opportunities for creating good environments and accommodating large amounts of traffic. But such large-scale comprehensive development presents great difficulties when building sites are in many separate ownerships. If it is to be secured in such conditions, then either the public authority must purchase the whole area, probably requiring the use of compulsory powers; or the owners of the separate pieces must be ready to co-operate in a new way, with a readiness to pool their properties and then to re-share them.

3.10

Implementation

Even granted that plans can be drawn up for the handling of motor traffic in urban areas, they will be of no avail unless they can be implemented. Here arises the most formidable difficulty of all, for it seems virtually impossible to devise plans that can be implemented except over a long period of years. No public authority, no matter how well-intentioned and even assuming all opposition is swept aside, can hope to reorganize an urban area in anything less than several decades. Yet traffic problems are endemic now, and growing rapidly worse as the ownership and usage of vehicles increases. In other words there is an urgent, immediate problem for which there is only a long-term solution. How is this dilemma to be surmounted? There is no very satisfactory answer to this problem, but the remedy can at least be seen in principle. It must lie in the control of traffic volumes to the levels that existing urban areas can reasonably accommodate *in their present condition*, but with the controls being gradually eased as capital measures are executed enabling more traffic to be handled. The problem is to devise a policy which is viable politically and administratively, which will enable this to happen. This may not be beyond solution, and it could well be a contrived variant of what is already happening in a "natural" way in cities, namely that congestion is acting as its own constraint.

Bruges, a magnificent civic square spoiled by cars.

4. APPLICATION TO HISTORIC TOWNS

4.1 *Introduction*

We have considered it necessary to present this brief review of the urban traffic problem, and the lines along which remedies must be sought, because these are the kind of problems that are arising in historic as well as ordinary towns, and these are the kind of remedies which must be applied. If there is no understanding of the problems in ordinary towns, then there cannot be understanding of them in historic towns. The fact that a town has historic and architectural value in certain parts does not alter the nature of its traffic problems, it merely gives them a different slant and makes them more difficult to solve. The rest of this report will be concerned with a discussion of the peculiar ways in which the problems are slanted in historic towns.

4.2 *The Main Difference*

The main feature which, from the point of view of traffic problems, makes a historic town different from an ordinary one is that some of the physical fabric is inviolable. It may be a matter of there being a considerable area of streets and buildings which is valuable as a whole, and cannot be altered except in minor details. It may be a matter of an area being "staked out" with valuable buildings whose presence prevents any comprehensive redevelopment even though much renewal of individual premises is acceptable. It may be a matter of a few isolated buildings whose existence influences the form of redevelopment or location of roads. Or it may be something as subtle as a medieval street pattern whose preservation is desirable even though none of the buildings are of any value. In broad terms the effect in all cases is the same — the capital measures which might be applied in an ordinary town, such as construction of new roads, road widenings, improvement of intersections, construction of car parks and comprehensive redevelopment etc. tend to be ruled out on account of the fabric of the area being unalterable. It follows, applying the "law" to which reference was made in Para 3.3, that some reduction of accessibility in historic areas is virtually inescapable. The problem is to provide sufficient accessibility to maintain the life of the area, yet not so much that the character of the area has to be changed. Within this context it is possible to set out a number of rules or precepts to be observed when plans are drawn up for historic areas. These are discussed in the following paragraphs.

4.3 *Deciding Acceptable Traffic Levels*

The general aim in a historic area must be to reduce the amount of traffic to acceptable levels. It is difficult to define "acceptable" but it obviously means that it should be possible for a person to see the area and to appreciate its qualities. In practice this means, as much as anything, that the person should have the freedom to walk around in personal safety himself and without his view being obstructed by traffic. This does not necessarily mean that the *whole* area should be "pedestrianized", though this could apply to certain streets and squares, especially if there also existed a case for pedestrianization from the point of view of, say, improving conditions for shoppers. The important point is that a conscious effort should be made to reach a conclusion as to how much and what kind of traffic is acceptable in the various parts of the area, and then to endeavour to devise a plan which will have the effect of reducing the traffic to the desired levels.

The factors which will influence the choice of traffic level will not be concerned solely with aesthetic or "visual intrusion" aspects. It will be a matter also of considering all the normal questions of safety, noise and fumes. Noise has to be considered not only from the point of view of people occupying premises adjoining the roads, but also from the angle of people wishing to converse in the street. All these aspects are combined in one important way, to which reference has already been made, namely that excessive traffic in a street of historical or architectural value, especially a residential street, tends to drive out the kind of occupiers who might be expected to cherish the buildings, and thus the cycle of decay and neglect is initiated.

4.4 *Diversionary Roads*
When considering how traffic can be reduced, a first and obvious need is to identify the "extraneous" traffic which has no need to be in the area at all, and to consider how best it can be removed. This may well involve diversionary roads on a sizeable scale, and care has to be taken that these do not indirectly harm the historic area by isolating it or ruining the approach to it. In a recent study of Bath, for example, it was found that the only acceptable method of handling the traffic extraneous to the central historic area was by means of a tunnel underneath the area.

4.5 *Sorting Out the Traffic*
The traffic "belonging" to the historic area will consist of all the commercial vehicles required for the servicing of the buildings, the buses, the cars of persons employed in the area (some of which may be used solely for the journey to work and others of which may be used for business purposes during the day) and the cars of persons visiting the area for shopping and a variety of other purposes including tourism. It is highly unlikely that all these, let alone their potential increase in the future, will be assimilable into the historic area without detriment to its character. Some degree of "sorting out and fending off" will be needed.

4.6 *Long Period Parking*
A first and very important distinction concerns the cars used purely for the journey to work. This is the category which has a very large potential increase in the future as car ownership grows. In general it will be desirable to arrange for these cars to be parked outside the historic area altogether, and for the access roads to the car parks to be similarly outside. If the car parks can be placed where pedestrian access to the historic area can be contrived, so much the better, but there need be no undue solicitude for the convenience of the all-day parker. Indeed, as already pointed out, in all but the smallest towns it is likely to be out of the question to meet all the demand for this kind of car usage, and some degree of reliance on bulk transport (most probably buses) will have to be sought.

4.6 *Parking for Shoppers, etc.*
Moving up the scale of "essentialness" one comes next to the shorter-period parker of whom the car-shoppers are the most numerous. It is not an unreasonable viewpoint for people to want the convenience of a car when shopping or paying other short visits, and to be able to park right outside the shops, or at any rate within a short distance.

50

Moreover, ease of parking may have a direct bearing on the prosperity of a shopping centre and its competitiveness with other centres. This is especially important in these days when there is a tendency for suburban centres with ample parking to open up. So any severe restraint on short-period parking, even in a historic area, needs to be approached with caution. To the extent that it is possible to generalize, it can be said that, provided the long-period parkers are kept out altogether, and given ingenuity and the construction of some modest structures and the use of some time-rationing system, there may be surprise at the amount of short-period parking that can be contrived. Even so, care must be taken to ensure that *access* to the parking areas can be organized without involving unacceptable traffic flows.

4.7
Residents' Parking
It may well be an important facet of a conservation policy for a historic area that people should be encouraged to live in the area. But it may be difficult to make a success of this unless parking can be provided. So residents' parking may have to be given a high place in the priority list.

4.8
Tourism
(Note the BTA contribution)
A historic town will, almost by definition, be a tourist attraction. All the indications are that tourism is likely to play an important role in the financing of conservation policies. But the success of tourism is bound to be linked to ease of access by car. In particular, hotels which do not have sufficient parking space could be a drag on the development of a tourist policy. Another requirement in the same field is for tourist information centres, with direct access for coaches. Whether the coaches can *park* at this centre, or whether they merely drop or pick up tourists and park elsewhere, will depend on the local conditions. But once again the approach routes for the coaches must be carefully thought out.

4.9
Servicing Traffic
Whatever controls or restraints may have to be involved in respect of private cars, there cannot be any question of preventing the access of commercial vehicles to the buildings they have to serve. The best arrangement, obviously, is for the premises to be served from the rear. This may not be as difficult to contrive in historic towns as it appears at first sight, because experience shows that the rear areas in many old towns are squalid, decayed and built over with single-storey additions. The clearance of these rear areas is a necessary part of conservation, and may well provide an opportunity for the provision of rear access and some parking. Even so cases will undoubtedly arise where servicing from the street frontage has to be accepted, at any rate for a period of years. If the traffic involved in such servicing seems likely to be excessive having regard to the character of the street, then one remedy is to arrange for the servicing to be carried out outside the hours when the public are "in occupation" of the street. This is now practised extensively on the Continent and appears to be a very simple and effective way of reserving shopping streets for pedestrians only during shopping hours. Another method of servicing premises, which so far has proved unacceptable to the retail trade but which might be capable of development in certain cases, consists of the establishment of a limited number of depots, themselves served by motor

vehicles but from which the distribution to individual shops, offices etc. is by trolleys, hand-pulled or electrically driven.

4.10   *Buses*
The point has already been made regarding the essentialness of public transport services. For practical purposes in the historic towns of this country, the bus is likely to be the system of public transport. This does not necessarily mean that the double-decker bus as it is known at present has to be accepted for all time in historic areas. The double-deckers tend to be overwhelming in size and excessively noisy, and there would seem to be a case for development of smaller vehicles more in scale with historic surroundings. This is a difficult matter because it raises questions of the need for interchange between large buses and small buses, and the whole subject of the economics of bus operation. There may be a line of advance in the possibility that if smaller and much quieter buses were to be developed, then they could be admitted on a privilege basis to streets from which all other traffic is excluded.

4.11   *Speed of Traffic*
Where it is necessary to use a narrow street for both pedestrians and vehicles, there would seem to be many advantages in restricting the speed of vehicles very closely — say to 10 or 15 m.p.h. — with the implication that the vehicles are admitted only on sufferance.

4.12   *Parking Policy in General*
Some of the points which have been discussed give a lead to the parking policy to be adopted in historic areas. In broad terms care should be taken that parking space is not introduced on a scale or in locations which will tend to attract excessive amounts of traffic into or across the area. In more detail, when buildings are redeveloped (which is bound to happen from time to time even in historic areas), then it will probably be best to limit the requirement for parking space within the curtilage to the needs of operational vehicles, including vehicles delivering or collecting goods. To the extent that short-period parking can be provided without damage to the character of the area, then some method rationing the space will probably be needed. Parking meters or disc systems are available and work reasonably well according to the circumstances. Opinions seem to differ sharply as to the appearance of parking meters — some people regard them as good examples of clean industrial design which, mounted on their slender columns, do no great harm to urban surroundings, but other people regard them as visually intrusive in all conditions. For ourselves, we think it is a matter of judging each case on its merits, and we would certainly not wish to take a firm stand on principle against meters in historic areas.

4.13   *The Long-Term Plan and The Implementation Plan*
Firstly, and most important, there is the fact that even if a plan can be drawn up setting out all the long-term objectives, there remains the problem of progressing towards it in useful, practical stages spread over a period of years. We think this calls, in effect, for an additional plan which might be called the "implementation plan" as opposed to the "long-term plan". An implementation plan is likely to comprize two distinct kinds of measures. First there needs to be a staged programme of capital works (new roads, car parks, etc.) each item of which, when carried out, will yield a worthwhile benefit. Secondly there needs to be

a traffic management policy closely geared to the capital works programme. The theoretical purpose of the management policy will be to keep traffic volumes under control and within the quantities which the area can reasonably accommodate; but, in practice, a well-designed scheme should be able to achieve more efficient circulation for essential traffic together with improved environmental conditions. The techniques of the management scheme will comprise waiting and parking restrictions, one-way streets and looped systems, elimination of awkward turns, street closures, restrictions on the passage of certain types of traffic in certain streets, and possibly the imposition of special speed limits. Provisions in the new Transport Bill should make it considerably easier to apply these measures than has been the case hitherto, and moreover it will be possible to apply them on an experimental basis until the best working arrangement has been discovered.

5. *SUMMARY*

To a considerable extent the problems presented by traffic in Historic Towns are similar to the problems in ordinary towns. There is the same distinction between the sheer difficulties of circulation and the anti-environmental effects of traffic. The same principle has to be applied of concentrating longer movements of vehicles from one locality to another onto a highway network, thus tending to relieve areas of development of all but their own traffic. The same analytical techniques can be used. The same phenomenon arises that in sizeable, densely developed areas there are fairly strict limits to the amounts of traffic that can be accommodated, which has important implications for public transport policy. However, in areas of historic and architectural importance, the environmental "constraints" are likely to be more severe, and the possibilities of making physical alterations much more restricted. This is likely to limit even more closely the amount of traffic that can be accommodated. Hence it becomes even more important to distinguish between the vehicles which are essential to the life of the area and the vehicles which can reasonably be kept " at arm's length". A long-term plan should be prepared for historic towns showing the final objectives, but it should be accompanied by an implementation plan showing how, by a combination of staged capital works and management methods, the final result can be achieved through a series of steps each of which yields benefits of its own.

Hotspur Tower, the narrowest section of the Great North Road, but an asset in stopping heavy commercial vehicles.

Alnwick, town centre, showing the proposed distributor road.

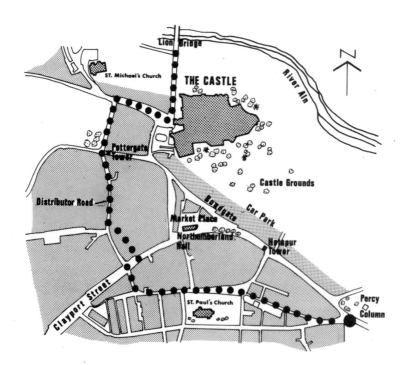

J. D. Nicholl

PEDESTRIANIZATION IN ALNWICK

Any views expressed are not necessarily those of the Local Planning Authority.

1. SIZE AND LOCATION OF ALNWICK

For those who know little of Alnwick, the town is one of Northumberland's important market towns. It is situated on the Great North Road about thirty-five miles north of Newcastle between the Tyneside conurbation and the Scottish Border Town of Berwick upon Tweed. The town owes its existence partly to its location on the early north-south communication system as a main staging post in the days of the stage coach, and partly to its function as a defence post. Traffic which helped to create the town's importance now provides one of the main problems in determining future planning policies. The function of defence post has given Alnwick much of its character, and one cannot mention the town without reference to Alnwick Castle which, more than anything else, dominates the town and, in some ways, its very existence. As a medieval walled town protected by the Castle, its military importance stimulated early economic growth, and it is perhaps largely due to the presence of Alnwick Castle that we have a historic town to protect.

Alnwick, which is a growth point in the County structure, has a population of about seven thousand.

2. PLAN FORM OF ALNWICK

An early feature of the plan form of Alnwick is the fork in the road system at the Bondgate/Market Street junction. In later times Fenkle Street was added and the central triangle created. This formed the "green" of the medieval village. It later became colonized with beer houses and shops. During the period of border warfare, when Alnwick became a walled town, the restricted space within the safety of the walls put a premium on the central location of properties and resulted in some infilling of the ancient market square. The line of the old wall still dominates the plan of the town and although the wall itself has for the greater part disappeared, the Pottergate Tower and the Hotspur Tower still remain, the latter surely representing (until the by-pass is completed) the narrowest section of the Great North Road. In some ways a problem, the Tower, with its restricted entrance, is also an asset because it already has the effect (without any planning magic) of stopping heavy commercial vehicles from entering the main street at this point.

3. TRAFFIC FACTORS AND THE ENVIRONMENT – WITH PARTICULAR REFERENCE TO PEDESTRIANIZATION

Three points must be examined :
(a) Is there a need for pedestrianization?
(b) Assuming that there is, to what extent?
(c) How can this be achieved without detriment to aesthetic and other

factors, within the limits of the financial resources available?
A fourth consideration, of course, must be that of programming the proposed development of the town centre.

3.1   *Is there a need?* Yes, there is! Perhaps at this point it is worth mentioning that more than a hundred years ago it was proposed that Alnwick should be by-passed to obviate inconvenience in the town centre. Plans can still be seen which indicate a road line not very different from that which has now been adopted. Constructional work on the by-pass did, incidentally, commence a few weeks ago.

When the first stages of the by-pass are completed, it will remove about 45% of the present traffic from the town. In five to ten years, however, it is likely that the volume of traffic, although of a different nature — i.e. a predominance of private car and service vehicle over the heavier type of commercial vehicle, will be back to its present level. Whilst volumes are not high compared with many towns there is, nevertheless, an acute car parking and servicing problem creating difficulties for the pedestrian and detrimental to the environment of the shopping and business centre, i.e. the historic core.

3.2   *To what extent do we want to remove the vehicle from the centre?*
A number of questions rise here too. First of all is it physically possible to remove completely all traffic? There are, in fact, difficulties in doing so, especially concerning servicing arrangements. Next we must assess the effect upon the aesthetic aspects if traffic is completely removed. Quite clearly a lot is to be gained, for example, more freedom for the pedestrian, more safety and more opportunity of enjoying the environmental qualities of the town centre. We would also hope that proposals involving a substantial degree of pedestrianization would, at the same time, provide more convenience for the car use provided, of course — and this is most important — that car parks are located in sensible places. One must, however, consider the scale of development in the centre of the town and the relationship between the "open space" and the buildings which surround it. It has been suggested that a case can be put forward for a very limited amount of traffic movement in the Bondgate Within/Market Street area, the inter-relationship of the space and buildings being of such a scale that it could perhaps benefit from some form of interest other than exclusively human activity. Perhaps there are examples in other towns where this consideration arises.

3.3   *How can we remove the motor vehicle from the town centre?*
The basis of any plan ought to be a new road which will distribute traffic from one part of the town to another and give easy access to car parks and service areas at the rear of the shopping/business area, i.e. the historic core.

A major consideration in selecting a line for this road must be the need to achieve a correct balance between easy access and adequate standards in an attractive setting. Although this road will effect improvements in the town centre, it must not be achieved at the expense of opening up and creating unattractive vistas which will be seen by people entering the town.

As previously mentioned, a decision has yet to be taken on the line of the distributor road, but there are a number of considerations which will have to be taken into account in connection with this road. Obviously, what would appear at first sight to be a most direct and convenient route for the distributor road is not necessarily that which will have the least damaging effect upon the environment. It is a balance which has to be very carefully determined.

4. THE PEDESTRIAN AND THE ENVIRONMENT

To achieve pedestrianization and convenience in the town centre, it seems to me that alternative car parking and servicing facilities are vital in order to achieve this aim. It may be necessary to plan the removal of cars in the town centre over a progressive period, for the gradual improvement of the environment.

The visual aspect of the town centre is completely ruined by the indiscriminate parking of motor vehicles on the cobbles. These cobbled areas play a most important part in the townscape, and it is absolutely necessary to adopt a positive parking or (a better description) "An Environmental Policy".

In association with the gradual removal of vehicles from the town centre and the provision of car parks, it is also essential to ensure that there are adequate pedestrian ways leading from these car parks to the shopping and business area. It is fortunate that a number of these already exist, even if some of them represent narrow passages of some four to five feet in width. These are an important element in pedestrian movement. The problems of traffic signs and the yellow "No Parking" lines which appear so readily in our town centres are often mentioned. Alnwick is no exception, but it is hoped that the implementation of a plan to remove the motor vehicle will also remove these elements which are detrimental to the townscape.

5. SUMMARY

An analysis of the problems relative to the town centre of Alnwick clearly indicates that the exercise must not be one of wholesale redevelopment. In this respect it is perhaps fortunate that surveys carried out on shopping requirements reveal that, even allowing for population increases, there is no need for an overall increase in the shopping area, and therefore future proposals can be based more on the adaptation of buildings than upon widespread redevelopment.

The need for change comes about from the familiar cause of the increasing number of motor vehicles, which results in traffic congestion and a most harmful effect upon the visual qualities of the town centre.

Decay and obsolescence have affected many buildings in the centre of the town and behind the main street facades there are large areas of underuse and dereliction. The condition of buildings is, of course, a major factor, and much more work will be necessary to get to the root of this problem. The preservation of the character of Alnwick, however, involves more than the retention of certain buildings. The intimate scale of the town centre needs to be preserved and in this respect groups of buildings can be of importance, even if individually some of the buildings in the group are not of outstanding merit. This aspect will be considered in some detail in our "An Environmental Study".

To sum up, it may be said that Alnwick has problems common to most town centres of its size in addition to the special features due to its historic character.

Alnwick illustrations by Northumberland County Council.

A. A. Wood

FOOT STREETS IN NORWICH

The urban fabric of Norwich, one of the major historic cities in Britain, is experiencing relentless pressure from motor traffic. It would be unthinkable to sacrifice the historic and architectural legacies of yesterday in order to cater for the unlimited use of the motor car - a relatively short-lived innovation. Perhaps the special problems of historic cities would receive more sympathetic consideration in monetary terms if their earning potential was more widely appreciated. It has been estimated that tourism contributed some £281 million to the national economy last year and it is our historic towns and buildings which many overseas visitors come to see. If the fabric of cities like Norwich and York are allowed to deteriorate then Britain will be financially as well as aesthetically poorer.

If wholesale reconstruction is inconceivable in historic cities then it is obvious that we have to accept some degreee of discipline and establish a clear division between those streets required by vehicles and those required by people. Any feeling that this approach is anti-motorist must be dispelled by making people fully aware of the situation which will shortly arise in our city centres if car ownership and use are allowed to multiply unchecked. The situation is rapidly approaching where it will be intolerable for motorist and pedestrian alike, and unless something is done to improve conditions, and that quickly, the stage will soon be reached where both will be deterred from using our city streets. The tragic result would be economic decline and corresponding deterioration in our city centres. This must not be allowed to happen.

In the United States where the amount of car ownership and use is greater than in Europe, an answer was sought in the development of out-of-town shopping centres. These flourished but usually at the expense of established downtown shopping areas. Accordingly, it has been recognized that out-of-town shopping centres will not solve the problems facing European cities and many town planners have advocated pedestrian/vehicular segregation as being the only practical remedy for the damage caused by ever increasing traffic congestion.

It is relatively easy to build traffic-free shopping precincts in cases where comprehensive redevelopment takes place, but the problems are much more acute when dealing with established shopping streets where the provision of rear access facilities is rarely possible. This is particularly the case in historic cities, such as Norwich, where the compact medieval street framework would be irrevocably damaged by the wholesale insertion of rear access roads.

Most planning authorities have plans to pedestrianize congested shopping streets but almost nothing has been achieved in Britain, many proposals being shelved after meeting opposition from shop-keepers who believe their trade will suffer if vehicles are excluded from shopping areas. Practical experiments which have been carried out in a number of enlightened continental cities have done much to disprove this popular fallacy.

In order to examine the practicability of promoting traffic-free streets in Norwich, visits have been made to Essen, Dusseldorf, Cologne and Copenhagen to examine the techniques adopted in the conversion of former all-purpose streets to pedestrian use. This research confirmed the practical benefits of foot streets and showed that, provided sensible and adequate periods are allowed for deliveries, the lack of rear access facilities is not an insuperable barrier to the creation of foot streets. Trading methods, servicing arrangements and other aspects of continental shopping streets are similar to those found in this country, and there appeared to be no reason why foot streets should not be put to the test in Norwich.

The Draft Urban Plan for Norwich has as two of its aims, the need to preserve the unique character of the city, while developing it further as a regional centre. These apparently incompatible aims are reconciled by the fact that there must be some discipline on the movements of the private motorist, coupled with ease of parking adjacent to the business centre. Motorists will reach these inner car parks by travelling along pre-scribed loop roads off the inner ring road.

Precedence will be given to the shopper and other short-stay parkers as their continuing presence is regarded as essential for the commercial health of the city. A preferential pricing system will be progressively used to achieve this aim and eventually long-stay parkers will have to park out-side the central area.

With a policy of some limitation on the use of private cars, every effort must be made to assure full use of public transport. To give it a significant advantage over other road users public transport will be allowed to cross the city centre on certain specified roads.

Two distinct pedestrian areas are defined in the central area - the shopping area and the historic area around the Cathedral. More attractive conditions for sightseeing and shopping will be created gradually by restrictions on entry of vehicles into the historic area and progressive prohibition of vehicles from central shopping streets during main shopping hours.

A nucleus of pedestrian shopping streets exists and the Plan proposes these will be gradually expanded to form the traffic-free shopping core. Stage One in the process has been achieved with the conversion of an existing all-purpose street into the first foot street - London Street.

London Street is one of the best shopping streets in the city and has considerable townscape value, winding between the Market Place and the Cathedral area. Prior to closure it acted as a short cut for traffic crossing the central area and carried up to 600 vehicles per hour. Being narrow and winding pedestrians were forced into close proximity to vehicular traffic and the stage was being reached where both the quality of the environment and the commercial health of the street were in jeopardy.

In the case of London Street, we did not have to convince the shop-keepers of the benefits of the proposals to create a foot street. They gained practical experience of the street closed to vehicular traffic when emergency sewer reconstruction had to take place in 1965. Although apprehensive at first, they experienced a slight rise in trade during the repair period and, accordingly, were not opposed to the scheme.

The legal powers used to create the foot streets in Norwich are contained in the Road Traffic Regulation Act, 1967. Section One of the Act gives powers to close a street for "avoiding danger to persons using the road." It must be appreciated that, as yet, there are no means of closing streets for purely environmental reasons, but it is hoped that legislation will shortly be forthcoming to make this possible.

In Norwich pedestrian projects are first initiated as experimental schemes (under Section 9 of the above Act) and this has proved to have three positive advantages. It is a democratic approach, it is cheap to install and avoids any possibility of abortive expenditure, and it gives room for manoeuvre, a facility found to be very useful in practice.

During the preparation of the scheme exhaustive consultations were made with the traders, business associations, suppliers' organizations and other interested parties, and a number of points arose which caused amendments to be made to the outline proposals. The need for full consultations and the creation of good public relations cannot be too fully emphasized when undertaking projects of this nature. Each successful scheme lays the foundations for future projects.

The experimental scheme was inaugurated on the 17th July, 1967, for a trial period of six months at a cost of £1,800. Because of the particular layout of the area two sections of London Street were completely closed to traffic and a further section of London Street and several interdependent streets converted to service access only. Servicing to the shops in the closed sections (which for the most part have no rear access) is by trolley or by carry, there being no distance greater than 120 ft. from a point where a service vehicle may stop.

Before the experiment London Street acted as a short cut for traffic and there was some anxiety expressed as to the effect of removing this link from the city's traffic network. In the event, apart from some difficulty on the first day, traffic smoothly re-adjusted itself to alternative routes, many drivers re-routing themselves in the outskirts of the city.

In practice, as found in the Strøget scheme in Copenhagen, only about 40% of the traffic formerly using London Street diverted to the surrounding network. It appears that Professor Northcote Parkinson's law can work in reverse and that lack of good alternative routes should not necessarily be a barrier to experiments of this kind.

With the removal of vehicular traffic there was a marked increase in the number of pedestrians using London Street. Some 300 shoppers were interviewed on a Saturday shortly after the start of the experiment and, predictably, 94% were in favour of the scheme. It is interesting that some 52% of the persons interviewed were motorists, and 83% of these said they had not been inconvenienced by the street being closed to traffic.

The shopkeepers' reaction to the scheme was one of wholehearted approval. They considered the removal of vehicular traffic created a greatly improved business atmosphere and better working conditions. The street became quieter, cleaner and free from diesel fumes. Customers are no longer harassed by traffic and this has led to an increase in impulse buying.

There are thirty-two shops in London Street and thirty of these have given an indication of the effect on trade during the six-month experimental period. Twenty-eight shops did more trade and in twenty cases percentage increase figures were given. Two increased by something under 5%, six by 5%, eleven by 10% and one by 20%. The two shops which recorded decreased sales were less than 5% down. When interviewed one of the shopkeepers revealed there had been a fall in trade in all their branches last year and he did not attribute their slight loss to the experiment. The other shop showing a slight loss was a high-class costumier, some of whose clientele are wealthy, elderly people who expect to be able to go everywhere by car. This appears to be a minority class who can never be accommodated in pedestrian streets.

With the consumer boom which has been experienced recently, it is difficult to determine to what extent the increases in trade can be attributed to the experimental closure. London Street contains a predominance of high-class and specialist retailers whose share of the boom is not likely to have been as great as those selling hardware, electrical goods and furniture. Two department stores attempted to separate their increase in trade from the national increase and felt that about 4% to 5% could be attributed to the closure.

Clearly, on the evidence of the London Street project, fears of loss of trade through pedestrianization are groundless, the reverse being the case. The servicing arrangements have proved satisfactory and in the service-only streets the traffic flows have been so reduced as to make them virtually pedestrian streets in main shopping hours. The experimental scheme proved to be a great success; the dramatically improved environment giving better shopping and working conditions with the added bonus of improved trade.

No objections were received at the end of the experimental period and the Minister of Transport confirmed the Order making London Street a permanent foot street. Loan sanction for the financing of the permanent scheme has now been granted, and the permanent works will commence as soon as the summer influx of tourists is over. The permanent scheme is estimated to cost £17,000 and includes repaving the closed sections of the street to a uniform level, new street lighting, street furniture and semi-mature trees. Showcases and continental type cafes will be introduced as outdoor extensions of the shops.

Besides the refurnishing of the street, the shopkeepers are being encouraged to collaborate in a face-lift scheme. A colour scheme, together with fascia designs and lettering styles has been prepared to assist the traders. A similar face-lift project in Magdalen Street, Norwich, in 1959 proved a remarkably successful experiment in environmental improvement.

Following the success of the London Street experiment, two minor shopping streets, Lower Goat Lane and Dove Street became experimental foot streets on the 24th June, 1968.

Vehicles are totally excluded from Lower Goat Lane (except in emergencies) but Dove Street became the first foot street to be tackled on a time service basis.

The concept of limited-time servicing is a basic principle in the creation of a traffic-free core in central Norwich and the problems are currently receiving further examination in a more complicated situation in an important street - White Lion Street. The conversion of White Lion Street

London Street, Norwich, before 17 July, 1967. Pedestrian/vehicle conflict and danger. The child in the push-chair is within an ace of death. The potential quality of environment is not exploited.

After 17 July, 1967, the same street is quiet and safe. The environment is immeasurably improved. Shopping turnover has increased by an average of 6½%.

Photographs by A. A. Wood

to limited-time servicing will establish a valuable precedent in the extension of the idea to other central shopping streets in Norwich.

The London Street project has proved that pedestrian streets can be created without the need to construct rear service networks or relief roads, given *full* consultation with affected parties and given the will of the local authority to effect environmental improvement. It is hoped that experience in Norwich will present other authorities with the practical proof that foot streets can have considerable economic advantages as well as environmental benefits and thus provide the weapons to attack the present inertia on this subject.

LEGAL AND FINANCIAL MATTERS

1. *INTRODUCTION*

    The impact of road traffic is possibly the greatest problem facing those
    concerned with the conservation of Historic Towns. The statutory powers
    which are available and the financial arrangements which have been made
    to provide for the needs of road users can help to promote the interests of
    conservation. It is therefore necessary to study these matters because
    prompt and effective action in the interests of conservation can be serious-
    ly hindered by uncertainty about the complicated procedures of central
    and local government and obscurities of highway law.

2. *JURISDICTIONS*

    Jurisdiction in traffic regulation and parking is vested in different author-
    ities which may not necessarily be the authorities responsible for planning
    of highways. In some cases an authority is responsible for all these functions,
    but in others, only for some of them. In the latter case formulation and
    implementation of policies which co-ordinate traffic control and town
    planning can be complicated.

3. *THE HISTORIC TOWNS*

    In 1964 the Council for British Archaeology published a Memorandum
    drawing attention to the implications of "Traffic in Towns" and produced
    a list of 324 towns of special historic interest in Britain. Of the 267
    Historic Towns in England and Wales, 19 are County Boroughs. These are
    large towns like York and Bath. 173 of the smaller Historic Towns are
    either Municipal (i.e. non-County) Boroughs or Urban Districts whilst the
    remainder are in rural districts and exercise no powers per se.

4. *THE SPECIAL CASE OF COUNTY BOROUGHS*

    In County Boroughs the County Borough Council is the sole authority for
    traffic and parking, planning and highways. There are only a very few
    trunk roads in County Boroughs. The situation is therefore at its simplest
    administratively. But this only applies to the 19 Historic Towns which are
    County Boroughs.

5. *PLANNING (OUTSIDE COUNTY BOROUGHS)*

    The planning authority for an area other than a County Borough is always
    the County Council. The planning authority is able to delegate some of
    its functions to local borough and urban district councils; appeals can be
    made against the planning authorities' decisions to the Minister of Housing
    and Local Government.

6. *HIGHWAYS*

6.1   Highway responsibilities vary according to the status of the road as well
        as the status of the district in which it is situated.

6.2   *Trunk Roads*

Trunk roads are the responsibility of the Minister of Transport who pays in full the costs of highway improvements (including improvements to other roads which benefit the trunk road) and the maintenance of road. In exercizing this function local authorities act as his agent and are paid 100% of the costs of doing the work plus a sum for administration.

6.3   *Other Roads*

(a) *County Boroughs*

The authority responsible for the maintenance of all non-trunk roads in County Boroughs is the County Borough Council.

(b) *Large Towns*

In municipal boroughs and urban districts both having populations over 20,000 the County Council is responsible for the maintenance of all "county" roads (i.e. those classified as classes I, II and III) and county bridges. The borough or urban district council are responsible for the non-county roads. However, the borough or the urban district can "claim" the responsibility of maintenance of county roads in their area. In this case they make arrangements with the County Council for the financing of these operations. Boroughs and urban districts who do this are called "claiming authorities".

(c) *Small Towns*

In those municipal boroughs and urban districts which have populations of under 20,000, the situation is the same as in large towns except that they cannot become claiming authorities.

(d) *Rural Districts*

In rural districts the County Council is responsible for the maintenance of all non-trunk roads.

7.   *HIGHWAY FINANCE*

7.1   Since the coming into operation of section 21 of the Local Government Act, 1966, grants from Central Government are paid on the following basis:

7.2   *Trunk Roads*

100% of all maintenance and improvement costs plus a grant to cover administrative costs.

7.3   *Principal Roads*

75% of all improvement costs. Maintenance is helped by the rate support grant (otherwise from the rates). Grant is also paid on traffic management schemes for the benefit of principal roads.

7.4   *Other Roads*

The costs of all maintenance and improvement is met out of the rates and the rate support grant.

(The rates support grant is made as a "block grant" to local authorities, and each decides how it will use this money. Where appropriate the County Councils make detailed arrangements with the county district councils).

8.   *TRAFFIC REGULATION*

8.1   Traffic regulation comprises the restrictions and compulsions on the movement and stopping of vehicles (except at parking places). Here again, the responsibility depends on the type of road and the status of the authority.

8.2	*Trunk Roads*
	(a) The Minister of Transport exercises the power of traffic regulation on all trunk roads. (In Wales the Secretary of State for Wales). Local authorities do not act as his agent.
	(b) *County Boroughs*
	County Borough Councils have the power over all non-trunk roads in their areas.
	(c) *Large Towns*
	Urban District and Municipal Borough Councils both having populations of over 20,000 may exercize these powers over all non-trunk roads within their area.
	(d) *Small Towns and Rural Districts*
	In all other cases (i.e. rural districts and municipal and urban districts of populations of less than 20,000) the power is exercised on non-trunk roads by the County Council.

9. PARKING

9.1 The power to provide parking places both on and off street is exercizable by the appropriate local authority — i.e. County Borough Councils for their area and the appropriate county district council for the rest of the country (i.e. the local borough, urban or rural district council without restriction on population). The Minister of Transport's consent is required for parking places on trunk roads, otherwise he does not normally exercize powers to provide parking places on roads. Until recently the Minister made orders designating parking places where parking meters might be used, but this has now been delegated to local authorities.

9.2 Parish Councils are empowered only to provide parking places for motor cycles and push bikes.

9.3 It can thus be seen that the majority of Historic Towns will fall into complicated administrative situations. For example a town may contain a trunk road for which the Minister is responsible, motivated by considerations of national traffic policy. And the County Council may be the highway authority for some roads and also the planning authority while the Town Council is the authority for other highways, traffic and parking.

10. ROLE OF POLICE AND TRAFFIC WARDENS

The police are allowed to regulate traffic and parking only in an emergency. Normally the police only control traffic in accordance with the regulations made by the traffic and parking authorities. In this situation the role of the police is to enforce the various measures — traffic regulation, parking and speed limits and it is important to remember that police co-operation will only be secured where orders can practicably be enforced. Attempts at enforcing an unrealistic order are likely to bring the law and the police into disrepute. Traffic wardens are police auxiliaries employed by the police authority with certain police powers to control traffic and on-street parking. On-street parking may also be controlled by attendants employed by the local authority but these have no police powers.

11. POWERS

11.1 *Traffic Regulation*
The Road Traffic Regulation Act, 2967, contains the powers for traffic

regulation. Broadly, these amount to the control of traffic by such means as :

(a) One-way streets

(b) Prohibition of waiting and/or loading and unloading

(c) Prohibiting the use of roads by through traffic and

(d) Overtaking restrictions.

Certain of the orders may be made by local authority without reference to the Minister although others require his confirmation or consent before they become effective.

It is essential to realize that traffic regulation orders can only be made for the purposes defined in the Act. These are mainly concerned with promoting road safety and easing vehicular congestion, although traffic can be controlled for preventing damage to the road or to riparian property and to preserve the existing character of the road. (The next stage would be to widen the reasons for which traffic regulation orders can be made to include the preservation or improvement of the amenities of the area through which the road runs.) There are thus constraints on the exercize of these powers and these are further limited by the fact that it is only in demonstrable cases of danger or damage that reasonable access can be denied. The existing character of the road has been regarded as including the traffic on it and so its preservation would not extend to the exclusion of all traffic which might be desirable on environmental grounds.

Experimental orders, extending to a maximum of eighteen months, may be made for the same reasons as permanent orders.

11.2 *Speed Limits*

The Road Traffic Regulation Act empowers the Minister and local authorities to impose speed limits on roads. These are largely imposed on safety grounds and must be enforceable — it is therefore clear that speed limits of less than 30 m.p.h. will only be authorized in quite exceptional circumstances. If a local authority wishes to impose or alter a speed limit it must obtain the consent of the Minister.

11.3 *Parking Controls*

The Road Traffic Regulation Act gives local authorities power to provide parking places both on and off-street. Where a charge is to be made for parking on the street the local authority must obtain the Minister's prior consent to the scheme of control. Where no charge is to be made, the Minister's consent is not required, but the Minister must approve any "device" used, e.g. a parking disc. Off-street parking is in the hands of the local parking authority.

12. *TRAFFIC CONTROL FOR AMENITY*

12.1 Existing powers are largely concerned with promoting road safety and traffic flow and very little can be done for environmental reasons.

12.2 Various local authorities have appreciated the need to control traffic for amenity reasons and have anticipated national legislation by introducing private Acts of Parliament. Leeds did so in 1966 and was followed by Manchester, Portsmouth and Guildford in 1967. In general these powers provide for the control of traffic to improve amenity and environment in both residential and shopping areas.

12.3   New legislation proposed for the Transport and Planning Bills, 1967/68 seeks to remedy this lack of general powers. It will allow for the partial and permanent closure of streets to vehicular traffic on amenity grounds and will thus allow traffic to be regulated for a purpose not directly bearing on the traffic itself.

13.   *TRAFFIC SIGNS*

Traffic signs are an essential ancillary to traffic, but are frequently regarded as a major source of visual intrusion. This depends on how intelligently they are sited. Signs are designed and intended to give information to the motorist and the prime consideration in their siting must be to fulfil this function. The Ministry's "Traffic Signs Manual" gives guidance on how this can be done efficiently, effectively and aesthetically. The Minister has powers to authorize special signs (including those of a different size to normal). These powers are only likely to be used in exceptional circumstances.

14.   *PUBLIC RELATIONS*

14.1   Road traffic statues and their subordinate procedure regulations lay down a mandatory procedure which binds local authorities in the way in which they make orders. The procedure is designed to ensure that the public have an opportunity to make representations about the measures under consideration. In general the following patterns of events have to be followed :

(a) the local authority must consult with the police and may also consult with interested parties
(b) the proposals are advertised, nationally in the London Gazette and locally in the local press and on the roads concerned
(c) objections may be made by the public and are considered by the local authority; a public inquiry may be held
(d) the local authority decides whether or not to make the order.

14.2   Any person has the right to object to a proposed order provided that he does so during the statutory period provided. Such objection can be made either to the local authority or, where the Minister has to confirm the order, to the Minister. Objections must be considered before an order is brought into operation.

14.3   Where a public inquiry is held any objector may be heard in person or be represented.

15.   *ROLE OF THE MINISTRY OF TRANSPORT*

15.1   Apart from being directly concerned in making orders on trunk roads and in prescribing traffic signs, the Minister is concerned in confirming and giving his consent to orders made by local authority. In this respect the Minister must consider any outstanding objections and thus is the ultimate arbitor of the citizens' rights. The Minister has the right to amend or revoke any order in the light of objection or other considerations. It is essential to remember that, under existing legislation, the Minister (except in Greater London) has no right to direct a local authority to manage its traffic, but this is likely to be changed.

15.2   The Ministry of Transport provides advice to local authorities on the use of powers by means of publications, liaison and through its regional Divisional Road Engineer organization.

Mismanagement! The fine classical market at Exeter empty and disfigured.

management

Graeme Shankland

CONSERVATION THROUGH PLANNING

Conserving our historic towns and cities is the best way of ensuring the individuality of our urban inheritance; of seeing that our towns are of themselves; different from each other and from those of other countries. This tangible link with the best of the past, through the buildings, streets, spaces, trees, views, the way the town fits the landscape, all these make up the total personality of a place. And it is through the impact of this on us as individuals that we make contact with our community.

This power and magic given by a vivid sense of place has even more importance for the modern world than it had. This is seen most sharply at moments of crisis when the passions of a community and nation are deeply moved. Warsaw was almost totally and systematically destroyed. In 1945 a cost-benefit study of where to site the future capital of a reconstructed Poland might well have proposed a new site or an expansion of historic and undamaged Cracow. The people, though, moved back to the site of Warsaw and made makeshift homes in cellars and rubble. The new government to symbolize the identity of national rebirth with that of the historic capital re-erected the column of King Sigismund, the founder of Warsaw, as almost its first act of rebuilding and went on to reconstruct from almost nothing whole sectors of medieval and renaissance Warsaw.

More recently, France, in a deliberate act of state policy intended to raise national prestige, has embarked on a policy of cleaning and restoration and conservation in Paris and a selected number of other historic French cities. The French, since Louis XIV, have been more self-conscious of the international importance of French culture than we have of our own and are today pursuing this splendid, expensive and centrally inspired policy as much, I suspect, for their own self-respect as for the enjoyment of tourists.

The identification of tourist development with a programme for the conservation and restoration of monuments, towns and archaeological sites, is a rapidly developing objective of countries which take tourist development seriously as an economic objective. Developing countries like Greece, Jugoslavia, Tunisia, Iran, all have important programmes which would not exist were it not for their conviction that conservation of their unique heritage was central to the business of attracting tourists and winning their proportion of one of the world's most rapidly expanding international industries.

We have a very odd attitude in Britain to tourists. Foreign tourism is growing rapidly, but we have done little so far by planned action consciously to encourage it. Anyone who can afford to travel for pleasure outside his own town or village is a tourist and this is the first thing most families save their money for. So the growth of tourism is directly linked with the increase in the standard of living. No country can afford to neglect tourism today, least of all one with a balance of payments' problem and a need to replace imperially-orientated markets.

Tourists, too, are not all foreigners! In making our historic towns more attractive we should win more visitors from home. Nor are the benefits simply economic; by the time every Japanese leaves school he will have visited all the important historic places, shrines, temples and gardens in Japan. Those local authorities in Britain who organize school trips and exchange visits at home and abroad are doing a most important and valuable educational job in an imaginative way.

UNESCO is helping to organize conservation programmes throughout the world. I have been studying Isfahan, perhaps the least known of the world's twelve most important and intact historic cities. Iran starts this month on its new five-year economic development plan which, inevitably, has urbanization and communications development as the chief physical means of raising the standard of living. As every existing town in Iran, except the capital, Teheran, is historically and architecturally unique, they face the problems of conservation in their most acute form.

But so does most of the world, because city and town building, both as a means and an end of economic and social growth, now confronts the world on a gigantic scale and the spectre of failure moves towards us at an accelerating pace. We cannot escape from urbanization, better or worse; either we harness these forces for social ends or our cities, historic or shanty-town, will be submerged in chaos and us with them.

It is not enough just for a nation to be rich as the crisis in the cities of the United States shows, if you do not spend the money on social objectives and are reluctant to accept physical planning as a means to this end. Today in most western countries it is the mis-spent wealth in development which is the biggest agent of the destruction of historic cities, not physical decay.

Our historic towns and cities will not get the attention they must have until out political leaders, national and local, are seized with their import-ance. Few in Britain are - at any rate at national level. Why do they not care? And so long as political perspectives are limited to a few weeks and months ahead, this is not surprising; so it is our job to help extend these perspectives.

* * * * * * * *

The most important task in conserving historic towns and cities is to arm all those in any way interested with the knowledge and understanding of the nature of the problem and of the processes, money and ideas necessary to tackle it, especially those carrying considerable political influence locally. From this basis we can then seek to win further under-standing among those who decide our destinies; wherever they are, in the Treasury or in City and County Treasuries, in private or in public enter-prise.

Much of the difficulty lies not so much in the complexity of the subject, but the proliferation of powers and bodies available and involved in tackling it. Patrick Abercrombie, in the context of local government organization, once described Lancashire as "looking like a moth-eaten blanket". This term could apply to our problem. We are bound to try and make conservation work with the powers and bodies we have and are

The Luxembourg Palace, Paris, before and after cleaning and restoration.

shortly getting, but there will still be plenty of holes in this blanket and anyway it is put together out of a patchwork of legislation still being stitched up. We have the Civic Amenities Act last year and now two very important Bills, the new Town and Country Planning Bill and the Transport Bill.

I will concentrate my efforts on trying to lay bare the essentials of the problem as a whole to help interested people in considering ideas about the long term all-round strategy needed for any particular town over the next ten years or so. For powers, leaders, Ministers, economic crises come and go and local government boundaries and functions will all be in a state of flux as never before during this period and we will all be put to it to keep our eyes on the main objectives.

* * * * * * * *

Perhaps the most fundamental point of all is that the processes of change and renewal in our towns and cities never stop. The cycle of renewal is always turning, however slowly, as the standard and mode of life of the people rises - and at a rate directly related to the activities they generate.

What is new in recent years is the greater rapidity of the revolution of this cycle. The motive power of renewal, effective economic demand, bottled up during wartime, restricted by building licensing for some years later, was unleashed in the mid-1950s on the centres of historic towns in Britain when most were unprepared to cope with it. The old type Development Plans and the old type planners and politicians were shown wanting and much needless destruction and shoddy development has been the result, despite the elaborate development control "policing" provisions of the 1947 Town and Country Planning Act. I would say we were caught napping because too much of our planning effort has been taken up with the purely negative aspects of statutory planning given prominence in the legislation itself. We should be drawing the lessons of these episodes while we have a short breathing space (the Chancellor's "two years' hard slog") during which to organize ourselves better.

Because urban renewal is a continuous process, so must be the planning policies to guide it. It is not just redevelopment, but also improvement and rehabilitation. Every historic town must be equipped therefore, with a programme, short and long term, for conservation and "revitalization". This programme has to be made up of complementary aspects, be costed in economic and social terms, and cover every aspect of the work from traffic management to building extensions.

At this point we run into the second problem, the all too common failure to see planning as a total activity embracing movement as well as buildings. Planning process and planning policy must be equally concerned with what happens in the spaces between the buildings - above all the roads - as with the buildings themselves. Roads and pavements are the means of experiencing the buildings, not just means of access to them, and if we cannot move about on foot in ease and comfort and enjoy this experience, the buildings might just as well not be there, for anyone save their occupiers.

Traffic in this sense is, and will be for some years, by far the biggest single menace to our historic towns - for the simple reason that motor vehicle ownership and use is still outstripping the funds available for by-passes, secondary road construction to facilitate precincting, car park construction and other means needed to channel and contain the motor vehicle.

The new Planning and Transport Bills should give us important new tools for conservation. Until they become Acts and regulations are made under them, local authorities will not know how best to use them. I would, though, like to make some proposals.

First, I think all historic towns should have "Structure Plans" prepared for them under the new Planning Act, whatever size they are. I mention this because the material on the new legislation suggests that only larger towns will get "Structure Plans" in the first instance.

Once this is done, historic centres within these towns should become "action areas" leading to the early preparation of detailed local plans within them.

This is necessary to give effect to Part I intentions of the Civic Amenities Act; such areas can be designated "conservation areas", but under the Civic Amenities Act, and conservation areas, listed buildings, preservation policies and urban design objectives and transport plans can all become integral parts of a town's overall planning programme.

The Minister has himself referred to the Conservation Areas as the "jaws", the teeth being in different Acts, including the 1962 Local Authorities (Historic Buildings) Act.

Because of this, we must therefore face the problems of interlocking our new transport plans with the Structure Plans; traffic management with action area proposals, all under an umbrella of a single planning and conservation policy. This task will not be made easier by the fact that this combined task is divided between two Ministries whose approval has to be sought separately and up to eight different officers in local authorities each usually serving his own committee. For all historic towns which are non-county boroughs - that is the great majority - there are two authorities involved in planning decisions, sometimes antagonistic and often unequally effective.

It seems surprising, considering this, that anything gets done at all. It does so when key people care and take trouble, when there is a decisive leadership either by local political figures or by town clerks and other officers and preferably by both. All this usually happens when there is active local opinion, even from a small group, agitating for the right things. Often, too, the most effective way of getting things moving and making a fresh start, is calling in a planning consultant who, if organized on a proper interprofessional basis, in addition to bringing his own ideas to bear, can act as an effective catalyst among otherwise inactive agents.

There is also one important principle about planning as an effective public and political activity. In planning, like photography, painting a picture, or playing the piano, you must employ both the positive and the negative. You must not only say "no" and give reasons and suggest alternative ways of achieving the same objectives, but say "yes, - this is what we must do" with these provisos. And not just wait but go out and find people to do it. The public will stand for tough restrictive policies if it also sees positive planning and development going on. In fact, the success of planning and its reputation with the public often lies in striking the right balance between restriction and activity, and in practice this really means we need more power to the elbow of positive planning and the positive planners.

To take a closer look at the relationships between these two sides of urban life and activity - and therefore of urban planning and conservation - the "static" and the "mobile", the "buildings" and the "roads". In total they make up the texture of our historic towns; they depend on each other just as the human body depends on the central nervous system, but the forces that operate upon them are different and hence the pressures that result have different effects.

The report of the Study Group on traffic sums up the situation with great lucidity and the minimum number of words. It concludes, rightly in my view, that the problems of traffic in historic towns is in essence no different from ordinary towns, but some reduction of accessibility in historic areas is virtually inescapable, and I quote :- "The problem is to provide sufficient accessibility to maintain the life of the area, yet not so much that the character of the area has to be changed." I wish to add a few points of emphasis.

First, parking: every historic town must have a comprehensive and com-prehensible parking policy based on the principle that there will always be a greater demand for parking space in the heart of the historic fabric than can ever be provided, so the policy must be restrictive and selective, pena-lizing the long term parker in the sense that he must walk further or change his mode of transport, in favour of the short term shopper; and preferring the tourists' cars to the locals' cars, especially in the tourist season - a common European practice, little followed here. Open car parks can be acceptable in the urban scene, at the edge and in the backlands of historic towns, provided they really are parks in the sense of being well planted with trees, pedestrian paths defined with them and they are broken up into small units. Multi-storey parking can pay its way in larger historic towns provided that the area is also an important shopping centre, but these car parking structures are potentially very large and intrusive in a medieval-scale town and are best sited outside the historic core.

While servicing traffic must have accesses inside the historic core, most customer shopping should not, whatever the Canterbury Plan may say! I could not help comparing Canterbury's practice in this respect with Avignon, a medieval town of much larger size and a flourishing regional centre which successfully excludes mass parking to outside the medieval city walls.

We need to consider the question of precincting by time and whether the powers, and new powers are being made available, will enable this to be done, and how to win the co-operation of retailers for this. If Copenhagen and Amsterdam can precinct selected key shopping streets and confine servicing traffic to between 4 a.m. and 11 p.m., I do not see why we cannot do it. If we did this kind of thing, in very few years we could make an immense and most valuable change in the use of our town centres, with some imagination, co-operation and perseverance, at very little money cost.

In the physical sense, the essence of conservation is maintaining the fabric and texture of cities and adapting it to changing needs and demands. While the street network within historic towns is largely "given", it can

78

and must be adapted by environmental management (not just traffic management). Some roads must be closed and pavements widened; just as others can be made one-way and extended to provide servicing arrangements behind shopping facades. So far most of the objectives of purely "traffic" management have been directed to squeezing more traffic through the network; but this is only part of the job - and in most historic towns should be subordinate to the task of reducing the impact of less essential traffic to levels which make a visit to the town attractive and residence tolerable.

If we take the same formula, that we must "provide sufficient accessibility to maintain the life of the area ...." one can use it, like an equation, in reverse. That is, we must determine the moment in time and place when the "life of the area" or of a key building is changing and see if we can or should use or deflect or stop this change. In this way we can help generate change by coaxing market forces and by administrative action.

The moment of truth for every building, when its life hangs in the balance, occurs when the site value becomes sufficiently higher than the building value to make redevelopment economic. This is how the market works. But as no market situation exists in a vacuum, action can be taken either by influencing the operation of the market in a surprising number of ways, or using planning and administrative processes. Plot ratio, building density as well as land use controls, should be used to boost redevelopment where it is needed and suppress it where it is not.

Then there is the deflection of demand. It should be the function of every town planning and municipal action to enable effective economic demand to be expressed in rebuilding, adaptation, modernization and extension of structure, provided, in the case of historic towns, the essential character of the place is maintained and preferably enhanced. Large industrial uses have normally no place in the built-up area of historic towns. They can be kept out altogether - as Cambridge did successfully for many years in the interests of maintaining the present predominance of its University town personality - without fear of the city's life and economic viability being threatened. Small workshops for craftsmen should, though, be encouraged.

Land for industrial development, if this is essential at all, can be zoned on the edge of the town. What is not sufficiently realized, though, is that historic towns often have an option open to them ordinary towns do not. They can chose tourist development instead of industrial development.

Shopping demand is perhaps one of the most difficult to deflect, yet it is often one of the most important to influence as the values it creates are the highest effective demand in renewal subject only to petrol filling stations.

In the plan we have drawn up for the expansion of Ipswich we have planned this in the form of two new districts each with its own shopping centre, roughly the size of those of the first generation new towns. This will enable the existing medieval centre of Ipswich to continue to develop as the main sub-regional centre without destroying itself in the process.

Another aspect of this is the selection of suitable uses to insert into historic centres and buildings bringing new life to them. There are great opportunities here for imaginative planning, architectural and development thinking. Lord Esher's new hotel in the precincts of Winchester Cathedral

Wessex Hotel, Winchester.
Consultant Architect, the Viscount Esher of Brett and Pollen.
Feilden and Mawson, Architects.
Copyright: The Architectural Review

New development bordering Worcester Cathedral precinct

is an improvement to that environment and brings more people to enjoy it. The whole peninsular fishing village of St. Stephen off the Jugoslav coast has been turned into a top class hotel. The Greeks have converted an island prison off Nauplia into one. The Spaniards have saved many palaces this way. All these, it should be noted, are government sponsored ventures, and it is to be hoped that the new measures of financial help just announced by the Government will enable the hotel industry here to embark on equally imaginative proposals.

Conservationists have to go into the business of finding new uses for old buildings, some not so obvious. The upper storeys of old buildings used for shops have great potential and as the environment is improved, the older buildings in historic centres can be adapted for living. Some relaxation of the bye-laws and a more generous use of grants and loans to private individuals will be needed. I think it would help if certain grants for conservation and improvement in historic towns were made obligatory on local authorities, not discretionary. After all we had to do this with improvement grants under the Housing Acts. Such grants should be direct from the central government and not come out of the block grant. This would ensure the money went into historic towns.

Institutions, too, could move in. The demand for off-campus student living will be outstripping supply in many places where universities are expanding and polytechnics being set up. Old centres offer ideal opportunities for this and these institutions - in the case of polytechnics the local authorities themselves - should be encouraged to undertake this.

Offices, too, particularly the smaller ones typical in country towns - should be encouraged to move in and take over old buildings. They are easier occupiers to accommodate than shops and despite what may be said and despite the appearance of many of our new office buildings, offices can be made to fit into almost any building shape.

Conservation, then, has to be seen as the promotion of development, using the word in the wide sense, and conservation plans and proposals have to be cast in the form which will induce private and public development of the right kind.

The first need is for clear public policies, openly expressed. Here our officials and the form of their plans need to be more forthcoming. Good developers are never frightened off by strong, intelligent planning policies. Bad ones may be; so much the better. What exasperates developers is indecision and non-action. They often get little lead about what they will be allowed to do: have to spend much time and money formulating proposals only to have them rejected.

All our historic towns should have proposals in the form not just of land use and traffic, but urban design objectives indicated in terms of architectural possibilities. Gaps in streets need to be filled up. Sites where new buildings would be welcome need to be identified.

If the staff skilled in urban design techniques is not available in County Councils for this, private architects and planners should be retained by the planning authority to provide this advisory service to them. There is much untapped experience and skill here which should be used. It is not a question of doing the job of the developer's architect for him, but of creating the conditions and environment for him to do his job properly.

Finally, we must remember that a conservation policy must, to be successful, deal with areas and not just with buildings. If, for instance, we are concerned to improve the quality of a run-down area for living, it must be brought up in value as a whole. There are, broadly, two ways of doing this; a council must decide which it is to pursue. If rents are to be kept down and the social character of the area broadly maintained and most of the existing residents rehoused, then only public action and public subsidy will do this. The L.C.C. did this very successfully in the Brandon Estate in Southwark.

If alternative housing is to be offered elsewhere, if higher rents can be afforded by present tenants, or a shift of population is politically acceptable, then less public subsidy, if any. is needed. In such cases, though, private sources and private individuals can and will be prepared to invest their own money on renewal and this is happening, in potentially attractive environments, on an increasing scale. The same town can, and perhaps should, pursue both these policies simultaneously, though not, I suggest, in the same part of the town.

In smaller country towns, the continuity caused by town size and sense of community usually eases such problems of social co-existence. It is curious that social co-existence in this sense is more developed in London than in many larger provincial towns and cities and if we are to avoid ghettos we must plan for it socially and physically; but it will not happen at once and overnight and care and skill will be needed to channel social and economic forces in historic towns for the benefit of the community as a whole.

But more care and skill, time and trouble must be taken, organized and demanded in our historic towns. The costs in time and trouble will be high, represent a dispropriate effort in the economic short term, but a social, economic and cultural investment in the long term, that like all worthwhile goals in life, it is impossible to quantify precisely.

"No writer on economics has yet told us what are the limits to expenditure in public acts, whether a beautiful city is an investment, or an extravagance. The modern political economy of quantity should be corrected by a political economy of quality" - wrote W. R. Lethaby fifty years ago.

This is still true, but we can now be much more certain that historic towns will be judged of value both for their quality and for their economic worth. All other antiques are now much more valuable; our old towns whose beauty has survived changes of fashion and use are the community's heirlooms and, like good antiques, have the special quality of being hand-made and bearing the impress of loving care and use. In an age of machine production, we feel an increasing need for hand made objects in our homes; we will value our historic towns for the same reason as well as these others.

Except in the tropics, historic towns are not destroyed by an act of nature but by the acts of men. They do not fall down, they are knocked down.

1. *EFFECTIVE CONSERVATION – SOME MAIN OBJECTIVES AND METHODS*

1.1   *The main tasks of conservation*

If it is accepted that some towns and parts of towns have special qualities which make conservation important, and necessary, how is this to be done? Who should be the authorities responsible, how should they be staffed and advised, what should be their duties, and how should the expenses involved be met and shared.

The essential tasks are:
(1)   to define buildings, areas, and towns which merit this special consideration.
(2)   to provide adequate deterrants to anyone contemplating alterations to these places before consideration has been given to conservation requirements, and positive encouragement for constructive improvements.
(3)   to ensure that the future of these places is considered with the advice of properly qualified persons.
(4)   to prepare schemes and formulate appropriate policies for them.
(5)   to control development and to promote the realisation of these policies, and
(6)   to see that the financial burden is placed on those competent and willing to bear it.

1.2   *Some main objectives and methods*

In historic towns and areas change is inevitable, but it should be allied with conservation and controlled so as to enhance rather than diminish character. In these areas conservation should be studied simultaneously with the other aspects of planning, traffic, pedestrian circulation, trading, work, housing, recreation, tourism, and the general prosperity and well-being of the area.

Values will have changed in most of these areas, and the original uses will have died out or become no longer economic. Alternative modern uses should be found whenever possible, both to maintain values and to make an economical use of resources by adaptation rather than by wholesale destruction and new building. The building and areas thus adapted will of course be changed from their original purpose, and might in varying degrees, be considered as 'fakes'. But they will not be merely museum pieces. The aim should be to keep the atmosphere and character of the place, rather than an exact copy of the past, and to maintain continuity with the past traditions. It is in this work that expert and sympathetic guidance is so necessary.

Non-essential traffic in these areas will usually be fatal to this conservation of character and atmosphere. In most cases diversion of main traffic, and arrangements for pedestrian access only for the most of the day will be necessary, and the provision of car parks elsewhere. Such areas will be subject to pressure for change and they will have to continue to serve some useful purpose if they are to survive. There will be a constant battle between the two sections of the community having a different outlook on change, between those who wish to sweep away for purely immediate financial gain, and those who wish to conserve inherited values. The conservation section will need to be fully informed, active minded, realistic and steadfast, and able to command influence at the right level. Cost-benefit analysis could sometimes be of assistance to them in emphasising the real though often intangible values of conservation.

Other areas, such as those now referred to as "twilight areas" are on their way into history, and many may contain places which on balance should be conserved. These will need to be carefully watched by the planning authorities to ensure that values are not lost or damaged in the process of rehabilitation and redevelopment. The rehabilitation of such areas with proper regard to conservation of character can often be more economic than large scale redevelopment.

As part of the planning process historic towns should be identified and classified as being of national, regional, or local significance. The fact that they have been so identified should be a fundamental consideration in the preparation and implementation of regional and local development plans. At this level of planning the most important factor is the setting of historic towns, in both an economic and a landscape sense.

The aim of the development plans should be to reconcile the conservation of the unique historical qualities of these towns with the continuance of their day-to-day role as urban centres within the regional settlement pattern. In the same way that Conservation Areas will have little impact if they are treated as mere oases in an urban desert, so too, the appeal of an historic town is often partly dependent on its unity with its landscape setting. The importance of this factor is already recognized by the opportunity to prepare Green Belt proposals for historic towns. Often such towns are only one element in a uniquely harmonious pattern of sub-regional landscape, the whole of which, nearby villages and open landscape alike, constitutes an important part of the town's attraction. This emphasizes the need to bring urban conservation planning into a full working relationship with rural and recreational planning via some effective form of regional planning mahinery — e.g. historic towns and villages will often be key elements in National Parks, areas of outstanding natural beauty, or the Planning Advisory Group's suggested areas of special landscape and recreational policies. Together with the major ancient monuments for example, historic towns are often important nodes in the recreational pattern.

The view of a town from its surroundings, and the view outwards from the town to its surroundings, are often important elements in its total effect. In this connection the example of Oxford in relation to tall buildings in its vicinity is interesting. Details of this are given in section 7 of this report.

The implementation of the Civic Amenities Act will pose immediate administrative and organisational problems. There is need to develop the techniques which will be appropriate for identifying and designating Conservation Areas and deciding the appropriate principles of conservation for the particular circumstances. Besides matters of conservation and restoration, these principles will need to specify what modification of general standards of planning and building regulations will be necessary in order to retain the area's distinctive atmosphere, (e.g. when dealing with minor redevelopments, or traffic circulation). Day-to-day decisions can then be taken in the light of a policy framework. The four pilot studies undertaken for the Ministry will increase the body of knowledge on technique and costs of conservation, and the results of these studies are eagerly awaited by all interested in planning.

2. *AUTHORITIES RESPONSIBLE FOR CONSERVATION*

All these tasks can be rationally regarded as within the scope of the planning machinery. They are at present shared between Government Departments and the local authorities. This should continue but with some modification to procedure.

Conservation is all too frequently a minority interest. The public, and the public representatives, particularly in the smaller towns, are often insufficiently concerned, and many buildings and areas of merit have already been lost. It is essential, therefore, that decisions as to designation of conservation areas and the protection of buildings of architectural or historic interest should be taken by the planning authority, and not left entirely to the local authority itself, except where the latter has shown it is both concerned and competent. There are many cases where this concern and competence has been shown, and the local authority should be consulted, and should have powers also to bring forward proposals for conservation.

The historical and architectural value of buildings and areas varies from the purely local, through regional to national level. Although the value may be only local, the local authority is not always particularly interested. To ensure proper consideration it is suggested that the planning authority should be brought in, with an appeal to the Minister as final judge. Money, for purchase and compensation, is frequently not available at local level. This is often an additional reason for taking decisions at a higher than the purely local level.

A convenient classification of historic towns and areas might be as follows:

(a) Those of *national* concern — to be designated by the Ministry and to have priority in national grant assistance;

(b) those of *regional* importance — to be designated by local planning authorities, in consultation with Regional Economic Planning Councils and any Regional Standing Conferences of planning authorities;

(c) those of *local* importance — designated by local planning authorities, in consultation with local authorities concerned.

Opportunities for representation should also be given to amenity societies and individuals specially concerned. The local planning authority would often welcome assistance from private interests, civic societies and similar organizations, and particularly from those having special knowledge and experience. This help could well be given both in defining towns and areas which should be the subject of special study and policies, and in dealing with specific cases of immediate threats to such areas and buildings. It is often an advantage if co-operation between amenity societies can be arranged, one society acting as spokesman for all.

The essential requirements are to ensure that decisions on conservation are placed in competent hands; to provide for a reasonable interval of time while steps are taken to consider conservation aspects fully; to provide adequate deterrents against hasty and ill-considered action; and especially to promote a wider interest in conservation.

3. POWERS AND DUTIES OF PLANNING AUTHORITIES

3.1   Assuming that conservation is to be the concern of the Planning Authority, what organization and procedure are best fitted for the tasks involved?

Up to the present the procedures have been cumbersome, and to a large extent, ineffective. Improvements have however been effected by the Civic Amenities Act, and more are promised in the proposed new planning legislation.

On the two important points of the need for a reasonable interval of time for consideration before something undesirable and irretrievable is done, and a more adequate deterrent to hasty action, the Civic Amenities Act 1967 provides improved procedures. The Act extends from 2 months to 6 months the period of notice to demolish or alter a listed building. It also substantially increases the penalties for contravention of Building Preservation Orders or for failure to give the required notice. Experience will show whether these new provisions are adequate. Improvements are also effected in the procedure for making Building Preservation Orders and for listing buildings.

Powers are also given to local planning authorities to designate areas of architectural or historic interest, and to prepare schemes for their control and management. The procedure for Building Preservation Orders has been further simplified, and listing will now have the same effect as a Building Preservation Order. The proposed demolition of a listed building has now to be advertised in the press; and the responsibility for transmitting a notice of listing to the owner of the property has been transferred to the local authority. These are all improvements on the lines recommended in this report. Subject to provisions to ensure that decisions on areas and buildings of architectural and historic importance are taken by a fully informed planning authority, to ensure the proper sharing of the consequent cost, the above provisions are to be welcomed. They should be reinforced by a further power to local authorities to require the owner of a listed building to carry out specified works, or in default to do the work themselves and recover the cost from the owner.

Up to now a Building Preservation Order has been mainly negative in effect. It might prevent pulling down, but did not secure keeping up.

3.2   *Control under leasehold management*
Under the new leasehold legislation it seems likely that larger areas in a single ownership may be split up into individually owned properties. The problem connected with conservation of areas of buildings of architectural or historic interest or indeed of preserving individual listed buildings will in consequence, in these cases, be more complicated than hitherto when it was possible to negotiate with a single and sometimes financially strong owner.

Under the new leasehold legislation, which confers on a tenant holding a

long lease at a ground rent of a house not exceeding the Rent Act limits
of £400 in London and £200 elsewhere the right to acquire the freehold
compulsorily, provision is made for schemes to continue the landlord's
control in an estate recognized by the Minister of Housing and Local
Government or the Secretary of State for Wales as a well managed one.
To begin with the scheme will provide for the existing landlord to continue
the management but it may provide for the eventual transfer of this control
to a body of representatives or to a local authority. There are some opportunities for useful conservation work under this procedure. A note of a case
at Oxford illustrating possibilities is given in section 8 of this report.

3.3   *Unification of Ownerships*
If unification of ownership by local authorities becomes necessary,
compulsory purchase may be the most effective method, but the local
authority's role is more often likely to be as the agent for promoting
voluntary unification of ownership in any one of its various forms. There is
experience of some attempts in this field, for example in Cheltenham, but
there are indications that owners are reluctant to pool their freehold
interests. In some cases, however, they are prepared to become partners in
schemes of total exterior decoration and restoration schemes when grant
is forthcoming from local authorities and/or government sources condition-
ally upon such co-operation. This promise of grant at present seems to be
the greatest incentive for co-operation between owners of buildings of
architectural and historic interest.

Some details of Cheltenham cases, and of work at Jedburgh and Roxburgh
where CDA procedure has been used for conservation purposes, are given in
sections 9 – 11. A note is also included in section 12 on the interesting "Town
Scheme" now in operation in York.

4.   TECHNICAL STAFF REQUIREMENTS AND ORGANISATION

4.1   *The Skills involved in Conservation*
The skills that need to be brought to bear on the conservation of historic
towns cover a very wide field. The emphasis on any particular skill should
vary with the special characteristics of the place, e.g. topography; archaeo-
ligical interest; the significance of the architectural heritage; or the dimensions of the traffic problem.

Most of the larger local planning authorities can provide the necessary
team of professional skills from their permanent establishment. But there is
a very serious shortage of trained staff in all the professions concerned, and
the establishments of even the larger authorities are by no means always
filled. Efforts are being made to overcome this shortage, but in the meantime
the greatest possible economy in the use of trained professional staff is
necessary.

4.2   *From where are the skills to be drawn?*
As important as the team, are the sources from which it is drawn, the
machinery which takes up and implements its work, and the provision for
continuity after its initial plan-making task is done. The first Study and Plan
for the historic area of a town or city is on paper; its validity is greatest when
the last word is written and the last map is drawn. Even by the time it is
printed, subtle if not major changes are called for.

The continuing nature of the planning job means some kind of continuity of approach in the technical team that is responsible for the active process of initiating and controlling the forces of change. Planning teams at County Borough level can operate employed by and within their own local government unit. At County level a specialist team is sometimes drawn from Headquarters staff to visit towns and larger villages with urgent conservation problems, and carry out special studies. Alternatively when there is a shortage of existing staff, or it is felt that there is insufficient need or money to make permanent appointments, consultants in private practice are given specific tasks with particular terms of reference. The Consultants produce a report and, in most instances, are thanked, paid and dismissed, as though with a paper plan the job were ended.

In some instances, where a local authority has been particularly aware of its position as custodian of a regionally or nationally important heritage, an outside view has been sought deliberately in the knowledge that local opinion may be too close to a situation — may over or undervalue certain factors — and that those with a broader based experience would do a better evaluation job and find a solution less inhibited by detailed local factors of perhaps lesser actual, but more apparent, importance.

4.3

Continuity

Here is the difficulty; the local team can ensure continuity; the ad hoc team may bring a wider experience to the job but, to date, its use has often meant a lack of continuity; a wasteful duplication and considerable frustration, both within the permanent office which has to take over the consultant team's work, understand and implement it, and in the consultant's office, the latter loses touch with the policy and plan into which it has put months or years of careful study and thought; and loses touch at the most important stage, that of a Plan's slow and subtle adjustment during the continual process of implementation, when a knowledge of the reasoning processes behind it would have been the best equipment for taking it forward.

With the enormous task ahead, and the present shortage of the right skills, the use of the few consultants that there are, and of regionally or centrally based teams under ministerial or regional control, will be essential; with the advantages and disadvantages already mentioned.

The need for continuity must therefore be faced if the work of visiting teams is to have any long term significance and waste of effort is to be avoided; and if the same ground is not to be gone over twice, first by the visiting team and later by those left behind to implement the Plan, its main intention getting weakened in the process. It is a matter of integration, which comes back to the source from which the team is drawn.

Local planning authorities have the plan-making task laid on them as part of their normal responsibility. The adequacy of their staff varies from place to place, and its make-up and strengths also vary, depending on the salaries that can be offered, and the capacity and experience of the individual people employed. If a team can be built up in which visiting personnel can draw in permanent officers or vice versa, then the right situation will be established in which fresh minds can contribute while continuity is ensured, through the interest and understanding of permanent staff. In this way, local deficiences can be made up as necessary and without trespass or duplication.

There is a long way yet to go in the development of team work, not least within existing local authority staff structures and in particular between the Planning and Highways Departments. Added to this is an urgent need in the reorganization of the local government structure, to get rid of the situations which at present must be dependent on team work but have been proved not to be susceptible to it, e.g. the allocation of planning responsibilities between County Councils and non-County Boroughs. But there is no time to wait for all this, and it may be that an outside element, brought in to supplement local efforts, can act as a kind of catalyst to speed up this essential integration by drawing on the skills of the two departments or authorities alike. An interesting example of integration on these lines is given in section 13.

4.4

Voluntary assistance

There is also the fringe of interested people who exist in most towns; highly knowledgeable in a particular field — having studied some aspect of a town's history in greater depth than could any planning team. Any such assistance should be brought in at the earliest moment. As contributors they have a great deal to offer, and as understanding and fully informed people they are firm and valuable allies, while as people kept in the dark, whose point of view is not weighed and discussed, they can frustrate or delay the outcome.

4.5

Regional Assistance

The existing regional staff structure offers a variety of experience and contacts which sometimes is, and always should be accessible. The District Valuer ranks high among these and could share his knowledge within certain limits. The Ministry of Transport and Ministry of Housing and Local Government regional representatives can also help, though they sometimes tend to be noncommital because of the structures within which they work. Channels of approach for the free and productive exchange in views and the evolution of and education in policy, will be a vital part of any new regional and local government structure. In this respect the regional machinery set up by the Government for regional economic planning could develop into something useful. The Regional Standing Conferences of planning authorities, or similar organizations, should also help.

4.6

Conservation Committees

The democratic safeguard behind the professionals' work in the continuing planning process is the responsible committee. For the job of conservation, some special sub-committee of the Planning Committee will be wanted for a number of reasons. Among these are that the particular job of watching the fate of the built heritage does not get swamped by other planning business; and that, for public relations reasons, it becomes generally known that an active and wise committee exists with this special job. This Committee would also act as "Custodian" of the inherited historic wealth of the district; and there would be on it a niche for co-opted members drawn from local sources, e.g. a specialist in archaeology, the curator of a local museum, and representatives of amenity societies.

Such a committee is, in effect, part of the team, as will be the Committee Clerk, who can be a key man in terms of continuity and achievement of purpose if he has the right personality. It will be responsible to its main planning committee for continuity in promulgating a positive conservation policy. In fact its job will become most important after the first Policy and Plan for a city or town has been put on paper, because these are only means to an end, that of the promotion and control of development.

The Committee's job will be to see that the initial work on a conservation plan is not thrown away but becomes the start of a sequence of events; to initiate public works; and to stimulate and guide private work. It will deal with modifications to the plan as called for, following new circumstances; and will decide when to bend and on what to stand firm.

4.7
Briefing for Conservation and Complementary Development
A conservation plan must be the basis for a proper and thorough brief for prospective developers of every kind. This brings us back to the professional team, members of which will serve committees on the one hand and deal with public and private developers on the other, putting over this brief to both in a way to make certain its proper implementation.

In this capacity they are public relations men, but they need to be very near to the Plan and Policy; very near to its intention. When it comes to design standards and the control of new architectural work (quite as important as restoration of the old fabric if the latter is to be given a worthy context), they also need to be sensitive designers in current building practice — that is if they are to carry conviction with developers and be able to argue a case through appeal if necessary.

When a visiting team has been working with a local planning authority, the question must be how team members can continue to contribute their specialist skills in the implementation stage with their particular knowledge of Plan and Policy; how they can continue to inject a wider experience into the situation, both in planning and architectural terms. This continued use of regional and private consultants must however be done through machinery which gives them a chance to function. It will be no good their being called upon ad hoc at the discretion of the planning authority after decisions have been taken that they might have advised against.

There should be regular progress meetings so that permanent and visiting team members continue to work side by side, visiting members being called on to play an active part with the Planning Department's staff — say in briefing important developers — or in recommending major Plan modifications to committee. The visiting team should also play an active part in major matters where, because of its size and functions a local planning authority is not in a position to employ many highly qualified permanent staff, e.g. the field of architectural practice on occasions when a broader than local view is needed to assist in settling a controversial issue, or where special skills are wanted to re-assess an aspect of the Plan.

The Government can take an initiative in the conservation programme. Ministry of Housing and Local Government conservation teams could aid local planning authorities in identifying and classifying historic towns and areas. They should also prepare Planning and Design Bulletins setting general guide lines and standards for conservation work. These could well be produced in consultation with local planning authorities and amenity societies. The designation of particular conservation areas and the preparation and implementation of conservation plans may give rise to appeals to the Minister and inquiries. It would not therefore be desirable for ministry teams normally to be involved in conservation work at this detailed level.

5. FINANCIAL ARRANGEMENTS

5.1   The main stumbling block to any satisfactory arrangement for conservation is finance. Many small authorities simply cannot afford the costs involved. They are increasingly concerned with keeping the rates down and increasing the rateable value of their areas. When a conflict arises, as it often must, between increased rateable value and conservation, less tangible values tend to be pushed aside. This is inevitable as things are. The position can be met by alterations in the local government set-up, which may well be on the way; by making the larger planning authority the ultimately responsible authority, as recommended in this report; and by arrangements for sharing the costs more in accordance with benefit through a reasonable classification of cases into those of local, regional and national importance, and giving greatly increased grants from central funds for conservation purposes.

This is obviously the crux of the matter. Although under the Local authorities (Historic Buildings) Act 1962, local authorities are empowered to assist owners financially so as to ensure proper restoration of buildings of architectural or historic interest, the funds available to the average Local Authority are so small as to be virtually ineffective. It often is the case that the less well off authorities are national custodians of very large numbers of historic buildings; those in the areas of some of the more wealthy counties and the larger urban areas having been destroyed when they were in the way of development, particularly during the industrial revolution. The conservation of the national heritage of architectural and historic buildings cannot possibly be effected merely by legislation unless there is backing by sufficient funds. All the historical and architecturally interesting buildings, even those with primarily a local interest, have some element of national importance and should therefore be, to an extent varying with their character and location, a national financial responsibility. If any building is considered "not to be of national, regional, or local importance" then it follows, surely, that there is no real argument for its preservation.

5.2   *Payment for Specialist Skills brought into the Team*
Some of the smallest and poorest local authorities have the largest and most important conservation problems. To pay professional fees for an initial Study and Plan is sometimes acceptable to these authorities because the outlay has a known end. For the continuing planning process they should be encouraged to free money budgeted for permanent, and possibly unobtainable, staff which could be better used in employing, part-time, members of the original specialist team. But there is still a large gap between what some Local Authorities think this sort of work should cost and what it actually does cost, so that consultants who submit realistic estimates for jobs are still sometimes looked on as "racketeers" by councillors, and the idea of their appointment rejected.

With this background in mind, whatever its advantages, the use of outside professional services as a part of the continuing planning process seems likely to stand a poor chance of being adopted generally unless some kind of financial assistance is offered. Nor does this seem unreasonable if conservation in a town or city is deemed to have regional or national significance as well as local. From which it follows that all aspects of financial outlay on conservation should be carried at the appropriate level – national, regional and local.

There would be some advantage if, in relation to areas and towns of historic and architectural interest, all grant facilities for historic buildings, redevelopment, improvement, reclamation, roads and other cognate matters could be considered together and co-ordinated with the aim of conservation in view. The example of other countries could be studied in this respect.

6. THE PROMOTION OF PUBLIC INTEREST IN CONSERVATION

6.1   Conservation depends on public opinion, which in turn depends on communication. People have to be made aware in time of the special character and importance of specified areas and buildings so that they will be concerned with their proper care. It has to be brought home to the public and especially to owners and occupiers of historic sites, that these are valuable in themselves, and that once destroyed they are irreplaceable.

It is important that the organizational framework for conservation effort should, in addition to providing information and stimulus to the public generally, give full opportunity for public and voluntary involvement by voluntary bodies, the professions, young people, and teachers and others involved in education, and by owners and occupiers of historic buildings and sites.

6.2   *Stimulation of Public Interest*
Public interest in the historic heritage in its value as an essential basis for civic pride, and in the action needed to care for it properly can be stimulated in many ways. Newspaper reports and radio and television features on historic buildings could well stress the contribution which historic buildings have to make to good environment today. Signs and plaques on historic buildings should be used more widely, and walking tours arranged to help people to understand what they see in walking round a town and to stimulate a wider appreciation of good architecture and visual qualities.

People understand the significance of historic buildings more vividly if they can go into them and see them more or less as they were when constructed. Museums and Folk Parks provide such opportunities, and much more should be done in this way. There is a very good local example at the Castle Museum, York.

Models are particularly attractive to children. They can also be a significant tourist attraction; and an excellent educative tool; and at the same time the basis for sensitive development control.

6.3   *Voluntary bodies*
Voluntary bodies should be encouraged to take effective action in a conservation campaign. They can assist the conservation effort in many ways. For example they can stimulate public interest by carrying out surveys of historic buildings, writing booklets, making models and conducting tours of historic areas and buildings and by constant vigilance ensure that buildings are listed; damage noted; demolition prevented; and the design of new buildings kept up to an acceptable standard. It is difficult to over emphasize the importance of voluntary action in keeping the planning authorities up to date and alert on these matters.

Many skills exist in any community which can be used to assist conservation. They should be brought into the effort. The most obvious are: historians, who can assist on the educational and advisory side; archaeologists; teachers; architects; and draftsmen of all kinds.

The importance of arousing the interest of young people, teachers, and others involved in education cannot be over-emphasized. If people are trained in visual appreciation at an early age they are less likely to develop the virtual blindness to their surroundings which seems to afflict so many older people. School classes in civics, geography, history, even the new mathematics and other subjects, could well use historic buildings and town structure as visual aids. Older students can study local history and help to make models or to do improvement work in historic houses. In all these, and other ways the study and appreciation of the local environment should be an essential part of the educational process.

6.4   *Owners and Occupiers*
The owners and occupiers of historic buildings have a key role in conservation work. At present the chief impact which conservation makes on them is that they are told that their building has been listed or that a Building Preservation Order has been put on it. This is a purely negative point. They should be stimulated positively to care about and to maintain their property. This stimulus could be provided by: information about the building, its statutory position and its role in the planning and future of the area; assistance, both financial and technical; and encouragement to joint action.

Owners and occupiers should be informed by the local planning authority or the local authority, that their property has historic importance; that grants and loans are available to help them maintain the property; and that they can obtain expert advice on these matters and on architectural and maintenance problems from the local planning authority. Their pride in the property could be encouraged by putting a plaque on it and by arrangements for occasional group visits to the property.

Positive action in improvement and maintenance of historic buildings by owners can be greatly encouraged by the prospect of joint action. Examples of this can be seen in the Civic Trust improvement schemes in such places as Norwich and Haddington.

Owners and occupiers are not all individuals. There are other significant categories. Examples are commercial firms, national or multiple bodies, and public organizations, including the local authority itself. Commercial firms and multiples may be approached through the Chamber of Commerce as well as individually. The hard commercial value of historic character, in terms of both a civilised environment and also as a tourist attraction, should be emphasised to them. In the case of multiples pressures at local level should be accompanied by approaches at national level. Public bodies, including notably the local authority, should be stimulated to give example by playing a leading part in conservation.

* * * * * * * *

7.   *THE SITING OF HIGH BUILDINGS IN OXFORD*

The location of new high buildings in Oxford presents a difficult problem for two reasons. The city already possesses a skyline which is recognized as a precious national heritage, and due to its peculiar geographical situation in a valley surrounded by hills Oxford can be viewed as a whole. Every proposal for a high building must be considered in relation to the silhouette of the city as seen from the surrounding higher ground (landscape) as well as various points at street level within the city (townscape).

Oxford High Street. Photograph by Graeme Shankland.

Cheltenham.

Buildings of comparatively insignificant height which make no difference to the "landscape" can be of tremendous significance to the "townscape". Similarly buildings could be erected outside a Conservation Area, but adjacent to it, which could destroy the scale and meaning of the area itself. In particular tall buildings badly located could ruin the effect of a Conservation Area.

Accordingly the City Council has set down two general principles to be followed by intending developers.

(1)   Where the proposed building exceeds the level of Ordnance Datum, Newlyn, 260 from ground level 200-210, or ODN.240 from ground level 180 it has to be considered carefully both from the townscape and from the landscape point of view. If the excess height cannot be justified by purely visual reasons the proposal will not be approved.

(2)   In High Street anything added to or subtracted from the street can only have a detrimental effect on this unique architectural composition. It should be preserved as existing. Any new building should be modest enough not to create new accents and not to change in any way the street's character.

Unlike High Street the skyline of Oxford is not seen to be a finite composition. Within the last 100 years a number of new elements have been added to it without impairing its beauty. There is no reason why this process should not be continued provided the skyline's main characteristics of extreme fragility, compactness and the dominance of the tower of St. Marys are maintained.

8.   *CONTROL UNDER LEASEHOLD PROCEDURE AT OXFORD*

In 1850 the Guardians of the Poor of the City of Oxford purchased some ten acres of land about a mile north of the City centre for the purpose of building a workhouse. Shortly afterwards the Guardians built the workhouse on another site and the site left at their disposal was laid out as a high-class residential estate to ensure the highest possible income for the relief of the poor.

A self-perpetrating body of Trustees was set up in 1854 for the purposes of management and were empowered to levy a rate to cover expenses. The Trustees had complete 'planning' powers and their scheme was completed by 1858.

Nos. 68 and 70, Banbury Road were always part of Park Town but, possibly because of their misleading address were not included in the Minister's Supplementary List under (then) Section 30 of the Town and Country Planning Act.

The YWCA purchased No.70 Banbury Road and used it for their hostel and in 1965 they applied for permission to demolish the existing building and replace it with a modern four storey hostel. This being refused by the Planning Committee the YWCA appealed to the Minister who allowed the appeal. The Trustees then invoked their original covenant and opposed the proposal on this ground.

The YWCA put an application before the Courts of Law for a modification of the restrictive covenant in 1965 under Section 84 of the Law of Property Act, 1925.

The decision of the Lands Tribunal maintained that the proposed building would be of a quite different character in appearance to any on the Estate and agreed that the Trustees were justified in refusing permission for its erection owing to its unsuitability and probable injurious effect on the (other) properties. In particular there would be a most injurious effect upon No. 1 which would materially affect its value and the Lands Tribunal dismissed the application with costs against the applicants.

9. GLOUCESTERSHIRE COUNTY COUNCIL AND CHELTENHAM CASES

9.1   In 1962 the Gloucestershire County Council and Cheltenham Borough Council produced a policy memorandum designed to assist intending developers to formulate proposals which were likely to be acceptable, to assist the Borough Planning Committee when considering applications for redevelopment, and to provide a useful background against which any possible selection of buildings for grants could be considered.

Cheltenham Borough Council were parties to this memorandum and in January 1964 approved a consolidated version of it with a reference map of the Regency areas where the preservation policy applied.

During 1964 Cheltenham Borough Council and the Gloucestershire County Council negotiated a joint restoration grant policy for Cheltenham and the County Finance Committee approved the conservation areas map and the policy amendments the following year.

9.2   *The Policy Memorandum: Conservation and Redevelopment in Cheltenham – Regency Areas*
The Character of Cheltenham
The Regency area of Cheltenham is fortunate in having a distinct character of being spacious and gracious which is extremely pleasant and is the town's greatest asset.

While it would be folly for Cheltenham to allow this character to be destroyed, this does not mean that no redevelopment should take place. There is no reason why the spacious and gracious character of many parts of the town should not survive a good deal of rebuilding.

9.3   *Scale*
Large areas of Cheltenham have a satisfying homogeneity of scale which is the basis of their special character. This scale depends not only on the buildings themselves but also on their spacing both in relation to each other and to the road, and on the width of the road itself and on the planting. All these things are part of a single design concept and need to be considered in relation to proposals for redevelopment. In 'Regency character' residential areas, the over-riding consideration will be that new development shall conform to the scale and rhythm of its environment. This will normally influence height, site coverage, space about buildings particularly laterally, building line and planting.

9.4   *Quality of Building*
A significant fact about Regency building was its fragile and often down-right bad construction. It was carried out by opportunists and building speculators who wished to exploit the new "Spa Patronage" without much

regard to building permanence. It was a period when decoration and applied ornament were of paramount importance, whereas the structure of the building in most cases was only just good enough to carry the floors, roofs and splendid facades. It will be appreciated therefore that problems which may be peculiar to any Regency area are likely to be experienced in the conservation schemes in Cheltenham.

9.5

Conservation

Old towns reflect our history and Cheltenham has a contribution to make as probably the best example of the town design of one particular age.

It has already been suggested that it should be possible to retain the particular character of many parts of the town where the actual buildings may change, but within more limited areas the actual buildings should be preserved.

With a large number of good examples of the Regency style in the town, it is clearly impracticable to hope that they can all be preserved and apart from the obviously outstanding single buildings such as Pittville Pump Room, the most rewarding course is likely to be to concentrate on preserving a few selected examples, and wherever possible, complete streets, squares and terraces.

A lesser number of buildings in complete areas of Regency design and layout will ultimately be of more value than a much greater number of individual scattered buildings, even if such complete areas contain some buildings of less than the highest quality, for grouping and environment play a large part in giving the Regency style its particular distinction. In these areas wall materials should generally be light in colour and detailing should be delicate.

Where planting is an important element in the creation of the character of the environment, the Local Authority will expect developers to have regard to existing planting and in suitable cases to undertake new planting. The Local Authority will not hesitate to make Tree Preservation Orders where necessary.

9.6

Conservation procedure in Cheltenham

The Policy memorandum and the resolutions of the Cheltenham Borough Council and the County Council were highlighted at an important meeting of owners and tenants of Regency properties which took place at Cheltenham during 1964.

This meeting was convened with the specific intention of persuading the owners and occupiers of the buildings in the priority Regency areas to form associations determined to renovate and restore the Regency terraces. At this meeting the Historic Buildings Council's Secretary expressed concern about preservation of these buildings and gave assurances that grant aid would be forthcoming to restore crumbling and delicate stucco decoration and ironwork which were important elements of the Regency style.

The County Council were equally concerned about the conservation of the more outstanding Regency buildings and had given grant aid in a number of cases to enable the owners of Regency buildings to restore them under the Local Authorities (Historic Buildings) Act of 1962.

It was agreed that the best way to arouse public enthusiasm would be to initiate a pilot scheme with the help of the Historic Buildings Council and the two local authorities, by restoring a terrace of say 6 to 12 houses. If grants were made available both for restoration and modernisation together with mortgages, the public, it was felt, could be shown that it was not such a financial burden as had hitherto been believed.

A list of terraces was received from the Historic Buildings Council and 6 houses forming the smaller part of Oxford Parade were selected.

9.7 *Oxford Parade*

A meeting with the owners was called by the Borough Council and a proposed pilot scheme of restoration was outlined by the County Planning Officer. The proposal required interior conversion horizontally with dwelling units on each floor, as opposed to the six existing three-storey vertical dwelling units. The scheme also required a pooling of freeholds and a redistribution of ownerships, exterior restoration work and replanning of the rear garden area.

Despite general interest by the owners complete agreement could not be reached and eventually the project was abandoned.

As a result the Lansdown Parade Association, which was formed in 1960 with the object of restoring and conserving the fabric and structure of the 23 dwellings in the terrace of Lansdown Parade, asked the local authorities for their assistance in implementing conservation proposals.

9.8 *Lansdown Parade*

Lansdown Parade is included within the Policy Map area and on the Historic Buildings Council's list and is also a Grade II listed building on the Ministry of Housing and Local Government's list of architectural or historically important buildings.

While discussions were in progress the County Council agreed to make a block grant of £7,000 annually to the Borough Council which would be matched by the Borough Council and expended by them on the restoration of properties within the framework of a 'Town Scheme' whose area was delineated on the Policy Map referred to earlier.

In 1965 the report of the architect retained by the Lansdown Parade Association was considered by the Borough Council. The Historic Buildings Council agreed that the first grant by them should be offered towards this project and would amount to 25% of the cost of repairs (estimated at £34,000). The County Council and the Borough Council agreed to contribute 12½% each and the Association agreed to pay the remaining 50%.

Tenders for the first two units comprising twelve houses have now been received and it is hoped that the successful conclusion of this particular project will generate local interest and that the situation regarding Regency buildings can then be further reviewed in the light of this test case.

9.9 *Conclusion*

On the one hand is the case of Lansdown Parade, where a willingness on the part of an Owners' Association to work together for mutual benefit has produced the desired result, whereas at Oxford Parade, where a more drastic form of rehabilitation is needed, the whole project has been halted by the inability to reach common agreement between owners.

At present it is not possible to say which case is the more normal. In terraces and other compact groups of buildings it would appear from current experience of these two cases that the multiplicity of ownerships could present the most serious hindrance to renovation of such buildings.

10.   JEDBURGH – THE ROYAL BURGH ON THE JED

10.1   *Setting and Character*

Jedburgh, the County Town of Roxburgh, is situated in the valley
of the Jed Water, a tributary of the Teviot, within ten miles of the
English Border. It is set in attractive rural scenery and by virtue of its
geographical location forms one of the gateways to Scotland from the
south. It lies astride the main road running through the heart of the
Borderland from Newcastle to Edinburgh and has easy access to the
road system in the Tweed basin.

Jedburgh, although located in a rural area, is principally a small industrial
town in which, during the past two centuries, prosperity has depended on
the fortunes of the textile industry. The population has fluctuated from
5,800 in 1755 to the present-day figure of 3,647. The County Development
Plan envisages an increase to 6,000 within the next 20 years.

The following factors are at present having a prejudicial effect upon the
character of the town:

(i)   Congestion caused by through traffic principally in the High
Street,

(ii)   Obsolescence of many of its buildings, particularly the North
British Rayon factory and properties in the Canongate, and

(iii) Lack of definition of land use in the central area.

10.2   *Analysis of Problem*

In June, 1962, the Scottish Development Department, Rodburgh
County Council and the Jedburgh Town Council agreed to set up a
Joint Working Party of Technical Officers to consider and report upon
the development and redevelopment of Jedburgh in all its aspects.

The Working Party have identified areas which may be considered for:

Conservation   - where historic, architectural or commercial
values are relatively high;

Redevelopment   - where buildings are derelict or can no longer make
any worthwhile contribution to the form, function
or life of the town; and

Improvement   - where a general upgrading of existing conditions
is desirable.

10.3   *The Objectives*

After full consideration by the Working Party the following have
emerged as basic objectives to be achieved:

1.   The improvement of the environment, the proper arrangement
of land uses and a new road network providing for separation
in the movement of people and vehicles.

2.   The rehabilitation of the central area to provide conditions
suitable to modern ways of living and, in particular, create
a traffic free shopping area.

3.   To meet present needs and those of the projected increase in
the population to 6,000 provision should be made for the
expansion of existing industry and the establishment of new
industries.

4.   There should be more new housing at Howdenburn and more new houses built in the central area by the redevelopment of obsolete sites.

5.   For education there should be an Education Precinct and for additional recreation a linked system of public open spaces related to the use of the Jed Water as an attraction for boating, fishing and walking.

All these must be so achieved that the town retains its historic character but is at the same time modernized for the latter half of the 20th century. Proposals (not referred to here) made to achieve these objectives cover roads, the town centre, industry, housing and education.

10.4   *Preservation and Historic Area*
The Provisional List of Buildings of Special Architectural or Historic Interest prepared by the Scottish Development Department under Section 28 of the Town and Country Planning (Scotland) Act, 1947, contains some 36 buildings or groups of buildings.

A scheme should be prepared for the restoration (including possible rebuilding), repaving, painting and colour-washing of the Castlegate, which is an important historic element in the town pattern. Any new development would require to be in sympathy in terms of use, scale and materials and the retention of the existing building line will be important. The restoration and reconditioning of worthy buildings in this street should be encouraged and, if necessary initiated by the Town Council.
The Market Place, Upper Canongate and High Street shopping area should be revitalized by a comprehensive tidying up of all the features in these streets on the lines of schemes already carried out in towns of comparable merit.

An area (defined in the Technical Working Party Report) of Historic and Architectural importance should be defined to indicate the scope of activity in the preservation, renovation and maintenance of buildings regarded as essential elements in the town's historic and architectural heritage. The County Council should give effect to this by a submission to the Secretary of State under the Town and Country Planning (Scotland) Acts.

10.5   *Landscape Areas*
The proposals comprise improvement and full utilization of the River Jed with open space links to the town centre. In addition, the approach and grounds to the Abbey should be improved and existing wooded areas throughout the town should be conserved and also improved.

10.6   *Comprehensive Development Area*
The County Council should submit to the Secretary of State proposals for a comprehensive development area covering the town centre.

10.7   *General Conclusions*
The town as a whole had been in a depressed state and unable to tackle the problem of revitalization and deal with deterioration of historic buildings. Designation of practically the whole of Jedburgh as a CDA enables an overall review of long-term land uses necessary to revitalize or maintain historic areas and to "manage" environment.

Because of the limited resources of the burgh it is not possible for the local authority to buy historic properties for restoration, leasing or selling other than in a strictly limited number of cases.

Nevertheless there is considerable local enthusiasm for superficial effects such as replastering and colour washing and now that redevelopment of a key site in the town has commenced it is felt that other projects will be implemented.

The Scottish Development Department set up the Technical working party representing the pool of technical resources available, as well as co-ordinating the three regional/local authorities. The report was intended to act as an example for similar efforts elsewhere although the follow-up by other county councils has so far been disappointing. Maybe the renewed interest in conservation programmes will change this.

11. *YORK — GUIDE FOR DEVELOPERS*

Amongst the other historic cities of England York is unique, having such a complete cycle of buildings of all ages, lying mostly within the mediaeval city walls. York still retains the irregular pattern of its mediaeval street and when there is added to this the grace of Georgian architecture, old churches, the river and the proud dominance of the Minster, then York's prominence amongst European Cities can be readily understood.

Because York City Council is determined that this character shall not be lost but at the same time wishing to encourage new development where this is appropriate, a guide has been drawn up for the benefit of intending developers. The Council think it important that new designs should reflect the essential character of York which is the mixture of historical styles, the tight grouping of buildings, the informality of street compositions, the absence of symmetry and formal or rectilinear groups, the broken sight lines and profiles of buildings and the refinement of silhouette at the sky-line. It follows from this that the addition of good modern buildings will enrich the already varied character of the City and new buildings should be contemporary in style. Developers should however observe fundamental limitations concerning scale, materials, detailing and finishes.

Particular emphasis is laid on scale. York's character depends profoundly on the relatively small scale of its buildings and streets. This is a human scale, and is related to the movement and comfort of pedestrians. Within the City Walls an increase in the number of passageways and pedestrian precincts is to be encouraged and the associated buildings should be of appropriate scale and the original proportions of the street should be retained. In other areas where new major road plans are in being, the scale of buildings can be suitably larger.

The traditional materials of York are facing bricks, limestone, slate and pantiles, together with timber framing and rendering. Any new materials used should be considered against this background. Because York buildings are seen at close quarters and usually in perspective, the detailing of the building is important. Shop fronts, lettering and trade signs must be suitable for the environment, the signs designed with the building. Window openings should not be too large, and their shape and scale must be considered in relation to neighbours.

The overall massing of the building must be right in relation to the general

Micklegate, York, part of the "Town Scheme".

Grants will be available to owners or prospective purchasers who would not otherwise be able to meet the exceptionally heavy burden of repairing an old structure.

When making these grants from public funds various concessions must be agreed by the owner. These safeguards include that the building concerned must not be sold after the repairs are carried out, that the repairs must be carried out in full within a specified time, and that where grant is made for the preservation of some interior feature the public shall have access to the building at certain times. Grants may be recovered in full if the person receiving a grant disposes of his or her interest within three years.

3. CONSERVATION AND DEVELOPMENT POLICY IN WORCESTERSHIRE

Worcestershire County Planning Committee has instructed the County Planning Officer to carry out in seven country towns the work of preparing conservation and redevelopment policies already started at Stourbridge and Bromsgrove in association with consultant architects. The Committee is of the opinion that the interlocking problems of conservation in county towns and at the same time providing for redevelopment, cannot be satisfactorily settled in piecemeal fashion.

Towns in Worcestershire where problems are apparent include Malvern, Stourport, Bewdley, Upton upon Severn, Pershore, Evesham and Tenbury Wells. Within these towns are approximately 900 listed buildings where quality and grouping is such as to justify comprehensive study of streets or areas as a whole.

The work to be undertaken in each town falls into three parts:

(1) A central area pilot study to produce a broad appraisal of problems and possibilities and to lay down a guiding policy.

(2) Concurrently with (1) architectural advice may be required on planning applications which would (if approved and implemented) affect the character and appearance of the study areas.

(3) A subsequent and detailed study of particular buildings or parts of the central area which need special attention.

The pilot study will deal principally with consideration of aesthetics, structures, economics and environment. The work to be done is seen as a combined operation between the County Council, their consultant architects and valuers, and the local authorities.

The County Planning Committee have been fortunate in enlisting the help of Worcestershire architects who are known to be keenly interested and skilful in this particular subject. The effect of enlisting such a considerable weight of expert architectural opinion in support of the work of the County Planning Authority should be to raise the standard of building development in these towns and to widen public interest in the subject of conservation.

skyline, and the particular street or riverside character.

It is concluded that 'good design' is to the benefit of the building owner; the architecture of the city is a principal attraction to visitors and therefore new development to high architectural standards is important in increasing interest in shopping and commerce.

12. *SCHEME OF GRANTS FOR THE PRESERVATION AND RESTORATION OF HISTORIC BUILDINGS IN YORK*

12.1   *Scope of the "Town Scheme"*

At the outset of the preparation of the scheme, which was undertaken jointly by officers of the Corporation and the Ministry of Public Buildings and Works, it was decided that part of the unique character of York is in its historic streets, and that whilst these contain some relatively undistinguished buildings, they made such a valuable contribution to the environment and character of the historic core that the preservation of whole streets and groups of buildings was the problem to tackle.

It was further decided that a whole street could not be included in the Town Scheme for the sake of one or two architecturally or historically good buildings. The scheme therefore is concentrated on the groups of historic buildings. It is not however the intention that other historic buildings within the City will be open to unrestricted demolition and their sites available for redevelopment.

The scheme enables financial assistance to be given towards the preservation of buildings within defined streets, but 20% of the total figure contributed by the participating authorities will be available for buildings of merit not specifically included in the designated groups.

Twelve streets and building groups are included in the "Town Scheme" in the following areas: North Street, New Street, Colliergate, Stonegate, Low Petergate and King's Square, High Petergate and Precentor's Court, Minister Precincts, Goodramgate, Bootham, Micklegate, Blossom Street and St. Saviorgate.

It will be necessary for the Local Authority to reinforce its existing powers of protection of historic buildings by requesting the Minister of Housing and Local Government to give statutory listing to those buildings contained within the Town Scheme which are not already so protected.

Despite these moves by the Corporation towards preserving the historic core of the City and the incentive given by this scheme to assist owners in renovating their buildings, it is recognized that there may still be a need to take further action towards successful conservation. In these cases the Council will pursue its policy of imposing a Building Preservation Order on a threatened building.

12.2   *Basis of the Scheme*

The basis of the grants to be made under the Town Scheme is for an initial experimental period of two years, commencing on 1st April 1966. The Ministry of Public Building and Works and the City Council have each agreed to make a 25% contribution under the Scheme, thus leaving the owner of the building to be restored to meet 50% of the total cost of the works to be undertaken. During the experimental trial period the Local Authority and the Ministry of Public Building and Works are each making available a sum of £7,500 per year from which grants can be allocated.

WINCHESTER – A CONSERVATION AREA

Winchester in 1939 was a typical English Cathedral City – the headquarters of a County of average size with its Cathedral and Close, a famous
school, barracks, a good shopping centre and a few hotels. But all was not
well. The City's largest hotel, "The George", had been bought by the
Ministry of Transport for a trunk road widening scheme in the City Centre –
the writing was on the wall. There were many worn out or empty small
houses, an almost complete lack of modern industry and much dilapidated
development in a City centre which was totally unfitted for modern traffic
demands. But, for most people, it was still a very pleasant place to live in.
The City Council had made real progress with Council house building and
had prepared a preliminary planning scheme. Numerous ambitious proposals
for road widening under the Restriction of Ribbon Development Act had
been adopted by the Council. Many of the problems of the historic City
had still to be faced.

Since 1945 Winchester has experienced two decades of rapid growth and
change. Whilst the population of the City itself rose only from about
23,000 to 30,000, housing conditions have changed markedly. Of the
9,500 dwellings in the City about 40% have been built since 1945.
Immediately outside the City boundary, several large private housing
areas with a predominantly professional population have developed rapidly, adding another 2,500 people. There are signs that the City is becoming
increasingly an attractive place in which to live for those who can travel to
work in Southampton and elsewhere.

About eighty acres of industrial land have been developed. The shopping
centre has been almost completely modernized and now serves, including
its hinterland, some 75,000 people. The City Council has begun on the
redevelopment, mainly for housing, of twenty-eight acres of the most
worn part of the centre. The County Council – growing out of all recognition at the centre of one of the fastest growing Counties in the country –
has had to plan a large programme of building, for new offices and courts.
A new ninety-bedroom hotel built by Trust Houses under a Local Act promoted jointly by the Corporation and the Dean and Chapter is a sign of
the growth of tourism, national and international. Winchester has, therefore, been subject to continuous and growing development pressures –
pressures which will increase now that its train service to London has been
electrified (in one sense, if not entirely in both) and a new road to motorway standard has been built linking the City to Southampton. These
pressures may increase still further when the M.3 is built and as development in the Southampton/Portsmouth conurbation, whether planned or
unplanned, presses ever more obviously on the environment of South
Hampshire. This is the background of growth, common to so many cities
today.

Despite the changes, and again this is perhaps still typical of most of our

Winchester, The Buttercross, 1896 and 1968.

historic cities, the essential pattern of the centre has changed very little —
indeed in Winchester the survival of its street pattern in particular is its
most marked feature. The traffic still grinds tortuously through the
centre, although now past a forest of traffic-lights and signs. Nor does
the centre alone suffer; by 1891 the fourteenth-century "Old Blue Boar"
was in a quiet back street, but before a start could be made on a proposed
restoration scheme, it was hit by the jib of a passing mobile crane.

Some may say that the City's character is not what it was. There have
certainly been changes, some regrettable, but it is easy to exaggerate.
For example, the area around the Buttercross at the City's commercial
heart has hardly changed. The horse-drawn carts were doubtless almost
as much a nuisance as today's motor traffic; the buildings are certainly
better maintained; the Victorian commercial clutter brings a positive
shudder — with apologies to Mr. Betjeman. Nearby, Minster Street
illustrates the quality of what has already been conserved. We do not need
to ask whether Winchester will remain a pleasant place in which to live;
but without wishing to paint too rosy a picture, what grounds for optimism
have we?

First, and probably of fundamental importance, there is an increasingly
close and friendly co-operation between the City and County Councils —
of which we hope this joint paper is some evidence. Too often the County
Town has been the bone of contention. In addition, both Councils can
rely by and large on the help and goodwill of the Dean and Chapter, the
College, the Chamber of Commerce and the Winchester Preservation
Trust. All these are actively helping in their own fields, and we doubt
whether any policy of conservation can be successful without this sort of
co-operation between the most important elements in the City.

Secondly, the City Council has always tried to seek the best advice.
Professor Sir Patrick Abercrombie prepared the first plans for the redevelopment of the Brooks and St. Georges Street, where Sir Hugh Casson
has since designed a small shopping scheme for the City. In 1962, Mr. S.
J. Garton, the first Chief Investigator of Historic Buildings, carried out a
survey which was the first attempt to look at areas of special character and
has proved a valuable guide since. Now, the City is advised on architectural
matters by Peter Shepheard.

Thirdly, the City Council, backed by a considerable body of official and
private opinion, has been determined to pursue an *active* policy of conservation. By this we mean a determination to clear slums, open up
attractive riverside walks and redevelop the most worn-out areas; to buy
land and buildings, restoring or rebuilding with the best available advice;
and, finally, to tackle the traffic problems of the City. All these have led,
in their time, to strong conflicts between the redevelopers and the pre-
servationists — a conflict inevitable and valuable, which made everyone
think, which has probably done much to crystallize a balanced policy of
conservation.

Fourthly, the City and County Councils have agreed on a plan — a four
year process of arguing out, between them and with the public, a basic
traffic pattern, a land use philosophy and a conservation policy. All these
are now put together in a Town Centre Map.

Winchester, Minster Street (see p.107) and Kingsgate.

Photographs of Winchester from slides by Hampshire County Council.

Traffic within the City, despite a pre-war by-pass and an extension shortly to be built, is expected to be double what it is now. The City Council published a Traffic Plan, prepared by the City Engineer and the County Surveyor. Needless to say, it caused a good deal of discussion. This was invaluable in paving the way for the proposals now embodied in the Town Centre Map, which although modified in detail, retains the principle of the same traffic plan. The map is intended to be diagrammatic to illustrate policies rather than precise land uses. Some areas are shown as requiring a comprehensive plan, whilst others (shown for "mixed uses") are subject to special policies in the statement which lay down the degree of change which will be permitted, according to the character of each area. The High Street and streets adjoining are shown as "principally for pedestrians". A three-quarter ring of roads, now accepted in the Ministry of Transport's advance preparation programme, will allow traffic to circulate round the historic heart of the City, but not through it; leaving the fourth quarter — the Close, College and best preserved part of the City quite undisturbed and linked still with the quiet meadows of the Itchen. Car parks will be close to the shopping heart, served by "loops" off the three-quarter ring. The growth of shops and offices will be strictly controlled, both as regards quantity and character.

To help formulate a conservation policy, Garton's 1962 survey was supplemented by a careful visual survey of the whole central area. Visually important buildings were noted, whether listed or not, as well as important views, trees and landscape, pedestrian routes, eye-sores and badly designed or sited buildings. The result of this survey was a "Control Policy Map" as we called it, intended to supplement the Town Centre Map with detailed policies for the areas of special character. Before the Map was finally adopted late in 1967, it was recognized that the Civic Amenities Act provided an even better framework for such a policy. Practically the whole of the medieval city is now therefore designated as a conservation area, together with another smaller area at Hyde outside the City walls. The map shows the boundaries, identifies listed buildings and other of architectural importance, visually important trees and open spaces and streets where "existing building frontages and road lines should be retained".

But perhaps as important is the conservation area policy which is written into the Town Centre Map. It provides that planning permission will not normally be given in outline form, and for the submission to the Minister of an Article IV Direction for some parts of the area. Policies covering the replacement of buildings, uses which generate undue noise or untidy sites, the choice of materials and the retention of trees are included. For example, new buildings or additions, unless entirely unobtrusive, will be required to make a positive contribution to the design of the area. Finally, the policy refers to the scheme of grants towards the repair of buildings and also to the work of the City Council itself in acquiring land and buildings in order to make positive improvements.

These are not really new policies, although this may be the first time they have been consciously and systematically expressed.

These policies reflect the practical approach of the City Council at the present time. There is a strong resistance to opening more than very limited new areas for shops or commercial buildings. A large part of the

City's twenty-eight acre Comprehensive Development Area could have been sold or developed for commercial purposes. It has not, and this has meant that those who wish to buy or build a new shop, a bank or a Building Society office, have in most cases had to find sites or buildings – often historic – in the City's ancient streets. Nor is permission to rebuild easily obtained; several of the largest and most recent commercial schemes have involved extensive, and no doubt expensive restoration – without a grant. These include premises for the Anglia Building Society, the National Provincial Bank and Boots chemists. A local newspaper office is another example.

At the same time a joint scheme of grants or loans for buildings of special architectural or historic interest is in operation, aimed not at businesses but at those cases which really need help. The Historic Buildings Council contribute 50% of the grant, the County and City Councils 25% each. Amongst buildings which have benefited are the old Church of St. Peter Chesil, restored as a theatre by the Winchester Preservation Trust, and a number of private houses. The City Council have restored many buildings themselves, including the Old Chesil Rectory, the Westgate, the Bargees Cottages at Wharf Hill, the Abbey Mill (used by a well-known firm of Architects), and the City Library, once the Corn Exchange. They hope shortly to restore Hyde Abbey gateway and to purchase and restore other old property nearby. The Dean and Chapter, necessarily preoccupied with the Cathedral itself, have nevertheless done much work in the Close, particularly the restoration of the Old Pilgrim's Hall and Priory Stables. Winchester College, under the guidance of Mr. John Harvey, has, since 1949, been engaged on a most thorough programme of restoration of its fine range of buildings, some dating from the fourteenth century. A particularly charming piece of work is the restoration of the Kingsgate and the little church of St. Swithun above it, a joint effort by the City Council and the Parishes themselves. Nor must one forget the work of individuals, resulting in the more modest but still valuable conservation of residential streets such as Canon Street. Some fifty-eight Improvement Grants have assisted this type of conservation.

Of course, some buildings have gone. In the last twenty-two years, of 439 Listed buildings in the City, 9 on the Statutory List have been wholly or partly demolished, 9 on the Supplementary List. Most of these losses were inevitable although there was room for argument about a few of them. A few could be turned to good account as was done with the site of St. Maurice's Church; the tower was retained, and an attractive new walk between the High Street and the Close opened up. It is not a disheartening record, even if mistakes will occur occasionally. But we cannot afford to be complacent and it is clear that the struggle to conserve must go on. Buildings now in fine condition, restored and in good hands, may turn out to be neglected and decaying in twenty to twenty-five years' time. We cannot be sure which buildings will be most valued in fifty or a hundred years' time.

But the preservation of individual buildings is only part of the story. What of the difficulties of conserving the character of the City as a whole and how is one to reconcile conservation with a thriving economy? The same pressures which will give a financial incentive to restore and repair, which allow the City to be used by a vigorous community, bring also the destructive forces of change, commercial self-interest, traffic and the new mobility of its citizens. To avoid disaster a strong system of checks and balances is needed, which we believe only a policy with popular support backed by a practicable plan can give.

It is sometimes claimed that excessive development pressure should be "siphoned off" elsewhere, but it may well be that too much pressure is better than too little. In 1439, for example, the cirizens petitioned Henry VI, complaining that through pestilence and loss of trade, 11 streets, 17 churches and 987 houses had fallen into ruin in 50 years. If, therefore, we must welcome some development — a better choice of more modern amenities, the need for bigger buildings — a strong planning control is essential. We must be tough with the developer, not reject him altogether.

Nor do we feel that to ban all traffic from the centre is necessarily the right solution. In some streets there may be no alternative, where crowds of shoppers make pavements hopelessly inadequate. Even there, pushing through new rear service roads could be disastrous, especially in a closely knit medieval street pattern. Loading and unloading at special times may be the answer or perhaps a municipal goods depot. We do not yet know whether peripheral car parks and a special bus service will prove either attractive or economically viable in a City of Winchester's size — although it may be worth trying. It should be possible to serve car parks close to the centre by "loops" which return cars to the main road system without letting them penetrate through the central area. The difficulty here is to judge the environmental capacity of the central area; we have had to admit that we do not know, and that we should not plan for very large increases in parking capacity until we do. It is important that the plan should be flexible enough to allow this.

A familiar problem in any old City or town is that of fitting into the old pattern a large modern supermarket. The difficulty is not only a physical one. The City authorities cannot prevent the Metropolis Goldblock Corporation, for example, from buying the sites of several small and ancient buildings, hoping to demolish and build yet another super emporium. There may be far more suitable sites, but one wonders whether the Local Authority should be made to pay for their subsequent refusal to allow the development, on the basis that the best economic use of the site is for a supermarket. And if they do, must they do so again on the next site the same corporation acquires? The shifting value for this type of use now strikes at any central site coming on the market. Perhaps the value of a listed building should be limited to that of its present use and condition, as for example, a farmer's agricultural land in a "white" area. Another possible solution is to remove the right to serve a purchase notice following a refusal of planning permission if the planning authority is prepared to give permission to restore or even replace a listed building with an equivalent one.

These are comments on a most difficult subject and do not necessarily represent, I need hardly say, the policy of our authorities. The planning policy for Winchester does, however, stipulate that, where considered undesirable, proposals for the redevelopment or amalgamation of smaller shops will be resisted. At the same time some provision for additional shopping in the long term must be made, although any calculation of its size is peculiarly difficult in at least one respect. It is possible to measure future shopping demands, even if with many uncertainties, but the effect of trade derived from tourists or visitors is an unknown factor on which more research would be welcome.

Another real problem is the design of new buildings in a conservation area. What is a "positive contribution to the design of the area"? Should new buildings be a facsimile, brutally modern, or merely polite? Winchester can, we think, show examples of all three! On the whole the City Council have pursued a catholic policy, which has permitted a fairly wide range of styles from the traditional to wholly modern. In several cases complete rebuilding behind the old facade has been carried out. Historically, it is clear that many of the City's old buildings have been largely rebuilt at one time or another, and the mixture of old and new, new-this and modern-that, is a very real part of the City's character. Despite the purists on both sides, we think there is a good deal to be said for a liberal attitude towards new buildings once a good case for rebuilding has been made. It is probably more important to insist on a careful choice of materials and attention to the scale of the building in relation to its site and surroundings.

This brings us back to the point that change cannot wholly be resisted, and may even sometimes be welcome. A new use cannot necessarily always be found for an out-dated building, and not in every case can preservation for its own sake alone be justified. Nor are the funds at present available for grant-aid sufficient for more than limited help in important cases. We believe that what success can be claimed for the results achieved so far is due to three principal factors :
1. A very strong business and residential property demand with pressure for change;
2. A strong, almost ruthless policy, backed by a sympathetic plan, opposing undue change;
3. Limited financial grants in extreme cases.

We welcome the designation of the conservation area as a very important addition to these three factors, the weakening of any one of which would, in our view, be a serious threat to the conservation of the City.

K. W. Grimes

CONSERVATION IN THE LONDON BOROUGH OF SUTTON

The London Borough of Sutton came into existence on 1st April, 1965, as a result of the combination of three existing Authorities; the Borough of Sutton and Cheam, the Borough of Beddington and Wallington and the Urban District of Carshalton. It is an Outer Borough with a total population of approximately 166,000 and is primarily a dormitory for those who work in the City, although it has limited industry of its own. The district developed rapidly following the coming of the railway during the last century and very substantial growth this century. It is hardly the place where one would expect, in relation to such historic cities as Lincoln, York and Norwich, conservation to be an issue.

Surprisingly, however, the London Borough retains areas worthy of conservation although now engulfed in sprawling suburbia.

There is the old village of Cheam which, although largely rebuilt in mock Tudor style in the 1930's, still retains much of a village atmosphere with characteristic shopping centre. In addition to Whitehall, which is an old mansion dating from 1500, it retains a complete street of old cottages, many of which are of timber frame construction with timber cladding and also a small half-timbered dwelling which is some hundreds of years old. It is owned by the Council and now leased as a fine arts and materials shop.

Carshalton retains even more of the village atmosphere with an old church, winding village streets, large areas of public open space, including some acres of waterways and many buildings of architectural or historic interest. This village was selected by the Civic Trust for particular mention in their booklet "The Protection of Areas of Special Importance" prepared for the commemorative conference at the Guildhall, London, to inaugurate the coming into operation of the Civic Amenities Act, 1967. Immediately north of Carshalton Village is a small area, where many roads meet, known as Wrythe Green where there is a former eighteenth century tollhouse of a most unusual timber frame and timber cladding construction.

At Beddington there is another historic area comprising an old church and adjacent manor house now used as a school, a park keeper's lodge which is a fine example of Victorian Gothic architecture, and octagonal dovecote, and many acres of typical English parkland which is in the ownership of the Borough.

The idea of conservation was fostered, long before the Civic Amenities Act made the idea respectable, by two local amenity societies, the Sutton and Cheam Society and the Carshalton Society. The latter, in particular, have fought strenuously for many years to preserve the remaining character of Carshalton Village and its historic buildings and last year prepared their own plan for preserving the village as a Conservation Area.

In 1965 the new Local Planning Authority inherited no firm conservation policy from its predecessors. The former Borough of Sutton and Cheam had purchased the historic mansion of Whitehall and its grounds with the intention of restoring the mansion itself and developing its grounds for housing purposes. Within the land purchased was a detached cottage and a terrace of four smaller cottages, all of timber frame and timber cladding construction in an extremely dilapidated condition. The former Authority intended to demolish the cottages as part of the redevelopment scheme. This led to a public outcry and the formation of an energetic preservation group which called itself the Cheam Cottages Preservation Society and launched a vigorous campaign to have the cottages preserved.

One of the first achievements of the new Planning Authority was to reach a compromise with the Preservation Society whereby the Council agreed to delay demolition for a reasonable period of time to permit the Preservation Society to find persons who would be willing to lease the cottages and restore them, at their own expense, in accordance with a scheme to be approved by the Council. This compromise, it was felt, would permit the cottages to be preserved without involving the Council in heavy expense - although they would suffer a loss as the land would have more value if redeveloped at a higher density with new dwellings. Unfortunately the Preservation Society were not able to find lessees who were prepared to take the cottages. The Estates and Valuation Section of the Planning Department, after some considerable effort, were however subsequently successful and the five cottages have now been leased to three persons prepared to carry out a scheme of restoration to the satisfaction of the Council. Mortgages were also granted by the Council in respect of the cost of restoration. The detached cottage is now in process of restoration. The terrace of four cottages has been converted into two cottages; both have been restored and one is already occupied.

Although the Planning Committee agreed, with some hesitancy, to the compromise suggested by the Preservation Society, the result has been so successful that I think it can be said that the whole approach to preservation, and conservation, in the Borough has been greatly influenced by this decision and even the members who were most reluctant to abandon the previous proposal for demolition and redevelopment now concede that the outcome has been most satisfactory.

The Council have themselves proceeded vigorously with the restoration of Whitehall which is now leased as an Art Gallery.

At Carshalton Village, spurred on by the interest of the Civic Trust and the Greater London Council, and the zeal of the Carshalton Society, a Conservation Area has now been agreed which will include the whole of the original village and comprise some 96 acres. This area should be formally designated at a very early date.

The major achievement at Carshalton has been the co-operation between the Local Authority and the Sutton District Water Company regarding the concreting of the waterways known as Carshalton Ponds, which are a focal point of the village. These have been gradually drying out as the water table drops as a result of increasing demands for water. In return for being allowed to extract further water from above the village the Water Company agreed to concrete the waterways and provide an auxiliary supply so that even in conditions of severe drought the Ponds will always be filled with water. The concrete itself is being covered with a thin layer of soil and gravel so that plant and fish life is supported and when the scheme is complete it will be almost impossible to tell that extensive engineering works have been carried out.

A small area of only fourteen dwellings at Wrythe Green has now been agreed for designation as a Conservation Area and the Council have also agreed in principle that further Conservation Areas shall be designated at Cheam and at Beddington.

The London Borough of Sutton, like most of the other London Boroughs, suffers from a serious difficulty in obtaining qualified planning staff. A special Sub-Committee of the Planning Committee entitled the Planning (Civic Amenities) Sub-Committee, has been formed to consider the problems of conservation in the Borough and one of its recommendations has been that additional planning staff should be appointed to prepare schemes for the Conservation Areas. Unfortunately the financial restrictions at the present time have obliged the Council to defer this proposal.

Interim progress is, however, being made which varies from moving an unsightly gritting bin to an inconspicuous position; the provision of a pedestrian route from a new shopping precinct to a public park and the replacing of concrete posts and wire mesh fencing with salvaged iron railings. At a later stage must come more radical schemes which will include solutions for the severe traffic congestion which is affecting the character of all the Conservation Areas, especially that of Carshalton Village.

Valuable liaison has been established between the Council, the Civic Trust, and the Historic Buildings Section of the Greater London Council. The London Borough of Sutton is, and will remain, a suburb of London but the conservation policy now being vigorously pursued will ensure that within the great sea of suburbia there will be islands of special character which will be preserved and enhanced.

The Maltings at Snape, a continuation of the photograph on the title page.
Photographs from the East Suffolk County Planning Department.

CONSERVATION AT WOODBRIDGE, EAST SUFFOLK

Woodbridge is a small market town, and population residential community, within eight miles of a sub-regional capital, Ipswich, which has at present a population of 120,000. Under the proposed New Towns Act expansion, this will be well in excess of a quarter of a million by the end of the 1980s. On the one hand, as new owners are buying up cottages and buildings in Woodbridge, they are also renovating them and so contributing to the general conservation of the town; but on the other hand, Woodbridge, with a population of only 6,000, can barely afford the money needed for conservation of the town generally.

The complex of tight-knit buildings with their surrounding areas does much to give the "character" of Woodbridge. High boundary walls make a necessary contribution to this character. Several dilemmas followed on the desire to conserve, not least of which was that of a proposal to preserve the front areas by making a rear service road to the shops run through the existing part to the rear.

The study commencing in 1965 was a major operation not to be carried out by the backroom boys at County Hall but with the full co-operation and participation of the community as a whole, hence the fullscale publicity: press, radio, television, talks to youth clubs and all types of club and society. There followed a fairly typical present-day story of survey appraisal, draft plan, passing through the mills of the local council and County Council committees; a public exhibition; more press; more and more meetings. The interest of the public had to be aroused — a public, moreover, grown accustomed to its surroundings, a little spoiled, and certainly frustrated in its desire to use to the full modern motor transport. A plan evolved focussed on the need "to preserve and to enhance the historic and architectural of the centre of Woodbridge".

All the fine words are written and spoken and duly incorporated in the Written Statement submitted to the Minister. A fundamental feature of the plan was to retain intact a horseshoe of considerable historic and architectural interest — an environment of very high quality. In an attempt to meet realistically the understandable desires, indeed demands, of the local and visiting population for adequate vehicular access, modest road proposals were introduced to carry terminating traffic to the town centre, to the riverside recreational area and from one side of the town to the other. Now, however, we find an unwillingness on the part of the population to agree that traffic and its trebling is unacceptable in the heart of a conservation area: a rigid rejection of any attempt to channel vehicles away from the shopping and high quality environmental area. In other words, "leave our town as it is thank you — and that includes leaving us free to ride where we want to (train the children to be more careful), letting us grow". Is this perhaps something that sounds familiar?

Another aspect of traffic control, rear service to shopping streets, can be straightforward in new towns, in nondescript towns, but in historic towns it is a nightmare. The back is not all tatty, but an equally important part of the mixed land use environment which makes the place, and which gives the town its quality. Also, car parking standards become a real problem when future economic use of old buildings arises. Relaxation in a conservation area can lead to strong pressure and appeals against the enforcement of standards just beyond where the same use is involved: the traffic should not be there but the areas must remain alive.

Woodbridge, however, is known for an industrial building of some size, the Maltings, which had fallen into disuse. Instead of being allowed to slip into decay it was listed and eventually divided up for re-use by another industrialist and as the Aldeburgh Festival centre: an example of conservation on a sound economic basis.

MANAGEMENT AND DESIGN IN A HISTORIC TOWN: KINGS LYNN

1.   *The Chesterton Report*

The value of designating a "conservation area" lies in the opportunity it gives the local planning authority to "pay special attention to the desirability of preserving or enhancing its character or appearance" when a planning application comes in: but an energetic authority can do this in any case and can count on public sympathy in the process. In Kings Lynn the authorities had already prepared and published a survey of the kind envisaged by the Minister when he named the four historic towns: this was back in June, 1964, and the terms of reference from the County Planning Department and the local authority to Miss Chesterton were:

> "To carry out an overall survey of the whole of the historic core of Kings Lynn .... to make recommendations within the framework of the current proposals for the Central Area Redevelopment, as to which buildings should be (a) Preserved (b) Preserved with alteration (c) Redeveloped."

The authors were asked to produce a plan and a report which was to include an estimate of the likely cost and revenue of any development proposals.

In addition to reporting on these matters Miss Chesterton put forward a proposal for replanning the roads and car parking structure of the town, and a scheme for reconstructing a sizable portion of the very area it was considered might be preserved!

2.   *Brief History of the Town*

Kings Lynn grew slowly from an agricultural/fishing settlement in the tenth century, as a result of an increase of trade with Scandinavia and the lowlands. The Customs Duty arising from this trade went to the Church and financed the various Churches and priorities in the town. Further growth was stimulated in the thirteenth century by the diversion of the Great Ouse Outfall from Wisbech to Kings Lynn (which widened the shipping lane). Kings Lynn suffered a rapid decline between 1850 and 1890, as a result of the changeover from coastwise shipping to rail transport, and also of the general agricultural depression, which hit East Anglia especially hard due to its lack of other industries. This decline and slow recovery halted urban renewal, and when prosperity began to return, the new houses and industries went to the outskirts and not to the merchants' homes and warehouses in the historic part of the town. Miss Chesterton points out that, with the exception of the Churches, practically none of the buildings singled out as being of special architectural or historic interest is now used for the purpose for which it was built, although some of the most noteworthy have been adapted for various public uses.

From the original starting point (by Saturday Market Place) the town grew along a line parallel to the river, up as far as Tuesday Market Place.

The merchants' houses were built, fronting the streets, with the long narrow warehouses at right angles to them stretching through to the riverside quay. It is hard to imagine a simpler or more logical arrangement, and to a limited degree it still operates in places — though not in the original buildings, whose fabric would no longer be able to take the required loads.

3. *Nineteenth Century Development*
Kings Lynn has always been fortunate in that its structure allows for the addition of new types of development alongside the old, without unduly disrupting the existing fabric: and it was a simple operation to locate new development parallel to the original line.

4. *Twentieth Century Pressures — Motor Vehicles*
It is worth examining the nature of the threat that twentieth century pressures constituted to the fabric of Kings Lynn. First, the motor vehicle. It will be appreciated that the original layout neatly separated commercial traffic by river from residential traffic by road: consequently the general increase in road transport as opposed to water transport meant that commercial and residential traffic went on to the same road. The volume of this traffic continued to grow considerably, but a still greater threat to the historic area comes from the private car — for which it was originally proposed to build an inner ring road straight through the historic area on the line of King and Queen Streets. This would have been an impossible road to construct without demolitions at awkward points, and the heavy traffic would impose vibrations which the old building fabric could not have withstood. The ring road has now been officially removed from the Development Plan, and a new access structure for the town has been substituted. It is still the case that the best defence for historic areas is to ensure that incompatible development takes place elsewhere!

5. *Twentieth Century Pressures — Population*
The second threat to the survival of the historic buildings and spaces arises from the pressure of population. Kings Lynn is expected to be the home for about 54,000 people by 1981 and the regional service centre for about 115,000 people. The Development Plan had to provide services for these numbers and the corresponding demands for additional space in the centre of Kings Lynn can be summarized as follows: (from the Report of Survey)

New shopping floor area	—	80,000 sq. ft. (say 6 acres)
Offices	—	Not stated
Service industry	—	17 – 18 acres
Places of public assembly	—	About 1 acre
Car parking	—	10 acres
Bus and coach station	—	1¾ acres
Open space	—	2 acres

6. *Effect of Pressures on Historic Area*
The pressure exerted by new needs such as these on all existing historic areas is twofold; direct, through specific applications to demolish and redevelop, and indirect, by raising the scale of commercial activity generally. Some of these uses could well find a home in the historic areas (offices for example) and the best thing that can

happen to a historic building, if it cannot continue economically in its original use, is for a new occupier to be found who does not need to have the building demolished or substantially altered. A great deal of effort has been expended on this approach in Kings Lynn by various bodies, both public and voluntary, and what has happened in the historic part of the town is that while most of the more meritorious buildings have been found suitable caretaker-tenants, little or no redevelopment as such has taken place in the others. In consequence, some of the buildings are now in a shabby state and the problem is not so much who is going to repair them as, who is going to live in them, and keep them warm so that the pipes do not burst? If anyone wonders why the Tuesday Market, one of the great town squares of Britain, has remained as good as it is, he should take note of who lives in it: four banks, twelve insurance companies, four hotels, five building societies and five solicitors. There is, however, a limit to the number of caretaker-tenants like those, and to the amount of money available for purchase and maintenance by the local authority: consequently if the historic areas are not to become slums, redevelopment in other cases eventually becomes economically necessary. I suggest this is preferable to uneconomical preservation *provided that the architectural scale and flavour of the area is not changed.*

7.
Scale
The changing intensity in commercial activity in the town as a whole involves the introduction of new structures of a fundamentally different architectural scale and character, such as multi-storey car parks, modern shopping centres and bus stations. I would like to emphasize this point of scale because, although it is not easy to define, nevertheless it is far more significant than, for instance, the crude heights of buildings. To give an example, the Chesterton Report recommends the construction of a multi-storey car park close by the Custom House: the main bulk of this would not be apparent at street level, but by increasing the openness of Purfleet Street and by arranging the buildings into larger units, the scheme would change the character of this crucial spot far more than the grain silo nearby, which is at least 115 feet high. By comparison, the Custom House is about 65 feet to the top of the cupola, and the car park would be only 55 feet high. All the uses mentioned above, which arise one way or another from the ability of more people to spend more money, are potentially large and unable to be assimilated into the small scale intricacies of the historic area. Quite clearly this is a matter where the Planning Authority must give the lead.

8.
The Impact of the Development Company
So far, I have described the commercial pressures in the abstract: in July, 1963, however, two property development companies appeared on the scene. My firm was appointed by the first of these two companies (Second Covent Garden Property Company) and as I am more familiar with this scheme than I am with the other (Norwich Union) I will concentrate my description on the former: in any case, the partnership arrangements with the Council were broadly the same. The areas involved did not fall in the historic area, although there were a few buildings listed as being of architectural and historic interest in New Conduit Street and one building preservation order (on a Gothic archway).

9.   *The Getting-Together Process*
During the twelve months up to June, 1964, Second Covent Garden
purchased further frontage and backland in New Conduit Street and
Broad Street, and established the usual contacts with both the Local and
the Planning Authorities. At the same time the Kings Lynn Council took
advice from Mr. Henry Wells (as his title was at that time) as soon as it
became aware of the two Property Companies' interest to ensure that the
local Authorities would be involved in the quality of the built environment,
and to join a commercial enterprise which would assist the various road
works and car parks in other parts of the town to be carried out. In
September, 1965, the Kings Lynn Planning Committee agreed that the
scheme should henceforward be implemented "on a joint participation
basis", but it was not until April, 1966, that the first of a series of
working party meetings took place, attended by representatives of the
County Planning Department, the Borough Council (now being advised
by Alfred Savill and Sons), the Development Company and their architects. The design of the scheme then proceeded smoothly; demolitions
began later that year, and work on site actually began in March, 1967
(just before April 6th!). The first shops are now open and trading.

10.   *The Elapse of Time*
I have laboured the catalogue of dates somewhat, because (if you have
kept a note of them) you will have seen that three years and eight months
elapsed between the purchase of a building site and the digging of the
first foundation trench. Conceivably, the Development Company might
have been premature if they had built shops to let back in 1965, but
many things could have gone amiss in that time. The developers might
well have tired of having capital tied up in unremunerative properties and
moved off elsewhere: the Council might have been subjected to pressure
to build the car parks or accommodate local interests in the wrong way or
in the wrong places: local business might have decided that Kings Lynn
was never going to develop and so built the new factories elsewhere. It
is not easy for those who have to design the new environment to keep
enthusiasm alive. In Kings Lynn the Planning Authority had a good plan
but I am certain it should have started at least eighteen months earlier.
I am aware of reasons for this failure but, as Mr. Shankland said, the
chief problem in a conservation area is that of mis-spent resources, and I
would suggest that time is the resource most often mis-spent. The result
of delayed decisions can be seen in unsightly hoardings across demolition
sites.

It has been suggested that conservation areas can best be dealt with by the
"Action Area" technique. I would question this because it implies that it
is possible for a Planning Authority to prepare a "once-for-all" scheme.
A developer recently told me that if he has to build a scheme exactly the
way he originally planned it, it will be a commercial failure because the
occupants will not have had their particular needs catered for. One has to
have a framework on which to build but it should not be rigid: and the
recipe which seems to work best is an atmosphere of mutual trust between
Planning Authority, Local Authority, and the Developer with his architect;
the absence of preconceptions about urban form; and the liberal (and
unofficial) exchange of rough perspective sketches on A4 size sheets. This
works and is infinitely more acceptable to those involved than a dogmatic
attitude towards design.

11.

To summarize the points made

First of all, nothing can be done without an imaginative and comprehensive plan which has regard to both conservation and economic viability. This is the job of the Planning Authority and it is not the job of the commercial developer to worry about preservation — particularly if it is in another part of the town — and it is pointless to suggest that he should do so "as a public duty".

Conversely, the right type of developer has much to contribute on his own terms: he is skilled at realizing the maximum return from redevelopment and nowadays it is in his interest to share this with the community. It is doubtful whether the community which is blessed with a heritage, without an inheritance to go with it, can pay for car parks and schemes of pedestrian segregation without this aid.

Thirdly, the only person who can preserve a building is the person who is going to live in it. There are not many buildings so outstanding as to merit retention at any cost, and it is better to find and, if necessary, subsidize, caretaker-tenants for as many of these as possible (if they are not already in occupation) rather than to select a few special buildings and to spend money in cocooning them.

Fourthly, where good buildings are falling apart through not being lived in, redevelopment should be welcomed. Of course I do not mean wholesale rebuilding, but it is far better to approach the revitalization of the historic areas in this spirit than to go about pickling the facades.

Finally, where it comes to design in a heritage area, the emphasis should be on the retention of existing scale and quality, and not on the preservation of particular features, or on blanket restrictions for example, on heights, glass areas, colours or building materials.

This is not a task for the unskilled and the designer of the built environment must understand what the economic objectives are, before he can start to recreate the quality which has decayed. I doubt if the multifarious intricacies involved can be tabulated and mapped in any significant way: and I suggest that you will probably destroy the flavours you are trying to capture if you try.

Philadelphia, sensitive combination of old and new. Photograph by Graeme Shankland.

Limerick, Eire, part of one of the finest Georgian streets in the British Isles.

RT FOUR – HISTORICAL RESEARCH

REPORT OF THE STUDY GROUP
CONVENED BY THE COUNCIL FOR
BRITISH ARCHAEOLOGY

Chairman: Maurice Barley MA FSA FRHistS
Secretary: Miss B. de Cardi FSA

Group Members

K. Barton FSA AMA
   Curator, Worcestershire County Museum
Martin Biddle BA FSA
   Department of History, University of Exeter
. G. Dunbar MA FSA
   *Investigator, Royal Commission on Ancient and Historical
   Monuments, Scotland*
K. R. Fennell PhD FSA FRICS MTPI
   Deputy County Planning Officer, Kesteven
Alan J. Frost AADip ARIBA
   Donald Insall and Associates
. J. Garton OBE FSA
   Historic Buildings Council
Mrs M. D. Lobel FSA FRHistS
   Secretary, Oxford Historical Atlas Committee
G. H. Martin MA PhD FRHistS
   Department of History, University of Leicester
Michael Middleton MSIH
   Deputy Director, Civic Trust
D. B. Peace MTPI ARIBA
   *Deputy County Planning Officer,
   Cambridgeshire and Isle of Ely*
Peter Smith BA FSA
   *Investigator, Royal Commission on Ancient Monuments,
   Wales and Monmouthshire*
Professor H. Thorpe
   Department of Geography, University of Birmingham

Assessors

Antony Dale FSA
   *Chief Investigator of Historic Buildings,
   Ministry of Housing and Local Government*
. Rarity
   Scottish Office
. G. Parry
   Welsh Office

SURVEY AND RESTORATION OF TIMBER
FRAMED BUILDINGS IN COVENTRY

F. W. B. Charles MA BArch FRIBA

1. *THE PURPOSE OF RESEARCH*

In a world of growing complexity and elaboration, it is essential to make sure, when a problem is to be tackled, that the right questions are asked, in the right order; the questions must then be put to the right people. If we are to have a sound conservation policy for our historic towns, the basic question must be: *what exactly is there to conserve?*

Those who study the past are labelled as historians, or archaeologists. They have as yet no place in the planning machine in Britain. It is therefore all the more important that such specialists should be given the chance to explain how this basic question, what is there to conserve, can be answered.

The question certainly *can* be answered, quickly enough, for every historic town, provided that all our resources are utilised. This means human resources - historians, archivists, archaeologists, and any other specialists such as geographers and architects who care to turn their skills to the study of the past. It also means material resources - historical records of many kinds; maps, surveys, photographs. Here the problem is not a scarcity of material, but the organization of it - making sure that it is accessible and arranged, in the right place, at the right time. If research into urban history was treated as seriously as scientific research, results would certainly follow, because the raw material is abundant.

Much of the past is buried. As well as having historic buildings still in use, many towns possess precious ruins - a castle, an abbey or a length of town wall. Whether such remains are still visible is, for us today, a matter of chance, but they are a reminder that still more must be buried in every town centre. Given a chance to find them, archaeologists could fill in many blank areas in the story of our towns.

Out of such research will come accounts, presented in the form of maps, plans, photographs and words, of every historic town. We must be able to see each town *as a whole*: its street plan, open spaces, buildings, all in their landscape setting. Each town is unique, and each has gone through its own phases of evolution, every one of which has left its mark on the present.

This research need not always imply professional work, in the sense of staff employed full-time by a local authority. Given suitable initiative and direction, a large contribution could be made by amateurs - that is, historians, archaeologists and students of all kinds - placing their skills at the disposal of local authorities, working in their spare time, and spurred on by the pride and devotion that any town ought to be able to generate. The key here is *suitable initiative* - best taken by local authorities.

These aspects of research into urban history are discussed in the following three sections of the Study Group's report. The immediate object of this research is quite clear: to enable planning authorities to carry out their obligations under the Civic Amenities Act (1967). It requires them "to designate conservation areas, the character or appearance of which, because of their special architectural or historic interest, ought to be preserved or enhanced". The Ministry's circular 53/67 calls for speedy action, because "the need is very urgent in many historic towns". Conservation areas "may be large or small, from whole town centres or squares, terraces and smaller groups of buildings". They may centre on "an historic street plan, or a feature of archaeological interest", as well as on listed buildings. And, most important, "the statutory procedure is simple".

2. MAPS AND DOCUMENTS

2.1

The Object of Documentary Research

Research for conservation takes the researcher first to the library, to answer the question: What was the town's physical appearance in 1800? or 1600? or 1066? Very few books or articles have been written explicitly to answer this question. Historians of every age write to answer the questions uppermost in their minds, and this question about the physical appearance of a town has rarely been posed before now.

2.2

The Evolution of Towns

If the answer cannot be found, ready made on the shelves of a library, it must be built up from a variety of sources. Before those sources can be described, we must have a general idea of the historical development of British towns. In those of Roman origin, if the Roman plan has not already been discovered, further excavations will eventually provide the answer. In nearly every case the area of archaeological interest is already known. But few of any of our Roman towns still possess more than fragments of a Roman layout. Most were replanned, usually within the framework of Roman walls, at a later date.

Most of Britain's historic towns, as we have inherited them, were shaped in two great periods of economic expansion. The first began in the time of Alfred (about 900 A.D.) and lasted until the Black Death (about 1350 A.D.). To this age belongs the layout of streets, some of the open spaces and the oldest public buildings and institutions. Of the three hundred odd towns in the list produced by the Council for British Archaeology (reprinted in "Conservation Areas", Civic Trust, 1967), some were "new towns" in their time, as new as Cumbernauld. Many of the rest, when closely scrutinised, show traces of conscious planning in their layout.

After 1350 there followed a static period, or even decline. Old lanes were blocked up or became disused; suburban growth contracted; open spaces within the walls increased. Monasteries and other religious institutions disappeared, and much property changed hands. Some ancient cities, such as Nottingham and Bury St. Edmunds, had so much open space between 1550 and 1750 that they have been described as "garden towns". After about 1550 growth was resumed, especially in market towns.

The 18th century saw much new building, especially of good quality housing for professional people, merchants and traders. The second great age of town expansion, due to the Industrial Revolution, belongs to the years since 1800. As well as growth, there were often changes in street plan and land use, which gave us the towns as we know them.

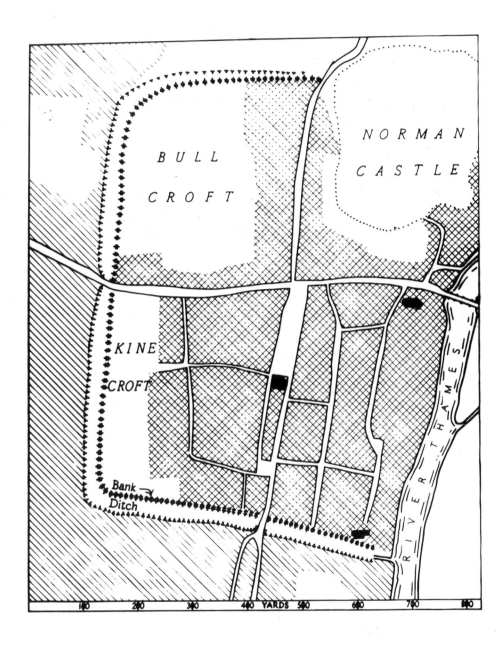

Fig. 1. Sketch plan of Wallingford, Berks., to illustrate the development of open spaces near the town centre. The defensive bank and ditch, and the grid plan of streets, belong to the time of Alfred (c.890 A.D.). Later, a Norman castle was planted in the north-east corner of the town. The built up area (cross hatched) shrank; open ground within the defences (Bull Croft, Kine Croft) became common, and recent development (hatched) was forced out beyond the defences. (Plan drawn by M. W. Barley).

Historic Town Maps

In the light of this sequence, it seems that period plans of the historic town ought to be produced, especially for

A. The period 850-1350;

B. The Elizabethan Age (1600);

C. The Georgian Age (1800);

D. The Victorian period for those towns which have virtually been created since 1840.

The maps should be accompanied by notes on buildings and institutions, streets, local trades and industries, markets and also on the surrounding fields.

What sources can be used in the compilation of these historic town plans?

A. *Older maps.* Working backwards, there are first the large scale maps (25″ to the mile and in some cases at a scale of 1:500) of the Ordnance Survey (about 1870 onwards). These are very valuable, but they may show towns only as the Industrial Revolution had transformed them.

B. *Local maps.* Many of the larger and wealthier cities commissioned maps of the highest quality: for instance, Nottingham (1744), Boston (1742), Norwich (1789) and Hereford (1757). Some of these go back even further, such as Ipswich (1674) and Bristol (1673). The War Office and the Board of Ordnance produced in the eighteenth century plans of many garrison towns and ports; they are now in the Public Record Office.

C. *Local surveys.* In many towns, statutory undertakings compiled their own surveys in the period 1830-70. For instance, the earliest accurate plan of Gloucester was prepared for the public health authority in 1835. Many of these maps and surveys are still in the departments now responsible for particular services, and are little known to historians. They should not be overlooked: indeed, they ought to be deposited in local record offices.

D. *The Oldest maps.* Map making in England goes back to the first Elizabethan age, with printed town plans like those of Speed (published 1610), and the many estate maps prepared for the new landowners of the time.

2.4

Historic Atlas of Town Plans

The model for modern maps of our historic towns will soon be available to the public. The Study Group has learned with great satisfaction of the scheme for an *Historical Atlas of Town Plans for Western Europe.* The British Section for this project is preparing a series of town plans, to be published in full colour, at a scale of 1:2,500 (about 25″ to the mile) - large enough to show individual properties. Each map will be accompanied by a text of about 7,000 words, and supporting maps. The map will show a town as it was in about 1800, with special conventions to indicate older features, such as town walls, and gates, which had disappeared by that date. Various scholars are at work, with a view to producing the first folio of ten maps by the end of 1968, with other folios to follow at yearly intervals. London will eventually have a volume to itself. This scheme has received grants from the British Academy and the Pilgrim Trust, whose support has been used largely for research and

Fig. 2. Part of a map of Boston, Lincs., published in 1741 by Robert Hall. It shows buildings and properties accurately, and also the line of the Bar Ditch, the medieval defensive system, which had in part been filled in or built over.

technical needs. Given more ample support, the scheme could go faster, though there would be a limit to possible expansion if the present high standard is to be maintained. Printers of the Atlas are Lovell-Johns Limited of 25, Caxton Street, London, S.W.1.

This scheme ought to be more widely known, and the Study Group welcomes the opportunity to draw attention to it. The honorary editor of the British section is Mrs. M. D. Lobel, 16 Merton Street, Oxford. For those towns with no immediate prospect of inclusion in the Atlas, the maps will be a model, in terms of scholarship and cartography, of what can be done.

2.5 *Documents*
Maps are not the only evidence for the historic street plan. Much evidence can be found in old deeds which begin to be plentiful from the 13th century onwards, and from a variety of rent rolls and surveys. For cathedral cities such as Canterbury or Lincoln, and for other places where record-keeping institutions such as abbeys had large property interests, it is possible to go a long way towards compiling a history of each property in the historic core. Even where this detailed knowledge is beyond reach, medieval and later deeds, which necessarily described a property so that anyone could identify it, can be used to identify streets which have vanished or changed their name, industries which have disappeared, market places which have been built over, churches long since pulled down, and fields now covered with buildings. Thus a picture of changes in land-use over 700 years can be built up, in outline and often in detail.

2.6 *Changes in Land Use*
These former land uses readily fall under heads similar to those used now in planning :
A. Public buildings or institutions, such as castles, abbeys and friaries, parish churches and hospitals.
B. Municipal and lesser public buildings — moot halls, guild halls, etc.
C. Commercial or industrial concentrations — butchers (shambles), tanners, potters, brick-makers, etc.
D. Public open spaces such as market places, burial grounds, etc.
E. Houses.

2.7 *Town Defences*
Last of all, as much information as possible must be squeezed out of documents concerning the defences of ancient towns. They are of intrinsic interest, and they provide a frame or limit for further historic research, as well as offering a possible boundary for the "conservation area". Some towns still possess a circuit of defences, either in the form of a standing wall, as at York or Chester, or an earth bank and ditch, as at Sandwich. Many other towns still have lengths of wall or some upstanding traces such as town gates. But for some other towns we still do not know whether defences were ever constructed, or when they were made, or exactly where they ran. In some cities, such as Bristol or Norwich, the circuit of defences was enlarged as the city grew. Each step in such a development needs to be established from documents. Archaeologists can then test these conclusions, and may themselves throw up further

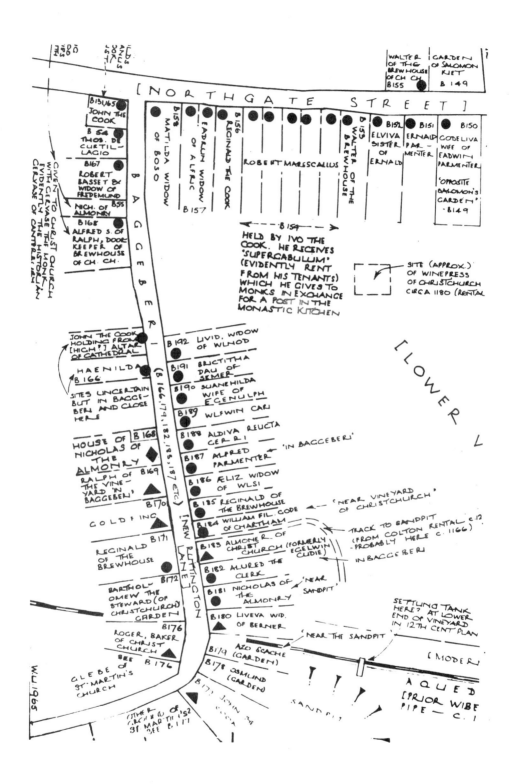

Fig. 3. Canterbury in the 12th century. Part of a map of the town compiled by Dr. W. G. Urry showing that, given plentiful documentary evidence, it may be possible to identify nearly every tenement 700 years ago. (From W. G. Urry, *Canterbury under the Angevin Kings,* London, 1967).

Fig. 4. Sandwich, Kent. This raised walk runs round the town on the crest of the medieval ramparts. Rampart and ditch still form the limit of the town. (Photo by M. W. Barley).

Fig. 5. Leominster, Herefordshire. Demolition has exposed the side wall of a timber-framed building (with the wattling still intact) encased in a nondescript Victorian structure. (Photo by M. W. Barley).

historical problems. Thus the two methods of research will constantly increase our knowledge (see Section 3).

(see Section 3).

.8 *Recommendations*

The proper exploitation of historical records, for urban history, on the lines here suggested, takes for granted some things that do not already exist for every historic town.

A. There should be a local record office containing all the relevant records. A large number of local record offices have come into being since 1945, but in many cases the records have not all been gathered into them. Departments of a local authority may be reluctant to deposit records which they consider they still need. In this sort of situation, photocopies or microfilms should be placed in the record office.

B. A large library of books would be useless without a catalogue. Without lists, catalogues and indexes, a large collection of records is also useless. The historian is in the position of searching through a haystack *in case* there is a needle in it. Local record offices ought to have enough staff to prepare the necessary aids to research.

C. Even when record material is so arranged and catalogued that it can be used with maximum ease, the task of sifting through it for all the evidence needed to prepare historic town maps is considerable. Dr. William Urry's great work on Canterbury, with its maps of the town and its streets and properties in the 12th century, represents a labour of many years. Very few other cities possess such a wealth of documents. In many cases it is more a matter of seeing that what is already in print, in books and articles, is organised and *presented in map form*. In other cases, an energetic attempt to organise group research on documents, by interested and qualified persons, could produce fairly speedy results.

D. This report started by pointing out that all researchers, whatever their subject, try to answer the questions uppermost in their minds. Local authority officers and council members must make sure that every local historian has planted in his mind the urgency of answering the question: What was the physical appearance of our town in the past?

3. *SURVEYS OF BUILDINGS*

3.1 Historical buildings are documents. If we can learn to read them, they will tell us things about historic towns that were never put down on paper. Reading a building means answering as many as possible of these questions:

When was it built?
Who built it?
Who paid for the building?
What was its function?
What was its plan and design?
What materials were used?

Why was it sited where it was?

What alterations has it undergone?

3.2

What is "special architectural or historic interest"?

The answers to these questions add up to the "special architectural or historic interest" of listed buildings. Usually, planning authorities try to define historic interest in terms of historical *associations* - the famous persons who lived in, or visited, a building; the famous events that took place in it, etc. It is often a matter of chance whether such associations can be established. In any case, history would be a poor affair if it had room only for famous people. Buildings are the visual expression of the life of a community. The houses of ordinary people ought to have a large place in our view of history, even though those ordinary people have left no documents behind.

Trying to measure the "special architectural interest" of a building means applying aesthetic judgments. These are largely subjective, so they are very treacherous weapons with which to defend a building. One party will say that a building is beautiful; the other party will simply deny it. But to put a building in its historic context - its time, its social class, etc. - is to define its "architectural interest" in a way that is beyond argument.

There have been enormous advances during the past twenty years in our knowledge of historic buildings in Britain. The question now is whether the information is adequate, and, more important, whether it is available to any planning authority, in a form lending itself readily to judgments by committees.

3.3

Ministry Lists

The planning officer, naturally and properly, turns to the list of "buildings of special architectural and historic interest" compiled by the Ministry of Housing and Local Government and Scottish Development Department, in accordance with the provisions of the Planning Acts of 1947 onwards. Our first task is to assess the value of these lists. With a few exceptions, only the outside of a building is described and, in towns, only the street frontage unless a building is free-standing in its own grounds. All buildings revealing or suggesting an origin prior to about 1700 are or should be included. From about 1700 to about 1830 any significant building that is intact is considered listable. But after 1830 the selection is much more restricted, and only buildings of definite character and quality are included.

The completion of the lists, in not much more than twenty years, represents a remarkable accomplishment. Once that is said, the shortcomings of the lists must be admitted. Some stem from the brief, with its inevitable emphasis on street fronts. Since investigators were not required to look inside a building, and have no right of access, a medieval building which was refronted in the Georgian or Victorian period may figure as belonging only to the latter age, and its history thus be overlooked. Many lists, especially for Scotland, are still only in provisional form.

The listing programme inevitably led to errors and omissions. The investigators were learning their job as they did it, and indeed learning to classify and date buildings which had never before h- closely examined. Errors and omissions have occasionally b(retrieved by "spot-listing". Today, the lists need revision, ideas have changed and new knowledge is available. Revisi more investigators, more clerks for the administrative work. Ministry and the Scottish Development Department each needs more staff of one kind or both.

Listing, as part of the planning process, and the division of lists into grades, have their own hazards. Obviously, omission from a list ought not to condemn a building as without historical interest, though in practice it inevitably does so. What is needed is an objective and accurate guide to the history of a building. Where can it be found?

3.4

Other Surveys

For more than half a century, various official and semi-official bodies have been at work. The *London Survey,* now run by the G.L.C., has produced thirty-four volumes combining documentary and architectural research. In some English counties, the *Victoria County History* has included accounts of buildings, though the degree of interest in architectural history is necessarily limited.

The one quarter to which we are entitled to look for definitive accounts of buildings is to the three permanent *Royal Commissions on Historical Monuments* (for England, Scotland and Wales). Each has now been in existence for nearly sixty years, charged with compiling inventories of buildings and other monuments "illustrative of the life of the people from the earliest times". The pace set by the Commissions (each with its staff of investigators, draughtsmen and photographers), and in particular by the English Commission, has aroused impatience which scrutiny of the output since 1945 cannot easily dispel. The Scottish Commission has published twenty-two inventories (i.e. volumes) of eighteen counties out of thirty-three, the Welsh Commission eight counties out of its thirteen (including Monmouth); the English Commission has dealt with nine counties completely and three others in part. One factor is rising standards: the more detailed the knowledge of building styles and techniques, the more meticulously every building must be examined. The limited staff has to deal with earthworks - castles, barrows, etc. - as well as buildings down to 1850 or even later. Surveys of this kind, it is clear, will not be available for every historic town within the foreseeable future.

3.5

Problems of Survey analysed

Before impatience leads us to thrust aside all such scholarly efforts, as irrelevant to our present needs, the nature and quality of surveys of historic buildings must be defined, and the practical elements of the task assessed. A bald statement that a building is listed as Grade I or II, without elaboration or photographs, does not answer the basic questions: how is the building *special*? Of what special *historic* or *architectural* interest? The character of a building must be described, in words, or photographs, or drawings, or all three.

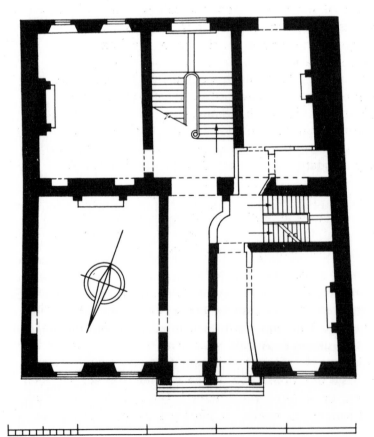

Fig. 6. Nos. 53/55 Micklegate, York, circa 1755, probably by John Carr of York, with alterations of c.1815.

This is a typical example of a drawing for reproduction produced by the Royal Commission on Historical Monuments (England) and is one of several hundred being prepared in their survey of York.

Systematic recording by photography offers a useful basis for historical and architectural judgments, but no complete surveys are at present available. Very few cities possess a systematic survey. The *National Monuments Record*, established during the 1939-45 war to record buildings threatened by bombing, has continued its work and is now a part of each of the Royal Commissions. The collections are available for consultation in London, Edinburgh and Aberystwyth, and are intensively used by government in day-to-day dealings with listed buildings, but can scarcely be used by local planning authorities.

The best photographs may miss essential features of a building. Knowledge of architecture is essential, and so is the architect's type of record: that is, measured plans and sections. For the last hundred years, the training of architects in this country has required students to produce such drawings to satisfy their examiners. Many such drawings have found their way into the National Monuments Record or into local libraries. But neither the collecting nor the commissioning of such surveys has yet been put on a systematic basis. It is high time that local authorities set themselves the task of gathering together, in public libraries, local museums or local record offices, all the photographs and drawings that have been made, for one purpose or another, of buildings in their towns. The result would be impressive and enormously valuable. It would include original plans deposited with the Borough Engineer since 1870 or so; surveys by planning and public health departments and older statutory undertakings, as well as the contributions of private individuals.

Archaeology, like photography, is a popular hobby in this country. Most archaeologists find their satisfaction in digging, about which we shall have something to say later, but there has been a significant growth, since 1950, in the number of men and women who prefer to study buildings. They have been specially interested in what they call vernacular building: that is, construction in traditional methods and materials, without benefit of an architect. Indeed many architects tend to despise such traditional buildings, or at any rate to regard them as of much slighter "architectural" interest than large buildings in a textbook style - "Renaissance", "Georgian", or whatever the label may be. Students of vernacular building have made spectacular advances in understanding of this part of Britain's heritage. Their work has been published in books, and in articles in county journals. Admittedly it has focussed largely on rural buildings, not on towns, and the results give no systematic coverage of the country. Nevertheless these buildings are the stuff of history, just as much as churches, castles and mansions. The study of their plans and details of construction, especially where they are timber-framed, is the only way to learn more than we know already, and more than any textbook on the history of architecture can tell us, about crafts and craftsmanship in former times, and about the homes and workplaces of ordinary townsfolk.

Examples are worth quoting to underline the importance and the variety of discoveries recently made in this field of study. They include buildings in Oxford which housed students before the development of the college system; large merchants' houses in Kings Lynn, a great medieval port, and

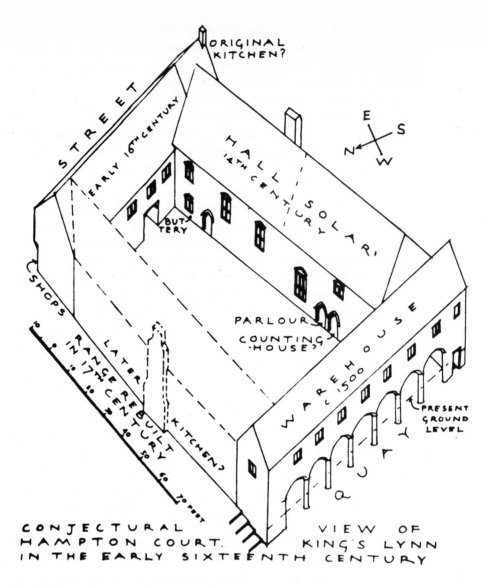

ORIGINAL KITCHEN?

STREET

EARLY 16TH CENTURY

HALL SOLAR 14TH CENTURY

E
N — S
W

SHOPS

BUTTERY

LATER RANGE REBUILT IN 17TH CENTURY

KITCHEN?

PARLOUR

COUNTING HOUSE?

WAREHOUSE c.1500

PRESENT GROUND LEVEL

QUAY

10 20 30 40 50 60 70 FEET

CONJECTURAL VIEW OF
HAMPTON COURT. KING'S LYNN
IN THE EARLY SIXTEENTH CENTURY

Fig. 7. Hampton Court, King's Lynn, recently restored by the King's Lynn Preservation Trust. This isometric drawing shows the development of the complex of merchant's house, shops and warehouse, alongside the river Ouse. (Drawing by W. A. Pantin).

a row of fifteenth century cottages in Coventry. Another striking example of a building whose date and importance were completely overlooked until it was threatened with demolition, is the Old Deanery, Salisbury. When examined on the eve of demolition, it was found to be substantially of the 13th century. So much of the original structure was intact, behind later partitions and inserted ceilings, that it proved feasible to restore it to its original condition. It now forms a splendid part of Salisbury College of Education.

In cases like these, it is frequently the roof construction which provides the best clue to the age of a building. This raises the problem of access. Ideally the investigator needs to examine every part of a building, and often to have time for a second look. Such practical problems can be minimized by, for instance, suitable publicity in the local press, and by competent organization of a survey.

Technical difficulties are as a rule more formidable in the case of urban surveys. Buildings have been modified more often, and more extensively, than in the country. In particular, properties in the historic centres of old towns have usually been more or less gutted at ground level. Changes like this mean that the original ground plan cannot be recovered. Properties may have been amalgamated and original boundaries obscured. Ancient buildings in towns vary much more in their plan and arrangement than those in the country, because of more diverse and specialized functions and the variety of site available.

It is a paradox that many of the striking advances in our knowledge of types of small houses and their construction would have been impossible but for the tempo of destruction since 1945. Assuming the goodwill of owners and contractors, buildings under demolition can be recorded without hindrance, and with the opportunity - with a pickaxe if necessary - of getting behind every partition or cupboard. Many archaeologists have done invaluable work in watching demolitions, recording buildings in detail and publishing their findings. The Royal Commissions allocate a small section of their staff to this same task.

.6
Publication of Surveys
In research of this kind, publication of results is essential. Apart from the needs of planning departments for convenient handbooks, the advancement of knowledge demands access to the results of research. Features of a building in, say, Yeovil or York may be explicable only by comparison with Kentish examples. A novel house plan or a newly discovered form of roof construction may, when comparisons can be made, prove to be widely distributed, and so characteristic of a region or period, rather than accidental or eccentric. The lack of published material is at present an obstacle to interpreting and classifying town buildings. There are in print no recent surveys of historic towns with substantial numbers of buildings of all periods, except for the Royal Commission's inventories of Oxford and Cambridge, Edinburgh and Stirling. The demolished buildings recorded by the Commissions would, if published in full, provide a cross section of Britain's legacy. Publication would facilitate comparative studies and spot-light regional variations. It would also reveal the rate and seriousness of our losses.

The ideal town survey then, is one in which every historic building is examined, described in words, illustrated as necessary by photographs and scale drawings, and then published. Such surveys would be essential tools for planners. They would also satisfy a widening popular interest in art and architecture, in crafts, in social history and in archaeology. Such surveys would be expensive to carry out, but without them, a conservation policy is to some degree blind or haphazard. No country can afford to neglect research. Britain is spending less, or spending less effectively, on research into historic towns than other countries in Western Europe.

.7
The Practical Problems
We have therefore on the one hand the *appraisal* of historic buildings in England by the Ministry of Housing and Local Government - speedy and cheap but superficial and fallible. At the other extreme we have *scholarly survey* - slow and expensive but definitive and accurate. Is there

Fig. 8. Halifax, Yorkshire. (a) The exterior of derelict cottages in Boothtown, due for demolition. The medieval core is completely hidden.
(b) Removing internal walls and stripping plaster has begun to reveal the beams of a medieval aisled hall. (Photo by Royal Commission on Historical Monuments, England).

any compromise between these alternatives? Only, at present, those surveys specially prepared or commissioned by planning authorities, such as Stamford (Kesteven), Tenterden (Kent) and Newark (Nottinghamshire). They are essentially concerned with planning policy: what is worth conservation and how this may be achieved. Such surveys cannot be expected to say the last word about historic buildings - their age, function, social and historic importance. They can, however, provide an architectural analysis, and pinpoint buildings which need closer scrutiny by specialists (Fig. 9). The initiative of the Ministry, in arranging for surveys of York, Chester, Chichester and Bath (to be published in 1968) should break new ground, in particular in exploring the economic and political problems of conservation.

Since planning authorities urgently need such comprehensive surveys, designed to produce results - that is, the retention of valuable buildings - it is much to be hoped that more surveys will be commissioned in the near future, and the results published.

3.8   *Conclusions and recommendations*
How can we learn, quickly enough, as much as we need to know about historic buildings? One solution would be a vast enlargement of the staff of the Historical Monuments Commissions and a modification of their county-by-county programme. For various reasons, this solution is probably impracticable, but the Commissions should be urged to arrange for speedy and complete publication of surveys made since 1955 of threatened buildings.

Another would be for planning authorities to take on to their staff specialists to carry out such surveys. Staffordshire County Council has shown how valuable this policy can be, and how quickly results can be obtained. It may be difficult to recruit suitable staff sufficiently quickly, but there is no doubt that this is the only adequate answer to the responsibilities of planning authorities for historic buildings and ancient monuments of all kinds.

3.9   *An interim solution* would be for the authorities to commission surveys, appointing interested and qualified persons from various walks of life. Their brief would be
      A. To adopt, without further research on a large scale, accepted accounts of churches, public buildings and houses of a textbook character;
      B. To concentrate on other buildings and features, especially
         (a) industrial buildings;
         (b) Victorian shops, offices, public houses, etc.;
         (c) smaller houses of all periods down to mid-Victorian times;
         (d) characteristic and traditional features such as materials used in walls, and ground surfaces, street-furniture, etc.
      C. To procure a photographic record of such buildings where none already exists in a local repository;
      D. To compile, in standardised form, a brief description of such buildings, along with sketch plans.

From our knowledge of the skills available among architects, historians and archaeologists and students of all kinds, the Study Group is of the opinion that such surveys, given brisk initiative and will on the part of

CHESTER

HISTORIC TOWN SURVEY
ASSESSMENT OF PROPERTIES

Date 16/2/67	Street Westgate St.
Time(s) 10.30 am st. level / 11.00 am row level	Number(s) 14, 16 street level / 12, 12A, 14 row level
Inspected by AF — Exterior ✓ Interior ✓	

OCCUPIED BY: owner(s) ~~tenant(s)~~ (empty)

BUILDING UNIT: extd (subdvd from 12) as origl combd wth

CONSTRUCTION DATES: origl (13) reblt 1718 addns 19 alterations (20)

BUILDING ELEMENT:
Check Exterior: front; ~~sides, L&R~~; rear; roof; addns.
List: Interior: cellar; gd fl; ROW fl; 2nd fl; ~~3rd fl~~; attic; ~~r. ex.~~

BUILDING ELEMENT:	1 ARCHITECTURE: quality, structure	2 CONDITION: A=urgent repairs B=soon, C=long term		3 PLANNING: use and fitness
Exterior front	4 storey 2 bay bk. with parapet and stone cornice. Doric cols. E.C.1. balustrade at row level. Mod. shop fts. st. level. 18 shop row level. Sash w/ws above with g.b. and orig. crown glass. bk. chimneys & slated roof.	settlement R.H.S. – watch some bk. decay esp. in parapet. Cornice in bad condition upper w/ws. poor several slates slipped roof poor	C B A A A	low beams at row level former access to row now blocked Incongruous mod. shop fronts.
R.H.S., L.H.S., rear	party walls in various bk.wk. motley assemblage with rear additions	bulge at 2nd floor level much bk. decay	C B	
Interior street level	mod. shop at front with med. rib vaulted cellar, partly rock cut at rear	back of cellar rather damp wet rot in rubbish on floor	B	shop well used, but fine med. cellars only as stores
row level	shop at front with rems. of med. timberwk. large central hall w. 18 cross stair. Room at rear w. 17 plaster frieze and fire pl. long rear addition	fairly well maintained, but rear additions poor and neglected – remove?	B	shop at front staff room at rear + WC additions empty
2nd floor	good front room with 18 panelling & doorcase. 2 rooms at rear with good stone fire places. Cross stair continues with large open well.	damp thro' ceilings and in party walls. some f.b. in floorboards window frames decayed	A B A	fine rooms now used only as stores for shop.
3rd floor	18 Chinese Chippendale screen at top of stair. Circular rooflight over.	water pouring through roof & parapet gutters. DRY ROT in floor next LHS party wall. rooflight leaks	A A	all empty and neglected.

SUMMARY				
1 ARCHITECTURE	Anchor bldg	(Minor s/scape) Group value Location value	Indispensable (Keep if poss) Dispensable	MOHLG grade III Recommended listing: II *
2. MAINTENANCE	Good Average (Poor)	Why Distant owner Disuse & neglect of upper floors	Grant H.B.C. ✓ aid County ✓ poss; Impmt.	Estimated cost of repairs: A £ 4,000 B £ 2,500 C £ 2,000
3 INTERNAL PLANNING	Good (Improvable) Poor	Rec. changes (incl. use) Remove rear additions. fire exit reqd. at top to use upper floors.	Replan (wthn bldg) " wth other " " " new extn.	Estimated cost: £ 3,000

ADDITIONAL COMMENTS AND RECOMMENDATIONS:
Potentially a fine building, under-used and suffering from resulting neglect.
Good med. cellar and 18 features should be preserved.
Upper floors could make attractive flat. Rear access required.

Further visit? (Yes) No. Made | Special photos? (Yes) No. Made

Donald W. Insall & Associates, Architects & Planning Consultants, 44 Queen Anne's Gate, London S

Fig. 9. Specimen of form used by Donald W. Insall and Associates for survey of historic buildings.

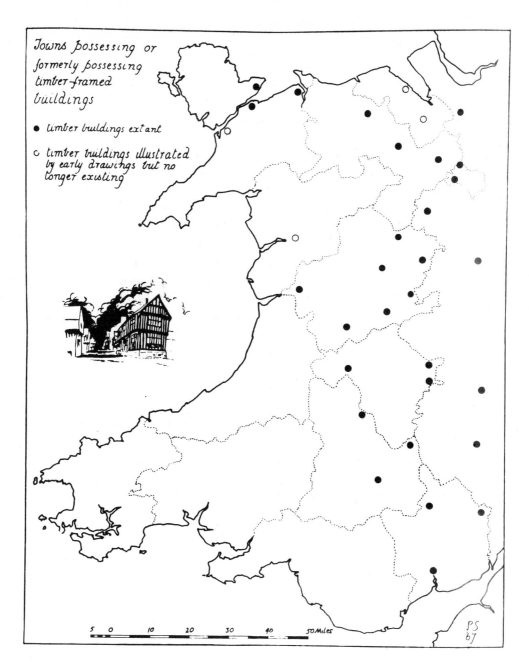

Fig. 10. Map of Wales, showing towns with timber-framed buildings. Towns should not be considered in isolation, and their regional value can only be assessed with the aid of maps like this. (Peter Smith, Royal Commission on Ancient Monuments in Wales and Monmouthshire).

local planning authorities and interested persons outside, could be produced within 5 - 10 years for most of the towns in Britain. The organisation of such speedy surveys ought to be the responsibility of those specialists in local planning offices referred to in the second paragraph of 3.8.

3.10   *Cost*
We have not referred to the *cost* of surveys of buildings. Towns vary so much in the scale of the work required that generalized figures would be of very little value. Within limits, the more a planning authority is prepared to spend, the more valuable the results.

4. ARCHAEOLOGY IN THE HISTORIC TOWN

4.1

The Necessity for Urban Archaeology

The origin and character of the historic town are rarely recorded in writing. Except in the case of the "new towns" of the middle ages, the first reference is probably no more than a passing mention; for instance, that a great Viking host went to Cambridge in 875, which reveals nothing about the origin of the town in the sense of exactly where, why and when it grew up. The written record is equally vague concerning the physical fabric and character of a town. Men had no occasion to describe the townscape, street-pattern, defences, public buildings, houses and daily life about them. Their documents dealt with different matters, the administration of justice, taxation and property.

The evidence of urban archaeology, of the physical remains of the past town, must be used to discover the origin and comprehend the fabric of the historic town at any time before the recent past. Archaeology and documents are essentially complementary: the written record preserves facts not to be deduced from archaeology; archaeology presents material evidence not recorded in the documents. The town archives are not only in the Record Office, but also below the pavement and in the structure of the surviving historic buildings.

An understanding of the plan and development of the historic town should be an essential foundation for modern planning; without it the former pattern and townscape, the very basis of urban character, may be needlessly and disastrously lost. But unlike documents, which today are carefully preserved, the archaeological evidence is being constantly destroyed by modern development. Many towns which give considerable thought and expenditure to the preservation of their written archives, do nothing, and are perhaps totally unaware, of the destruction of the equally important archaeological archive below their feet.

4.2

The Materials of Urban Archaeology

Archaeology studies all the physical remains of man's past activity, from a single potsherd to a cathedral. The study involves many independent disciplines, including art - and architectural - history, numismatics, historical geography and many of the natural sciences. Archaeological material may be buried below the ground; it may form patterns of streets, properties and buildings on the ground; or it may exist as structures above the ground. Any of this material may throw light on the past. A series of potsherds properly recorded has, for example, revealed more of the origin and earliest history of Norwich, than have either the Norman castle or the cathedral. Archaeological finds, however, only realise their full value if their association with other objects and structures is fully recorded. To carry their full weight as evidence, such properly recorded finds must, in their turn, be related to the total historical background, of the site of the particular discovery and of the town in general. Only in this way can the right questions be asked of the new discovery, the answers to which will throw significant light on the history of the town. Because of this need for a careful record, the destruction of the archaeological remains of our towns by commercial development is serious: the evidence is lost for ever.

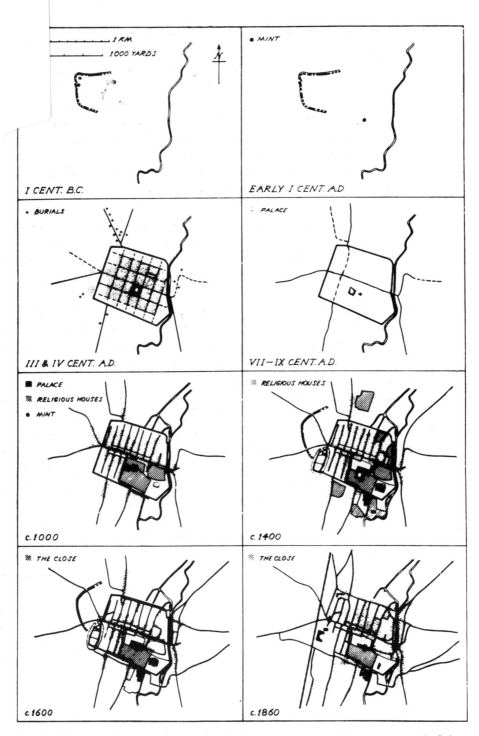

Fig. 11. Winchester. Phase plans showing the development of a planned Roman town by the 3rd century A.D., and the replanning of the interior in the middle ages. (Martin Biddle).

4.3

The Methods and Problems of Urban Archaeology

Archaeological research takes place both by excavation and by the study of finds. In any town it is inevitable that disturbances of the ground will produce casual finds. These may find their way to the local museum for identification or as gifts, or they may be collected and recorded by the museum staff as part of a deliberate policy. Although these are casual finds without a full record of their associations, they can be used to reveal a great deal about a town's development, *provided that* their

147

find spot has been recorded. The Ordnance Survey (Archaeology Branch) will have a record of many such finds, and should always be informed of new ones. To discover the exact location, extent and natural setting of the earliest town, it is necessary to plot on a map the geographical distribution of all known early finds. The relief of the ground, the soil, rivers and other natural features form the framework for this map, while historical facts, such as the recorded existence of a church or castle by a certain date can also be added. The essence of this approach is to plot every geographical locatable fact relevant to the period being studied. The method was first used at Cambridge in 1933, but was only fully developed by E. M. Jope for Norwich and Oxford in 1952. It is also possible by this method to follow the subsequent expansion and contraction of a town. At Oxford Jope showed that the origin of the northern suburb lay in a twelfth-century expansion beyond the Saxon town; while at Winchester M. Biddle has shown in a series of development plans that several periods of growth and contraction can occur in an urban history of two thousand years. Not all museums have a consistent policy towards making such a record; staff and finance are rarely sufficient to enable museums to contribute as much as they could to a lively understanding of the past; some contractors and site-owners, even when this is the local authority, have no awareness of, or concern for, the loss of knowledge which their activity causes. The collection of finds relevant to a town's history is a proper and essential function of the local museum curator. The actual collection need not hinder the work of a contractor, and provision for such collection and observation should be inserted into the contracts before the work begins. Such a policy is already being followed by some local authorities - e.g. Hampshire County Council in connection with the construction of their New Assize Courts in Winchester.

The collection and recording of casual finds presents few problems compared with excavations in towns. Sites which are threatened by destruction must be examined if their evidence is not to be lost for all time. The State, through the Ancient Monuments Inspectorate of the Ministry of Public Building and Works, has assumed a responsibility towards such threatened sites, and a distinction has grown up between "rescue" and "research" excavations, the latter taking place for purely archaeological reasons on unthreatened sites. Such a distinction is false, or at least only relevant when practical considerations of finance arise. In practice no site should be excavated unless there is good reason for doing so. In any town today, so many archaeological sites are threatened simultaneously that it is impossible to excavate them all, if only because staff and finance on such a scale are unthinkable. A choice has to be made and within the wide scope of potential "rescue" sites in any one town, a proper programme of research excavation can be evolved. The only practical difference between these sites and so-called "research" sites is that the former qualify for financial support from the State. In planning such a research programme, it is essential not to be dominated by an over-riding need to rescue all sites before development. It may be necessary to abandon some threatened sites (except for observation) and to excavate others which are not threatened, because they and they alone can answer questions relating to the history of the town. Like a good general seeking to impose his will on the enemy, the archaeologist must reduce the critical problems posed by the destruction of evidence to subordination to a properly conceived and carefully planned scheme of research into his town's history. Only thus can the expenditure of public money be justified, and the destruction of evidence minimized.

The problems of carrying out an excavation on an unthreatened site, apart from permission and finance, are the normal archaeological problems of proper supervision and record. The excavation of threatened sites is another matter.

(i) The site may be an open space, for example, a garden. Here excavation should be possible before redevelopment. The main requirement is that the archaeologist should be aware of the intended development sufficiently early to arrange a proper excavation well in advance of contractor's work. In this way no delay is caused. Sometimes the excavation may benefit the contractor by removing soil from an area which is to be a basement or by informing him of subsoil conditions. The presence of standing buildings nearby, and concern for the foundations of the new building, may sometimes impose limits on the extent and depth of the archaeological excavation. These limits are not always realistic and sometimes represent a mutual failure of understanding between archaeologists on the one hand and those concerned in the new development on the other. Everything must be done to improve such understanding.

(ii) The site may have been cleared of structures well in advance of rebuilding. In this case excavation should be possible in the interval. Most of the considerations discussed above will apply, but the developer's fear that the archaeological work will delay him is perhaps greater. It is only by the archaeologist showing his understanding of these reasonable fears, as well as his scrupulous observance of time limits, that such worries can be overcome.

(iii) The buildings on the site may be demolished and rebuilding begun at once. This case, where there is no interval for excavation, is perhaps the commonest and most difficult of all. Any kind of formal excavation is almost certain to delay rebuilding and is rarely allowed even in the most favourable situations. The most that may be possible is for an archaeologist to observe the site constantly, to make records of his observations and to collect finds. Much can be done in this way, as the work of the Guildhall Museum has shown in the City of London since the war. The situation has been, however, unsatisfactory from the archaeological point of view, and will remain so unless either the Ancient Monuments Acts or the Planning Acts be extended to protect *buried sites* of potential archaeological importance in towns. The act would need to impose a statutory delay between the clearance and rebuilding of these sites in order that excavation might take place. In Sweden the developer is sometimes obliged to contribute to the cost of the excavation and publication of such sites. Short of a statutory requirement, the situation in this country could be greatly improved by the insertion into contracts of clauses giving archaeologists right of access for purposes of observation and record (see record (see 4.3).

Excavation in towns may be directed to the solution of particular

Fig. 12. Nottingham. The medieval town wall, 7 ft. thick and built between 1260 and 1330, appearing among the rubble of a demolition site. This length of wall, standing about 10 ft. high at this point, is now buried under an internal ring road, Maid Marian Way. (Photo M. W. Barley).

problems, or may be designed to reveal in all its detail the general character and development through time of an area, such as a street or parish, containing many buildings of different kinds. In the former category may be placed excavations, sometimes by only a single carefully placed trench, carried out to investigate an area of early settlement relevant to the origin of the town, or to establish the date and sequence of construction of the city defences or streets. The examination of remains of individual buildings, important either in themselves, or for their influence on the town's development, also belongs to this class, although the excavation may be large and complex in itself.

Such excavations will produce a great deal of evidence towards a skeleton of the town's material history and topography, but they will not normally reveal the character of an area in such a way that the setting of life in past centuries can be reconstructed in much detail. To do this it is necessary to excavate large areas, revealing one coherent part of the historic town in all its detail of houses and shops, local churches, streets and lanes. By excavating in depth, it is possible to show the way in which such an area has changed through time from the moment of its first occupation. Such excavation is very costly and British archaeology has lagged far behind in this field. Only in the Brooks area of Winchester, and in the excavations at Thetford, can anything be seen at all comparable to and then on a much smaller scale than, the great continental excavations at Novgorod (Russia), Opole and Gdansk (Poland), Lund (Sweden), Bergen (Norway) and Hedeby (W. Germany). Such excavations are so large that they require an exceptional expenditure of time, money and other resources, including skilled workers. In the Winchester case, the site was made available for the period 1965-70 only by a rephasing of the city's redevelopment plan.

Excavation, observation and the study of finds, combined with a proper understanding of the written records, can trace the development and changing character of an historic town from its origins down to the modern period. By such a combined approach the nucleus and plan of the early town, together with its subsequent growth and occasional contraction, can be discovered; its streets and defences can be planned and dated, its churches and palaces seen in relation to the town that has vanished. Of that town, the houses of the ordinary citizens can be traced in plan and construction through the centuries, and all the detail of daily life, clothing, shoes, utensils and tools seen in their proper setting. The imported goods found in excavation can reveal much of the trading connections of the town, thus demonstrating that regional function which is one of its main claims to urban status. By excavation of houses, cess-pits, walls and cemeteries, even the physical character and bodily health of its former inhabitants can be discovered, while examination of animal bones and cereal remains can show the agrarian background to the town's life.

It is on the basis of such a well-founded understanding of its past that a historic town can develop carefully and thoughtfully in the future, but the very foundation of that understanding is being rapidly and at an ever increasing pace destroyed, usually without record.

4.4

The Destruction of Urban Archaeology
The destruction of the archaeological evidence for the history of towns

151

Fig. 13. Bird's-eye view of excavations in Lower Brook Street, Winchester, in advance of redevelopment. The very slight walls of cottages built in the 15th century have been exposed, showing for the first time in Britain the plans and quality of lower class housing in a medieval town. When these remains were removed, still earlier buildings were found below. Only *large-scale* excavation will make such structures comprehensible. (Photo Winchester Excavation Committee).

Fig. 14. The redundant church of St. Alkmund, in the centre of Derby, is to be demolished for the construction of an inner relief road. Excavation, sponsored by the Corporation of Derby, has revealed not only the plan of the earlier churches on the site but also this fine Anglo-Saxon sarcophagus, which may once have held the remains of St. Alkmund himself. The sarcophagus will be removed to the Derby Museum. (Photo by R. Marjoram).

affects all those kinds of evidence described in paragraph 4. The destruction of standing buildings has been discussed in Section 3. On the ground, the laying out of new streets and the closure of others, the amalgamation of properties and the removal of town defences all combine to obliterate the ancient pattern. Even though maps of the previous state may exist, they are no substitute for proper excavation with the relevant questions in mind. Below the ground, destruction is even more widespread and more serious. The digging of foundations, the construction of basements and underground car-parks, remove archaeological evidence totally and on a large scale. Even road widening, with its requirements for deep foundations and the relaying of services, usually destroys the vital frontage where for centuries the now vanished houses and shops have opened on to the street. Such a widening destroys the evidence of an area far greater than that directly affected. The construction of ring- and spine-roads wreaks havoc with the past of an historic town. In London such destruction has reached "the end of all hope of further information on the early past of the City within the walls" (W. F. Grimes).

Destruction is going on in every town. In England alone, at least fifty major medieval towns are currently the subject of massive central redevelopment plans. During the twenty-seven years, 1940-67, serious archaeological research took place in about sixty English towns, but in only twenty-three was excavation on anything other than a very small scale. Little has been done in Wales and scarcely any excavation has been carried out in Scotland, despite the numerous opportunities provided by major redevelopment schemes in the larger Scottish burghs. When excavation has been possible, it has usually either been concentrated on the Roman period or confined to the larger medieval towns - Bristol, Cambridge, Canterbury, Chester, Coventry, Hereford, Ipswich, King's Lynn, London, Leicester, Nottingham, Norwich, Oxford, Shrewsbury, Southampton, Stamford, Warwick, Winchester, Worcester and York. Of the total of well over eight hundred towns in medieval England, very few small and medium-sized towns have been investigated, probably because their present-day populations are too small to include by chance any interested persons and because they have no local museum and curator. Serious as is the case with the large towns, it is the archaeology of the small and medium-sized market town that is threatened with total and unrecorded destruction. And because each town is a unique reflection of its region, the loss of its history can never be repaired.

4.5

Some Possible Solutions
The basic requirement is an awareness of the critical situation of urban archaeology. Given that - and at present there are few elected representatives, local authority officers, planners, or developers, or even historians and archaeologists, who recognise it - action might follow these lines :

(i) The most important single action would be statutory provision for an interval of time, commensurate with the importance of the site, between demolition and redevelopment, so that excavation may take place;

(ii) Local museums should be encouraged to watch all building

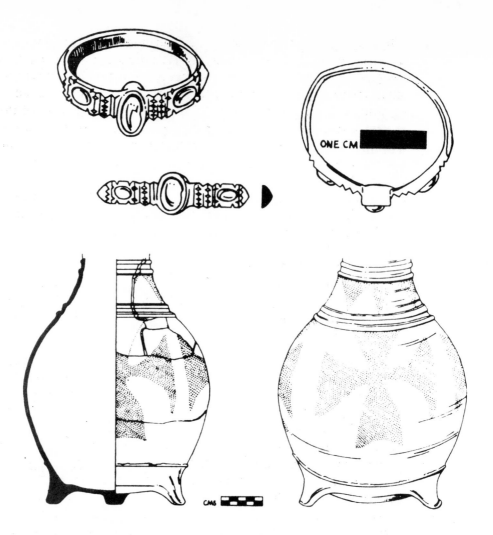

Fig. 15. Two finds from excavations in medieval Southampton. The first is a gold ring set with three amethysts, dated about 1200 A.D. The other is an earthenware jug, dated before 1200 A.D., with slip decoration in the form of crosses, and an amber glaze; it was made either in Northern France, or the Low Countries. (Southampton Museum).

sites in their towns, and to record the evidence revealed against a background knowledge of the possibilities offered by each site.

(iii) The authority concerned should consult the local archaeological society to discover the archaeological potential of each development site. Such action might lead to the establishment, as it has done in Canterbury, Derby, King's Lynn, Oxford, Stamford, Southampton and Winchester, of a local committee to co-ordinate research and excavation in the historic town;

(iv) Such a committee could by lectures and other information media, such as exhibitions, increase local awareness of the problems involved and make application to the Ministry of Public Building and Works for grants for "rescue" excavations.

(v) Local authorities should encourage or insist on the insertion into building contracts of clauses designed to allow, with proper safeguards, access to construction sites for the purposes of archaeological observation and record.

4.15   The destruction of the early fabric of our towns is the most serious problem facing British archaeology today. Town sites are the most complex and difficult of all archaeological sites and consequently the most expensive to excavate. In our urban civilization they are also perhaps the most important; in them are contained the seeds of modern Britain, and each town is a unique expression of the resources and character of its region. Yet these very sites are the most vulnerable to destruction.

5.   *THE LAST WORD*

The whole of this report on historical research for conservation has been written from a two-fold point of view. The first is that this research is an immediate and practical necessity. More knowledge of the past is needed for a proper implementation of the Civic Amenities Act.

The second point, which readers may feel looms large in this report, is that knowledge of the past is worth having for its own sake. The Study Group hopes that it is justified in taking this for granted. Ever since Homer, man has wished to know about the past. A town whose history has been explored, and is presented in the form of books, photographs, drawings, museum exhibits and actual buildings, enriches not only the lives of its own citizens but also society as a whole.

A third point is implicit in this report. Research into the past is a matter of collecting data, and then interpreting them. With fresh knowledge, and those changes of attitude and interest that differentiate us from our fathers and grandfathers, interpretations and judgments will change. The buildings that we think little of, the archaeological sites that seem to us of no interest, these may to our children seem precious and significant. In our efforts to conserve and record the past, we have a responsibility that is wider than our own tastes and goes beyond the limits of our own vision.

POSTSCRIPT

National concern about public participation in planning is growing. The recommendations of the Study Group about engaging the help of local historians, archivists and archaeologists in the preparation of maps and surveys are entirely in line with the need to involve the public at the formative stage.

Does modern Coventry regret the loss of historic buildings?

SURVEY AND RESTORATION OF TIMBER-FRAMED BUILDINGS IN COVENTRY

Historical accuracy is no less important in the repair and re-erecting of timber-framed buildings than it is in the survey of towns, as Maurice Barley emphasized in his paper. The original design of a building, though confused and disguised by alterations and accretions, must be discovered. This involves research beyond the detailed survey of the building itself. It is necessary, however, not only for the sake of dating and placing it in the context of the town's history, but also because the original structure and form offer the only proper guide to a building's sound and economical restoration and future use. The age-old habit of patching and making-do, despite the views of the S.P.A.B., is not an alternative to radical reconstruction when the original structure has been so mutilated that, without its later insertions of brick-work, cast-iron columns, lath and plaster and miscellaneous props, it could no longer support the roof. This was, or still is, the condition of all the buildings mentioned in this paper. For them, and innumerable others throughout the country, the only alternative to thorough (and preferably intelligent) reconstruction is demolition.

1.

Cheylesmore Manor

The restoration of Cheylesmore Manor and its conversion into a suite of marriage rooms and offices was commissioned by Coventry Corporation in 1965. This followed a report on the history and condition of the building — its condition being only discernible through the hardest external stucco I have ever encountered, layers of wall paper and plaster internally, inserted ceilings, partitions, fireplaces and so on. My intention then was to make-do and mend rather than renew any part of the frame, obvious though it was that much of it had been replaced by brick in the eighteenth and nineteenth centuries. It was also apparent from documentary excerpts that Cheylesmore Manor had not survived its 700 year life-span unscathed. The first mention in documents is of its being built by the Earl of Arundel on the site of the ruined castle in 1232. A hundred years later, the manor passed to Queen Isabel and from her to the Black Prince. In 1385 it was to be enclosed within the city wall then under construction. In 1421 the house was decaying but rebuilt with timber from the park. In 1538 from a survey of Greyfriar's property we learn : "adjoining is an old manor of the king called Cheylesmore, where they say Edward IV kept a parliament. The hall is down and the lodgings might be repaired with tiles from the friary." Leland said at about the same time, "The king has a palace in Coventry, now somewhat ruined." From the mid-sixteenth century, ownership and occupancy regularly changed hands. Sir Robert Townsend "laid out much money" in repairs in 1661. In 1738 a weaver proposed to make a tenement of the great hall. Thirty years later a lease was granted of the "old ruinous building". At last P. B. Chatwyn in 1944 discovered a medieval roof, south-west of the gatehouse range, in a row of weavers' cottages, typical of Coventry's now nearly extinct "top-shops"; and in 1955 the corporation demolished it.

The surviving "manor" comprises the 3-bay gatehouse of c.1520 with bits probably added by Sir Robert Townsend after 1660, a south wing of two bays, and a 2-bay north wing. Both the bays of the former, though of remarkably different construction, are not later than the fourteenth century and the front bay of this wing might even be of the first build, i.e. thirteenth century. The north wing, of which again each bay is structurally different from the other, is fifteenth century. This wing was built astride what was probably a spur of the city wall as a 2-storey porch house, with upper chambers and open bays beneath, giving shelter to a great ogee-headed doorway with the manor precincts on the one side and the city on the other. The original form and purpose of this building could not have been discovered without complete removal of all relatively recent accretions, such as a range of topshops built onto its north face. These topshops, however, hid no medieval roof, but instead extensive remains of the city wall, now exposed and preserved. Many other discoveries of archaeological interest have resulted from the complete stripping of the building down to its bare skeleton — an operation not decided on in the interests of scholarship but through sheer structural necessity.

By doing so almost complete evidence of the original framing of every part of the building has come to light even where all the vertical members of an entire wall had been replaced by brick. In these cases sufficient lengths of horizontal members — wall-plates, rails, sill-beams, etc. — though bedded in brick, broken and decayed, still survived to give the information needed for authentic reconstruction.

Needless to say, there has been criticism of the amount of new oak used (there is no re-used timber, pirated from other buildings) and of the transformation of the building's appearance, from a mainly Victorian, rather picturesque composition to a clearly articulated group of powerfully framed structures. Whether the internal restoration, defining space by the structural bays and splendid roof trusses, again visible from the upper floor, will cause nostalgia for the previous warren of dark little rooms and corridors is less likely. The most fortunate aspect of the entire conversion is that the building's future use is compatible with its clear bay divisions. In those conversions where structure and modern function are at odds it is the latter which should be adapted to the structure, or a different use found.

2.

The Spon Street Scheme

This is the first attempt by any corporation in England to establish a historic area where the city's few surviving timber houses could be seen in sympathetic context, instead of isolated and generally battered by traffic among brazen shop-fronts and supermarkets. But it was also the last hope for this city, which had suffered, not only Hitler's bombs, but the far better planned destruction of post-war redevelopment, to retain any visible link with its medieval past in the shape of the ordinary citizens' or artisans' dwellings. A survey done in 1955 by R. Stanley Jones for the Victoria County History revealed over a hundred such buildings. My survey in 1966 of the same streets (where they survived) accounted for only thirty-four. The rest had gone. Seventeen survivors were in the severely truncated length of Spon Street which it was intended to preserve, the rest scattered individually or in small groups. I said in my report, "Few of them are any longer complete houses as originally built (or even as they stood in 1940); most of them are in their final stages of decay; several of them are vacant; none is easily recognizable for what it was, or even as a timber-framed structure. Indeed, two of them are already demolished, their timbers in storage for future re-erection. Yet not one fails to make a signal contribution to Coventry's architectural history, and several of them are of profound importance to the history of timber-framed architecture."

The proposal to move buildings was condemned by the S.P.A.B., and could not under the Ancient Monuments Act be financially supported by the H.B.C. Nevertheless, the Corporation has refrained from demolishing two medieval hall houses though their site is needed for new development. It has put them into moth balls of corrugated iron and boarding to prevent destruction until funds are found to transfer them to Spon Street. Another splendid though mutilated building would also have been demolished but for the Corporation's approval in principle of the scheme. Meanwhile, nearly all the buildings to be preserved have been acquired, and much now depends on whether the H.B.C. will circumvent the humble unpretentiousness of each of the Spon Street buildings, taken individually, by assessing them as a group-unit large enough to qualify for aid.

The problems in moving timber buildings are best illustrated by one already moved. This previously stood in the main street of Bromsgrove, Worcestershire. It was a late fifteenth century hall house with solar cross-wing jettied over the street. As so many others it was scarcely recognizable as anything but a worn-out relic of no architectural significance. Its one interesting feature for the antiquarian was a well-preserved internal chimney, timber-framed with infill panels of wattle-and-daub. In 1961 a public protest meeting against the local authority's demolition order resulted in the gift of a site outside Bromsgrove and about £400 for the building's systematic dismantling so that. re-erection as a museum would be possible. Four years later an association, the Avoncroft Museum of Buildings, had come into being and the timbers were taken from store. The chimney had stood practically unprotected in the open throughout this period. The timbers were fractured, decayed and incomplete. The survey drawings showed only the building as it was before demolition. These failings were the result of working under crisis conditions and the lapse of time between dismantling and re-erection.

Yet the skill of one carpenter, with only intermittent help and the sub-contracting of such trades as plastering the wattle panels and tiling the roof, resulted in the opening on midsummer's eve, 1967, of a medieval house exactly as first built. The cost, allowing for gifts of oak and the occasional skilled help — amateur labour is not suitable for work of such engineering precision as timber-framing — was £7,000, or about 90/- per square foot. For modern use, that is, providing glazing, heating and insulation, but without destroying the space and openness of plan or doctoring the natural surfaces of oak and plaster inside or out — it is still not fully recognized that chemically treating oak is a modern commercial racket, or that "black-and-white" was a Victorian one — must be added a further £4 per foot. Even this compares not only with the cost of restoration in situ but with that of modern building for offices, showrooms, committee rooms and the like. Only in terms of time can reconstruction not compete with building new, for precision carpentry cannot be hurried.

Other lessons are that not even a trained imagination can grasp the architectural potential of a timber-framed building until its transformation from its present state to its true original has been experienced. Demolition spells not only historical and architectural loss but waste of capital assets and use-value. The Spon Street Buildings so restored are ready-made for showrooms, studios, shops and living rooms overlooking what is to be a pedestrian street, requiring only the addition of a modern rear wing, for the kitchen, bathroom and garage, to become the most sought-after dwellings in Coventry.

Lastly, the Avoncroft Museum has already acted as a training school for other carpenters, a centre for research and a powerful influence for conservation. And it has hardly yet begun.

design

PART FIVE – THE ARCHITECTURE OF CONSERVATION

*REPORT OF THE STUDY GROUP CONVENED
BY PROFESSOR P. E. A. JOHNSON-MARSHALL
(Chairman of the RIBA Town Planning Group)*

Secretary: J. A. Finlay DA(Edin) Dip TP (Edin) ARIBA

Group Members

Ian Begg DA(Edin) ARIBA
Kenneth Browne AADipl ARIBA
T. T. Hewitson DipArch ARIBA AMTPI FRIAS
Town Planning Officer, Edinburgh
Hew Lorimer RSA FRBS
Col. J. W. A. Lowis
Colin McWilliam MArch(Cantab)
Secretary, Scottish Georgian Society
R. F. Pollock
Secretary, Scottish National Housing Town Planning Council
J. H. Reid DA(Edin) ARIBA RIAS FSA(Scot)
R. W. C. K. Rogerson BArch FRIBA FRIAS FSA(Scot)
Councillor R. A. Raffan
Aberdeen
F. P. Tindall MA MTPI
County Planning Officer for East Lothian
H. A. Wheeler BArch(Strath) ARSA FRIBA AMTPI

Assessor

G. L. M. Goodfellow
Scottish Development Department

LANDSCAPE DESIGN IN CONSERVATION
from a paper on behalf of the Institute of Landscape
Architects by Jocelyn Adburgham LRIBA MTPI FILA

SYLVAN SUBURBIA
from a paper by D. W. Lloyd BA AMTPI

LIVING CONTINUITY IN CONSERVATION

J. G. Mackley
North Regional Officer, Housing Corporation

1. *WHY SCOTLAND?*

Our Towns, the urban part of our landscape, represent one of the composite forms of art-and-life (the novel, the countryside, the country house) at which we have been notably good. The present agony is because so many of the natural and social factors which helped to make them have broken down. We have to bring to their aid a new science; Townsmanship, in all its branches from the widest kind of planning, through architecture to the smallest details and furnishings.

Townsmanship involves all sorts of things which are not only against the British grain, but often contrary to the very spirit in which some of our towns were created; analysis, calculation, the substitution of reason for intuition. But it is only by this new and still rather esoteric science that we can retain and make the most of our irreplaceable town architecture - and even, in time, attain a language of renewal comparable to that which we admire and envy in our urban heritage.

By looking to Scotland for a Report on the Architecture of Urban Conservation, the Royal Institute of British Architects have drawn attention to a wide variety of projects on which it has been possible to assemble a quantity of vital detail.

It may seem odd for a Report on the Architecture of Conservation to be devoted entirely to Scotland. Yet this restriction has certain advantages. Chiefly, it has given an opportunity of presenting the complete picture of Conservation in the Historic Towns of a whole country. This we have tried to do.

Always excepting Edinburgh and a handful of picture-postcard places, Scottish Towns are not well known for their environmental qualities. Many deserve recognition - indeed they need it if they are to survive. In some the quality is latent and in others, unfortunately including a lot of places well known to history and tourism, completely non-existent. They have something to teach, and much more to learn.

Of the historic materials used in Scotland, wood has now become the rarest and is almost forgotten except indoors where wooden construction (sometimes decoratively painted) has recently become the subject of intensive recording and conservation. Sir Patrick Geddes, with his picturesquely improvised housing developments built in Edinburgh at the end of the nineteenth century, reminded us of this lost element in our townscape.

It is stone which has established the substantial, monochrome image of the Georgian and Victorian towns of Scotland, from the sooty grey of Edinburgh to the silver granite of Aberdeen. In the latter city, the brick spire which Archibald Simpson set over the junction of the three Free Churches in 1844 is an extraordinary incident; an exception to the rule of stone which was virtually unchallenged till late Victorian times - and then not often. Caithness flags and Ballachulish slates fill in the grey picture. Regional variations - the warm brown of East Lothian, the pink of Angus and the red of Dumfriesshire, are in a minority.

In complete contrast, and a surprise to most newcomers in Scotland, is the charm of the late mediaeval vernacular. Its vocabulary is tiny; gable, wall and window, with an occasional turret. Its quality, in most surviving examples, relies on one universal material, low-cost rubble walling harled with an all-over wet dash. This is maintained by periodical washing in white or colour which on the grander buildings is set off by stone margins.

This simple formula was adaptable to all sites and all needs. It gave unity of character to town and village centres, but avoided monotony in the long roadside development of a place like Linlithgow. It was always individual and personal, yet the balance of solid and void gave it an abstract sculptural quality, very close to the aspirations of many architects today. Thousands of such houses have been replaced in the "normal" process of redevelopment, especially near town centres. Thousands more, having lost their immediate charm for want of painting and other maintenance, have been needlessly condemned as ugly and unfit.

In 1937 the 4th Marquess of Bute, one of the fathers of Scottish preservation, sponsored an inventory of the "little houses" in Scottish towns. This not only formed a partial basis for the comprehensive lists prepared under the 1947 Planning Act, but also led to the series of group-restorations pioneered by the National Trust for Scotland at Culross and Dunkeld. Many of the case-studies in this report are in this category.

We have given case-studies pride of place because we think that any statement of standards and ideals is most useful if it is backed up by experience of how something can be done, and by continually asking how the next job can be done better.

2. THE TRAINING OF ARCHITECTS FOR CONSERVATION

2.1   All Schools of Architecture include historical studies in their regular courses of training. These establish an essential background of architectural styles on a continental or world scale but tend to overlook examples nearer home - often the very buildings on which any architect (let alone a conservation specialist) may be asked to work.

With the increasing realisation that so many of the buildings and towns of Britain deserve a second lease of life (and that so many of these are disappearing or losing their identity), the study of conservation has a strong claim to a bigger share of students' time. Maintenance, townscape and the basic procedure for work on existing buildings, all merit more attention than they get in most schools.

Conservation is a special study in that it demands a special state of mind - the development of a well worked-out attitude to existing buildings and landscape. But in one sense it is not special; that is, it must not be limited to a few architects only, since nearly every architectural job is related to the existing environment. All students must be made aware of the fundamentals, though some of course should specialize in the subject.

2.2   *Specialization*

Specialist training in conservation is available at some Schools as a subject for "Diversification" (the scheme by which a student develops a particular interest within his general course). Bristol and Manchester Universities and the Edinburgh College of Art all offer the option of diversifying in this way, and the School at Liverpool University is among those which have undertaken conservation or urban renewal projects.

A two-year course on the Conservation of Historical Monuments (leading to a Diploma) is run by the Institute of Archaeology, University of London. The Society for the Protection of Ancient Buildings has a one-week annual course for architects and other professions connected with conservation, and the Institute of Advanced Architectural Studies at York holds similar Courses in the Spring. All these activities are organized in consultation with the Standing Joint Conference on the Recruitment and the Training of Architects for the Care of Old Buildings (83 London Wall, E.C.2) and with the R.I.B.A. who held a conference in Bristol in November 1966 for School staff members concerned with training in conservation through regular or specialized courses.

At the Edinburgh College of Art the Diversification Course begins with two weeks' intensive study of the history, theory and practice of conservation through lectures and visits to buildings and architects' offices. The rest of the year is devoted to a single area of Edinburgh, chosen in consultation with the Planning Authority not only so as to offer a good range of conservation problems but to give the opportunity for work which will be of practical use. Survey work is undertaken by the whole team of students together, and individual thesis subjects (involving conservation, improvement or the filling of gap sites) are selected from those which appear to be necessary within the area.

2.3
The Selection of Architects for Conservation
The Standing Joint Conference (mentioned above in connection with Training) maintains a Register of Architects specialising in conservation.

For existing buildings just as for new ones, the choosing of an Architect is the most important decision the client has to make. Very few Architects have experience in full-dress operations involving scholarly and practical restoration. In the wider field, including that of new building in existing surroundings, both cases and Architects vary enormously and it is worth a lot of trouble to find the right men for the job. Visits to executed projects of a similar kind can be very useful; the things to look for are a consistent and intelligible outlook (has he made the most of the building, in itself and in its context?) and satisfaction on the part of client and user.

3. THE ROLE OF URBAN DESIGN

3.1
Three-Dimensional Planning
The land-use and traffic proposals which form the main part of any town Development Plan are devised with the object of making the town work. Three-dimensional Planning is concerned with how it looks as well.

It is impossible to separate these two kinds of Planning. A functional plan worked out in two dimensions cannot be imposed on an existing town without causing unforeseen damage to its appearance and even conflicting with any functional balance it may already have. Equally a scheme which works from a basis of appearance and townscape alone will obviously fail when it becomes clear that changing functions will not fit into the existing scheme; the visual qualities themselves will suffer through the pressure of increased traffic and other unsuitable uses.

3.2 *Standards for Development Control*

The Planning Officer's function in historic towns (and that of his Planning Committee) is to establish and use the machinery at his disposal, which is mainly negative and restrictive, to obtain a positive result.

The basic instrument of planning is the careful allocation of land uses in a Development Plan. With appropriate allowance of floorspace for particular uses, strict development control based on three-dimensional planning can make for viable projects at reasonable costs. Where existing buildings are concerned, and especially in Conservation Areas, the machinery of use-zoning is severely tested. On one hand it must be sufficiently rigorous to exclude undesirable uses, or those tending towards deterioration of a building or area. On the other, it must be flexible enough to embrace (or modify, or even develop) the diversity which gives life and character to many towns. Some of the design issues involved, both for new and existing development, are discussed elsewhere.

The Civic Amenities Act 1967 expresses new ideals and gives some assistance towards a more positive interpretation of previous Acts:

" ....Conservation Areas represent a shift of emphasis from negative control to creative planning for preservation." (Scottish Development Dept. Memo. No. 57). The Memorandum quoted also asserts the importance of the integrity of these designated areas, and that other planning considerations must respect it.

These provisions, though obligatory, depend on local authorities for their implementation. Even those who are willing will have to decide where to find the necessary funds and qualified staff. In spite of this difficulty, the Act does confirm the efforts already made along these lines, which included the selection of Bath, Chester, Chichester and York as subjects of special Conservation Studies. It also confirms another innovation from the period of the Crossman Ministry: the new emphasis on group preservation.

As it is obviously a pity to use public - or private - money on the restoration of a building and then see unsuitable works (even small ones) being carried out on its neighbours, all efforts at urban conservation demand an intensification of control; i.e. they will fail if they are not thorough. In this sort of control, a strong and well-informed voluntary element is essential.

Technically, any works which "seriously affect the character" of a listed building are subject to planning permission under the 1947 Act. While maximum enforcement is certainly desirable as a safeguard, the most immediate and positive solution is that the Minister or the planning authority should take steps to explain the meaning of the to all owners of listed buildings. Alternatively, the owners may form proprietors' associations and observe certain rules by mutual consent.

3.3 *Liaison - with Developers and Owners*

A serviceable procedure is now established for the consideration of proposals once they are submitted, but it often happens that developers are (or pretend to be) unaware of the importance of the building or site in question and may already be committed to large design expenses for a completely unsuitable proposal. Planning authorities should make the implications of listing and the designation of conservation areas widely known and be prepared for advance consultations with developers and the advisory bodies concerned.

The completely intractable owner's ultimate weapons are time and decay, and it is hoped that good use will be made of the provisions for the compulsory purchase of listed but neglected buildings by Planning Authorities in the terms of the Civic Amenities Act.

Both central and local authority could do more by sending out special negotiators to work out an answer to difficult cases on the spot, a difficult but rewarding task. The county of East Lothian has done much in this way. On an official level the Scottish Development Department (at present miserably understaffed in this sector) should give a lead.

3.4

Liaison - with the Public

Planning authorities seldom seem to have the confidence of the public; indeed they are the Aunt Sallies of modern life. The vast number of negative complaints against them is a symptom - at least - of a failure in public relations. It is also worth remembering that they are blamed when a good building has suddenly disappeared, but are seldom praised when by their efforts it is still there.

Edinburgh Corporation mounted an excellent Civic Exhibition in 1961 and another for the New Town Bicentenary in 1967. On the other hand they incurred the wrath of the majority of citizens when the Inner Ring Road proposals were published as part of the latest Quinquennial Review of the Development Plan, and the environmental implications of the Road became known. (The Secretary of State rejected a large part of the Road in 1968, after a Public Inquiry).

The most useful contribution which can be made by amenity organizations (though they must reserve the right to adverse criticism) is the expression of positive attitudes towards the whole environment, whether in a street, an area, a complete historic town or the entire nation. They must also manage to be really representative; otherwise, as in two recent cases in Bath, they will agree on something with the authorities only to find a new wave of opposition going in over their heads.

The Planning Authority, who are often anxious to avoid seeming to be got-at by pressure groups, should none the less examine ways of improving liaison with the public, and building on firmly expressed public opinion. Information about listing and conservation areas and related planning questions should be made available quite openly so that the continuity and purpose of planning can be seen. Larger authorities at least should consider the appointment of a suitably experienced Historic Buildings Officer, who might also be the secretary of a Consultative Committee; this would have some members from the authority itself and some from amenity organizations, and could hear representations from groups with special interests.

On-the-spot information about buildings can help people to enjoy and appreciate them. Properties of the National Trust for Scotland are marked with a small cast-iron badge, and a similar mark is being discussed for listed buildings in Dunbar. Edinburgh Corporation commissioned a set of large open-air screens illustrating the development of the Georgian town on the occasion of the New Town Bicentenary in 1967.

3.5   *Models*
To some extent the Model is the three-dimensional counterpart of the paper plan. Probably the best known historic town model is that of central Bath, designed to show the relation of new proposals to the existing Georgian development.

A model is much the best and most honest way of showing the location and bulk of proposed development to committees, amenity organizations and the public at large, and giving a broad idea of effective relationships between buildings and/or spaces. It is also very useful as an aid to memory if successive developments and provisional decisions can be incorporated in a model of a whole town or area as a help to further decisions. In some ways it can replace (or even be more useful than) a visit to the site. In these limits, models often justify their cost.

However in addition to their dangerous miniature charm which can make a bad scheme look just as attractive as a good one, models have a tendency (especially on a small scale) to flatten out the apparent effect of the ground-contours which in some towns are such an important factor in the townscape. Also, as in the case of drawings, they cannot possibly give more than dubious guidance on important things like details, materials and textures, seen in their true context from all points and in all conditions.

Practical points are important too. Where is a model to be displayed, and will it need to be transported? Can it be kept in good condition, and if necessary repaired and kept up to date?

The "full-size model" on the site (usually made of scaffolding, to indicate the mass and silhouette of a proposed new building) should be demanded more often.

3.6   *Drawings of New Proposals*
The usual "artist's impression" falls far below the standard necessary for proper consideration of a proposal in its context; either ignoring the neighbouring environment or specifically emphasizing those points of difference which appeal to a client in search of spurious status. Perspective presentation-drawings should show proposals as honestly as possible in their whole context.

4.   TOWNSCAPE

4.1   Today we are threatened with an ever-increasing fragmentation of our environment; not just the disappearance of special "historic buildings" from a selected number of towns of special beauty, but a loss of meaning in the whole appearance of what we significantly (and accurately) call our *surroundings,* which are vitally important to us and are bound to affect us for good or for ill.

The situation in our towns calls for nothing less than architecture in the widest sense; for Civic Design embracing the whole three-dimensional form of each town.

4.2   *What is Townscape?*
It is the total landscape of a town; its natural and man-made ingredients,
and those which are a combination of both. As a science, townscape
consists in the studying and recording of all the elements (from buildings, groups, spaces and variations in level, down to details like street
furniture and lettering) which give a town its *individual character.*

Further, it shows specific ways in which this character can be safeguarded and enhanced. In its practical application, townscape is *not*
just the meaningless tarting-up of old towns with cobbles and flowerbeds
in any space which happens to be available, but one of the primary
factors in the making of planning decisions.

The standards of townscape are first the *sense of place* ("I know where
I am") the second the *sense of unity* - the town experienced not as a lot
of disconnected pieces but as a whole, with one recognizable area leading
into another.

4.3   *Why is Townscape needed?*
   - To avoid mistakes. Time and again some historic street or square is
ruined by unsuitable alterations and additions; clumsy concrete lamp
posts, gaps in the building-line, wastes of dreary tarmac, the destruction of a key building (not necessarily historic), the felling of trees, or
the sudden unforeseen intrusion of a large new building outside the area.
Valuable enclosures are smashed open for traffic, and strident new shop-
fronts wreck the scale of neighbouring buildings.

   - To realise hidden assets. Without attention to townscape, sound but
shabby buildings which are basically important to the form of a town
are in danger of being thoughtlessly demolished. Marvellous spaces which
are almost invisible on a map may be "tidied" out of existence. Effective
changes in level may be ignored. These hidden qualities and possibilities
should be identified and brought out.

4.4   *When is Townscape needed?*
   - Always, but especially at the outset, so as to influence decisions. The
townscape survey map will show where opportunities lie, and this evidence
should be considered at the same time as the requirements of traffic and
use.

4.5   *How is it done?*
   - First of all by a Townscape Survey. This is a careful street by street
examination of what exists now. The kinds of things recorded are :

(a) Buildings and groups of buildings which are important to the town.

(b) Significant street lines, spaces and shapes to be kept - where the
       proportion, height, alignment, etc., are important to the town even
       if some rebuilding takes place. Entrances to the town.

(c) Areas of unified character which should be safeguarded. Sequences
       of spaces.

(d) Important views, skylines. Views will include not only those inside
       the town itself, but those to the countryside beyond and also in
       reverse (the image of the town as seen from the countryside).

(e) Details: materials, floor space, street furniture, lettering, etc.

(f) Opportunities: scope for improvement which will at the same time reinforce the character (not one solution necessarily, but all the alternatives which emerge).

The information collected is recorded in photographs and sketches related closely to notes and survey map, and a very important part of this work is to convey information clearly (to architects, planners, committees and the general public) so that the situation can be understood; showing for example, how a scene looks today and how it might be improved.

4.6   *Who does it?*

- The necessary skill, while lying between that of a planner and architect calls primarily for an artist's eye. The specialist townscape consultant with a wide knowledge of other places and working closely with the planning team is perhaps the best answer. For example, townscape consultants have been appointed by Buckinghamshire County Council and the London Borough of Lambeth.

- Another useful contribution is made by the permanent member of the local planning staff who combines the necessary skill, and an ability to assess the town with the eyes of an "outsider", with a greater personal knowledge of the place and its people. He will also have the advantage of being on hand to give continuity of policy and suggest new answers in the light of changing circumstances.

5. *NEW NEIGHBOURS*

The challenge of designing next door to a historic building or within an existing townscape does not often seem to bring out the best in architects. There are plenty of reasons for this, but not so many excuses.

When a single building has to be placed in an architectural group which is all of the same period or character, there is a strong case for deliberate imitation, with careful reference to records of any building which may have been on the site before; the closer this can be followed the better. There is nothing wrong with a reconstruction of this kind provided it looks like the original (a matter of some skill in design and execution).

Nor is there necessarily anything immoral about "character" architecture - preferably in a context where the character has some point. The trouble is that the tradition of designing and building brilliant improvisations in defunct styles is now itself almost defunct.

The familiar directive to architects (and tranquillizer to objectors) that a new building shall be "in sympathy with its surroundings" is all right as far as it goes, but it can mean anything - from a genuine exercise in compatibility to a weak essay in applied character, with a few coy quotations from its neighbours. Random rubble, with its associations of honesty and antiquity, tends to crop up in the oddest places whenever the name of amenity is invoked.

Unfortunately there are no absolute rules for compatibility to cover all townscapes, and the architectural relationships within them. Height of frontage, building-line, materials and plot-ratio are commonly controlled by planning authorities. They can also under the Civic Amenities Act require the preservation and planting of trees. In addition to these clear and necessary restrictions, they can, of course, reject a design as unsuitable or suggest modifications. Yet obviously they cannot make a poor design into a good one.

Should materials and finishes be restricted at all? The answer depends on existing usage in the area; Aberdeen's local light-grey granite is the best example, but not all materials impose so strong and effective a discipline (it is difficult to avoid using granite in that city, or to design a really bad granite building).

In places where a larger variety of materials has been used, it is generally possible to select from them. Almost any newly introduced material will be wrong, especially if it is of strong character or colour. If the use of larger areas of glass has been established in an urban scene, this may be particularly useful to the designer.

Many new buildings in old environments are too conspicuous, not always in materials, but in unnecessary design features with no relation to neighbouring buildings or even to their own function. Assuming that a new design is free of this sort of thing, there are certain questions worth asking about it; no single answer is necessarily right, but whatever the answer is, it must have some point in relation to its surroundings. For example:

In what ways (if any) does it challenge comparison with one or more of the neighbouring buildings, or its surroundings in general?

Does it

- use the same/different materials/colour/texture?
- follow/interrupt an existing building line/height lines?
- have the same overall balance between horizontal/vertical: wall/window?
- have the same window treatment: small/large panes?
- assert the same degree of status/permanency?

The trump cards of today's architectural vocabulary are precision and adaptability. The former is very seldom out of place, and the latter, although it means that there are endless ways of doing everything badly, also means there is nothing which cannot be done suitably and well.

6. THE SURFACE

6.1

It is possible to give so much thought to the mechanics of conservation, with all the problems of structure and planning, that the final details are left to look after themselves. The result can be disappointing in itself, and wrong in its context.

Although a lot can be planned in advance, much has also to be done during the final stages and site supervision should if anything be intensified. This, after all, is the part of the work which is going to be seen.

Similarly, when the whole job is in the nature of surface improvement or maintenance, a lot of care must be taken to discover what treatments on details or accessories are most suitable - first for the building and its style and materials, and then to its surroundings. Superficial improvement is just as important (or at least, just as effective) as radical restoration.

Stone Conservation and Cleaning

Stone facework deteriorates for various reasons. Sometimes it is laid on edge and so exposes a weak face to the elements. Sometimes it is physically affected by wind-borne particles of dirt which erode the surface, and sometimes chemically by atmospheric pollution (especially in towns) which leads to a build-up of corrosive salts; these tend to concentrate in places not thoroughly washed by rain, or where water tends to hang (particularly under cornices). The soundest, best designed stonework can also become dirty, especially on a north-facing front where the natural cycle of washing-and-drying takes place slowly.

Stone cleaning as regular maintenance can greatly reduce or even eliminate decay by removing corrosive salts. It can also improve appearance by removing any build-up of dirt. In its simplest and safest form it involves no more than washing with water and brushes. It does not change the character of the stone and a building so treated will not stand out conspicuously in a terrace where other buildings have not been cleaned. This method is unreservedly recommended.

A second method, a little more drastic, involves lightly abrading the stone surface. This is often done by hand-cleaning, or just enough sandblasting to remove the surface dirt only (but sandblasting tends to blunt the sharp edges of carving and channelling which must be cleaned by hand). Some stone surfaces darken quite naturally in the course of time and a client who expects a "new" building at the end of the job may be dissatisfied unless he is warned beforehand what to expect.

The third and unfortunately the most common method is by severe physical cleaning which amounts to resurfacing, by grinding off the top surface with carborundum wheel or sandblaster, or re-working it with tools. Such treatment may well be a sign of pride in ownership, but a building subjected to it is architecturally devalued by the loss of the entire original surface and the substitution of an inferior one. It also sticks out like a sore thumb in a terrace, upsetting its balance.

Stone cleaning and repair is not at present subject to planning control but there is good cause to make it so - at least for listed buildings or in conservation areas. Advice must also be made easily available in these cases, and should also cover correct methods of re-pointing and stone repair.

Painting

Much excellent work has been done by co-ordinated painting schemes to give unity to a mixed development (e.g. in St. John's Street, Perth) but there are also possibilities for restoring unity to continuously designed terraces and rows of shops.

The painting of external stonework, except in the rare cases where it represents the original treatment or the surface has had to be patched with a dissimilar material, is to be discouraged. This is another practice which should be subject to control. It is usually a departure from the original appearance; it is irrevocable, except by undesirable physical methods of cleaning; and sometimes the result is not stable over the whole surface, because active mould or salts will break out through the paint unless the stone is properly prepared for painting.

The whole subject of colour in conservation and townscape deserves much more attention than most architects are able to give it. A greater respect for original treatment is also needed in interior work.

6.4

Shops

Shop-fronts (of any period) tend to be low in the order of conservation priorities, and to be overlooked both in official listing and in the consideration of planning applications. Nor have the demands of townscape come to satisfactory terms with the thin impermeable facing materials which seem to be part of the shopfitter's required vocabulary; especially difficult when they are part of the image of a multiple shop. Plainly there is room for much improvement both in the design of new shop-fronts and the realisation of the character and possibilities of old ones.

6.5

Lettering

Of all architectural accessories, lettering is generally the weakest, at the mercy of unnatural mass-produced forms on one hand, and sterile taste on the other. The names and notices which identify shops are, quite naturally, an important part of the identity of a town.

Apart from the brash and chunky forms of the "big-town" shop front (improvement here is important) certain reasonably good ranges of applied lettering are available, mainly in wood. But there is still room for a good series with the universality of the typical late-Georgian display-alphabets on which it would, quite reasonably, be based. The opportunities for a revival in painted lettering should also be followed up, and good signwriters (now mainly employed by coach builders for the lettering of buses and lorries) should be encouraged to do shop-lettering and to train apprentices for the purpose. Painted lettering has an immediacy, a closeness to the building without interfering with its form, which make it an indispensable part of the townscape vocabulary.

7. *A NEW LEASE OF LIFE*

Churches, town halls, schools and museums, commercial buildings and markets; these larger members of the townscape group have a way of becoming obsolete just as we are becoming aware of their merits and their contribution to the scene.

Sometimes such a building is internally remodelled, with or without a visible extension. Sometimes this course is not adequately or intelligently considered and the building is pulled down and replaced; possibly a symbolic act connected with the forming of a new image, or a curious preference for the contingencies of new work rather than the more dreaded hazards of alteration and restoration. Alternatively the user may simply move out, leaving behind him a problematical and depressing hulk. Our towns have far too many of these.

It is surprising how few owners seek advice on the feasibility of repair or alteration to extend the useful span of this kind of problem-building - and how few architects are prepared to consider this possibility seriously. Functional needs have changed and extended far more in public than in domestic accommodation, and the challenge (as well as the rewards in terms of results) is increased by the fact that in many cases a really important work of architecture is at stake, sometimes an interior as well as an exterior.

When the survival of a first-rate building is publicly argued in terms of "vandalism", "we can't live in the past" and so on, it is a sure sign of something having gone wrong at a much earlier stage; either maintenance and sensible planning by the owner, or appreciation of the qualities of the building itself. Where there is good architecture in a prosperous town it should be possible to take timely steps for its preservation.

Nevertheless most towns and all cities are faced with redundant buildings. It is something that they still exist - a fact which often owes something to preservation efforts or equally often to beneficial neglect. Too much is sometimes made of the difficulty of finding uses - especially by local authorities who find the whole responsibility (not always unjustly) laid at their door. With today's enormous diversity of need there is virtually no building for which, with imagination and persistence, a realistic use cannot be found (engineering monuments can be a difficult exception). It is the architect's job to marry this use to the physical form, the character, and wherever possible the detail, of the existing building.

8.   *THE WHOLE SCENE, AND HOUSING*

The strongest reason for retaining a complete urban scene is that it was designed or built as a whole. The weakest, but unfortunately one of the most real, is that we are worried about the quality or compatability of a new building in an old environment. Between these positive and negative extremes lie many others which are perfectly good, but need to be looked at very carefully.

Of the case-histories given in this section, Inveraray and New Lanark are classics; each built by a single master to a strongly unified design, in which any change would be an intrusion, and each restored by a single agency at the end of its *first* life-span, during which it had remained in common ownership. The only real difference is that the New Lanark project is more gradual, indeed still far from complete. As in many other cases, the first phase was an act of faith in the successful completion of the whole job.

Common ownership (in its enlightened form) has also been the key to the "natural survival" of many a village like Gatehouse-of-Fleet. In quite a different way it has come to the rescue of Culross, Dunkeld and Old Aberdeen. In its statutory form (compulsory acquisition) it has seldom been used, though there are Comprehensive Development Areas incorporating listed buildings in Haddington and one or two other Historic Towns in Scotland.

In places unified by design but not by ownership, the problem is acute. From Georgian Perth, the elegant and vulnerable outer shell of the Town, to Georgian Edinburgh with its two square miles of solid high quality development, such Towns have as many owners as street-doors. They were created by extraordinary feats of discipline and organization, and a similar effort will be necessary for their conservation; in both these cases, it is only just beginning.

Almost nowhere, as is shown in the case of Culross, has it been possible to contain a historic town within its existing boundary, un-extended. Considering the number of important villages which have contracted or virtually disappeared, this seems particularly unfortunate and unnecessary.

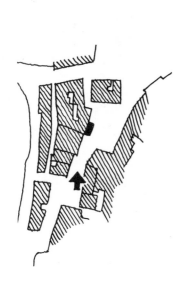

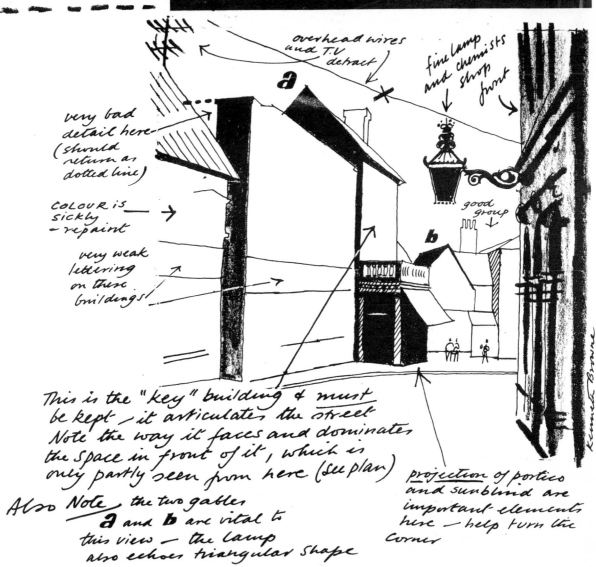

overhead wires
and T.V
detract

fine lamp
and chemists
shop
front

a

very bad
detail here
(should
return as
dotted line)

COLOUR is
sickly
- repaint

very weak
lettering
on these
buildings!

good
group

b

This is the "key" building & must
be kept — it articulates the street
Note the way it faces and dominates
the space in front of it, which is
only partly seen from here (see plan)

Also Note the two gables
a and **b** are vital to
this view — the lamp
also echoes triangular shape

projection of portico
and sunblind are
important elements
here — help turn the
corner

Kenneth Browne

Photographs and St. Ives drawing by courtesy of The Architectural

enclosure lost

The Market Place, St. Ives, Hunts — AS IT IS TODAY

the important sense of enclosure
has been squandered
by allowing gaps to be made in surrounding buildings.

enclosure regained

Kenneth Browne

way through to small
square
at back

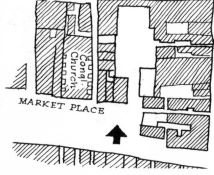

MARKET PLACE

AS IT COULD BE

with gaps filled and
a usable pedestrian space
formed — serving market,
pub, café etc.

But local authorities in general still have to be convinced that restoration of the town centre is any substitute for a prestigious fringe of new housing, or that the first is financially comparable with the second.

Towns which are historic in the literal sense, where not only buildings but the whole environment is expected to be old or (in some ways equally important) to look old, have even greater problems. The medieval parts of Stirling and Edinburgh show a gradual progress towards a satisfactory answer. Both had become depressed areas with numerous gaps. In Stirling, below the Castle, the town's enlightened restoration-and-rebuilding policy has engendered a curious product not lacking in trouble or expense but in life, the organic quality of use and design which gave the original its character.

Of Edinburgh's "Royal Mile" less than a quarter remains in its medieval shape. There is a great deal of plain Georgian tenement frontage, anonymous in design yet not without effect, but for the last one hundred and fifty years most buildings have been explicit attempts to preserve the old-town scene; the baronial Improvement Act tenements of the 'sixties and the picturesque improvizations of Sir Patrick Geddes in the 'nineties; both now contribute to the remarkably valid and consistent scene for which the small modicum of surviving pre-1700 buildings sets the tone, preventing the unhappy feeling of overall pastiche. Individual restoration projects (mainly by the City) and new buildings, which have so far tended to follow the unwritten principle of being "in character", are dealt with in the case studies which follow.

9. THE FIFE STORY

Partnership of Preservation Societies in a County
In 1938, only seven years after the National Trust for Scotland was itself founded, the St. Andrews Preservation Trust, first of the five amenity societies now active in Fife was brought into being. It was not until after the Second World War that the second of them was established in 1957 at Crail.

The comprehensive group restoration embarked upon by the NTS at Culross in Fife, which is now well advanced, led to the idea of "blazing the trail" for similar work urgently needed in other old Scottish Burghs. For this purpose the *Little Houses Improvement Scheme* was launched by the NTS in 1960 with a grant of £10,000 from its General Funds.

This formed the nucleus of a Fund that would be "revolved" again and again by a continual process of the purchase of little houses of character - their improvement and sale, releasing money for further work. It was soon "doubled" by a gift of an equal sum from the Pilgrim Trust to be likewise "revolved" with special application to that unique close-set chain of ancient little coastal burghs in the East Neuk of Fife, from St. Monance to Crail.

The NTS next appointed a Representative in Fife to stimulate and watch over these developments. In the following three years he helped bring into existence two further societies for the East Neuk and for Central and North Fife. These, together with the two already mentioned and that most recently formed for itself by Tayport, now cover the entire very important area of East Fife. Impressed by these developments, the Pilgrim Trust again came forward with a loan, interest free and for a specific use, of a further £10,000.

The local societies have each received loyal support from that minority in any community that really cares and is prepared to express itself. Local Authorities viewed their establishment at first with distrust, fearing obstruction, but have since had reason to welcome their influence. The NTS County Representative officially attends meetings of the Planning Committee. So far the Societies have not attracted the scale of financial support which was hoped for. The NTS therefore decided to offer to each a loan drawn from its own Pilgrim Trust loan so as to enable them to carry out for themselves specific approved Little Houses Improvements. These activities have served also to give the Societies added public recognition and status.

Each Society has published a short, historically reliable yet readable illustrated manual on its area. They have succeeded in arousing a measure of public awareness of this aspect of amenity and have sought to sow the seeds of future enlightenment by contact with the local schools. At least a beginning has been made.

10.   *HADDINGTON, EAST LOTHIAN*

10.1   *Introduction*
Haddington, County Town of East Lothian, lies in the valley of the Tyne seventeen miles east of Edinburgh. Built as a royal burgh in the twelfth century to promote trade and industry in one of the richest agricultural counties in Scotland, it was laid out as a long narrow triangle six hundred yards long with a base of one hundred yards, the properties lining the triangle having long riggs (gardens) reaching two hundred yards to the town walls and the common grazings beyond.

In the sixteenth century, the centre of the triangle was built up and now there are three streets lined with three and four-storey buildings mainly from the late eighteenth century and early nineteenth century, and still remarkably unspoilt. It was by-passed in the 1920's and so is not dominated by traffic, but by 1956 Haddington, like so many small Scottish burghs, was suffering from stagnation and the decay of its buildings.

Basic statistics:

	1951	1966	Forecast
Town Population	4498	6440	9500
Net Sphere of influence	9406	10870	14320
Travel to work	440 out	1150 in	

1966

Overall Density 12 p.p.a.   Rateable Value per head £28
Average Household Size 3.3   Product of 1d. rate - £775.14s.
Insured Population in Service Industry 60%
Sales per head (1951) £78

10.2   *The County Development Plan*
This Plan, approved in 1955, specified the policy both of building up Haddington as the County Town in order to unify the County (resisting suburbanization by establishing new industry) and of developing its

social life to check rural depopulation. It also specified the preservation of Haddington's fine architectural heritage. These two principles, far from being irreconcilable, worked to each other's advantage, as industrialists and new population were attracted to the town which had taken so much trouble to look after its heritage.

The Plan defined the centre of Haddington as an *Area of Great Architectural Value* and the riverside as an *Area of Great Landscape Value* and these zonings resulted in stricter control of development (in general, no alteration is allowed to the external masonry and roofing materials). They also justified considerable initiative on the part of the County Planning Department in preparing schemes for the improvement of these areas.

The Plan also defined a Comprehensive Development Area with the purposes of solving the future traffic problems, dealing with an area of obsolete development and, in particular, providing a new area for large modern buildings which would normally have broken into the old streets.

10.3   *Preservation*

The first need was to build up a "climate" for conservation:

1. Condemned and derelict house reconstructed by the County Planning Officer who also wrote a guide book extolling the town's architectural qualities.

2. Town Council restored the early nineteenth century Town House on occasion of Coronation in 1953.

3. Interest aroused 1954 by controversy over tarmacing of cobbles and erection of lighting columns (later replaced by fluorescent wall-mounted lanterns - first time in Scotland).

4. American industry attracted to town 1956.

5. Overspill agreement with Glasgow for 250 families 1958, some housed in restored buildings.

6. Completion 1962 (first in Scotland) of co-ordinated paint scheme for town centre.

7. Provision of land and services for private building. This and other efforts to increase the prosperity and attraction of the town have given basic stimulus to conservation.

The County Planning Department has always taken a special interest in *Listed Buildings*. Despite this, of the 184 buildings in the draft list of 1950, only 129 survived to 1961 to appear in the Provisional List, 75 of them in dire need of repair. The present situation is as follows :

Categories	A	B	Supplementary	Totals
Restored	4	27	12	43
Future Assured	2	40	18	60
Future in Doubt	-	8	9	17
In Critical Condition	-	3	5	8
Demolished	-	-	1	1
Totals	6	78	45	129

These 43 restored buildings are assured of a lifetime of at least sixty years and the powers available in the Civic Amenities Act, 1967, will enable those in a critical condition to be saved.

10.4   *Two of the Main Conservation Schemes*
South Side of High Street 1962-65

Prepared in County Planning Department (beginning with 1/32" survey and mainly carried out by Town Council under the Housing Acts. Scheme embodies rear access road into the largely derelict long-riggs where new houses were built. Garden ground was acquired to give foot access to High Street through Ross's Close.

Results: People brought back to live in Centre, historic properties restored and fine "backs" revealed, ruins and clutter removed.

	1 & 2 Apt.	3 Apt.	4 Apt.	5 Apt.	
1955 Inhabited Houses	18	13	8	12	51
1965	17	38	5	13	73
Awaiting Reconstruction	7	1	4	-	12

Costs:

Acquisition - 1.30 acres £3,100	31 new houses	£73,034
Accommodation Works and Demolition £9,400	Ross's Close 6 restored houses and 6 new houses 2 restored shops	32,500
Roadways and Site Services £8,000	Private restorations (Housing grants £1,600)	18,100
Rateable Value before £ 185	Rateable Value after	2,242

10.5   *Mitchell's Close 1963-7*

Carried out by County Council under C.D.A. powers (architect in charge, Hugh Small of Messrs. Campbell and Arnott), the scheme includes restoration of seventeenth century close to provide three houses and three craft workshops; new health clinic under construction; road widening to open up reserve area for town centre expansion. Restoration policy was to reconstruct the buildings in the form in which they had developed and grown familiar. i.e. neither strictly archaeological nor "no-nonsense" modern - though the work includes a bit of both.

Results: Many users of the health clinic will become interested in the neighbouring old buildings and the craftwork in progress. The restored houses are aimed to attract young professional people.

Costs:

Purchase and Demolition	-	£3,230
Reconstruction and Fees	-	£27,300
		£30,530

Less:

Sales of Land	- £2,120	
Historic Buildings Grant -	£3,800	5,920
		£24,610

Annual Charges			1,760
Rents	-	£1,085	
Housing Grants	-	125	1,210
		Deficit -	£ 550

Rateable Value before: £86   Rateable Value after: £426

The annual deficit of £550 will be reduced as the rents are reviewed but in the meantime it is carried on the Planning Account which is rated over the county as a whole.

10.6   *Town Expansion*

The growth of Haddington has meant new developments. Special care has been taken to get the best quality available and developers have responded to the quality of the town. No attempt has been made to reproduce the styles of the past but rather to work the new developments closely into the fabric of the old. One of the qualities of Haddington is the continuity of the townscape with one development fitting closely into the next. The retention of old sykes, walls, footpaths, old trees and other features has helped to tie the old and the new into this community of design. Care has also been given to the social development of the town.

11.   *DUNKELD, PERTHSHIRE*

Dunkeld became the ecclesiastical capital of Scotland in the ninth century. The cathedral is now part parish church, part Ancient Monument. The town is built on a T-plan, the cathedral at the base, approached down a street completely rebuilt after 1689 when it was burnt by the highlanders. Dunkeld was eclipsed by the building of Birnam, the railway-station town on the other side of the river, and thus survived. Its setting in the larch-clad valley of the Tay is one of the finest in Britain.

The National Trust for Scotland began work in 1954 on the improvement of derelict houses (all for local tenants) on the north side of Cathedral Street, given by Atholl Estates. Old houses were subsequently purchased to complete the scheme. The County (housing authority) have followed suit on the south side.

    40 houses stabilised and improved (about half by NTS)
    Costs: Uneconomic for piecemeal contracts involved in NTS work; increasing from 18/4d. to £3.10s. per square foot between 1954 and 1965 when the scheme was completed by opening of NTS Information Centre. All the later phases were aided by Improvement Grants and HBC Grants.

Dunkeld was the testing ground for many techniques and procedures painfully evolved but now considered standard. Its outstanding feature was willing co-operation between county authorities, NTS and other owners, but other points are of interest:

1. The first small contract had to be economic to be acceptable. Houses were not fully improved and had to be re-improved six years later.

2. Today the whole job would be tackled in fewer contracts, probably by means of a housing association loan although this would imply rents on an economic (not local authority) scale.

3. The only advantages of small contracts were (a) minimum disturbance of tenants and (b) a newly-finished house was often available as a show-house, with excellent propaganda effect, before the tenant moved in.

4. One unit was formed within each original house, though all woodwork was replaced and interiors re-planned. External appearance was unchanged on main frontages but extra (traditional type) windows added at the back.

5. Gap-site policy; original construction was poor and one house had to be entirely rebuilt in "reproduction" to retain integrity of character. This earned a rebuke from the Saltire Society Housing Panel when they gave their Award. On the south side of the street the county reproduced a free-standing house and managed to contrive by-law ceiling heights within the original eaves-height by a reinforced concrete floor on first-floor level.

6. Other townscape features; NTS staff mason laid cobbled margins: county consulted NTS on lighting, litter bins, bus shelter, parking.

The early nineteenth century Atholl Street (on the A9) which forms the crossbar of the T-Plan, was the subject of a successful "facelift" scheme.

Architects: Ian G. Lindsay and Partners, Edinburgh for NTS.
County Architect for Housing Authority.

12. *PORTSOY, BANFFSHIRE: SHOREHEAD*

This is an architecturally distinguished town whose sixteenth century harbour (with vertical-coursed wall) was later extended, but it declined towards late nineteenth century when the buildings of the Shorehead group became half-deserted.

The Town Council instigated the Shorehead Conservation Scheme in 1962 and began work in 1963. By 1967 the following were complete: blocks 1 and 2, 1 house each: block 3, 1 flat and 1 maisonette: block 4, 1 maisonette: block 5, 2 flats. Block 6 is being reconstructed as 3 houses. Costs were low, reflecting regional practice in Banffshire; from £2,000 to £2,500 per dwelling. Improvement Grants throughout, plus HBC grant for block 5. Architectural treatment: some roofs still sound: windows re-arranged in some blocks but retaining seventeenth/ eighteenth century character with uniform sash and case treatment. Walls colour-washed when existing pointing was in order: otherwise harled. Blocks 1 and 2, white: block 3, pink: blocks 4 and 5, off-white.

Reaction is favourable. Tenants enjoy individuality of houses and (contrary to gloomy forecasts) their situation; not surprising, for the living rooms look out to the Moray Firth. Neighbours have followed suit with similar colour-washing (accepted practice on this coast).

Architect: John J. Meldrum, Banff.

13. *EDINBURGH: CANONGATE*

The Canongate is the eastward section of Edinburgh's "Royal Mile", the main street of the Old Town. It gave its name to the Royal Burgh, independent of the City till 1856, which had its own church (1688) and tolbooth (1591) and a number of other outstanding buildings whose restoration began in the late nineteenth century and continued after 1945. These however occupy less than a quarter of the 700-yard frontage on each side and the remaining buildings and gap-sites have set a variety of problems in restoration and redevelopment, which grow more difficult as work goes on piecemeal.

A score of architectural firms has worked in the Canongate with different degrees of scholarship and imagination. Apart from half-a-dozen faithful restorations there is a considerable variety of approach which it would be all too easy to condemn as a historical hotch-potch; in fact it avoids the danger of dullness and (if the present concensus of policy continues) should provide not only a good environment for residents but a satisfying experience for visitors to this historic street.

Techniques vary from the straightforward "timeless" character of Nos. 70-80 by Ian Lindsay and Partners (this actually comes quite near to the Scots tradition) to the more quirky restoration-of-a-restoration at Whitehorse Close by Sir Frank Mears and Partners. But almost all the work has maintained the convention of short frontages of rubble and/or harling with conventional window openings (if not always old-type glazing), standing shoulder to shoulder along the old building-line. The city has successfully installed wall-fixed floodlighting in place of standards or brackets, but has unfortunately replaced the worn granite road-blocks (causeys) with asphalt.

The largest and most important section of post-war work in the Canongate is in three schemes carried out by Robert Hurd and Partners:

1952   Tolbooth area   27 houses   8 shops
        Instructed by Lord Provost Sir James Miller. 3 frontages were retained including Bible Land and Shoemakers' Land. Traditional glazing.

1954   Morocco Land   32 houses   5 shops
        Site cleared before commission. Frontage reconstructed, incorporating original figure of the Moor. Some non-traditional glazing.

1964   Chessels Court   60 houses   5 shops, nursery school and pub
        Two eighteenth century blocks back from street line restored, including some interiors. Street frontage part reconstructed, part re-designed with distinctly modern detail, including open arcade to give through-views of fine eighteenth century building from pavement. Modern block, not seen from street, to complete large internal courtyard where trees were unfortunately over-lopped and have to be replaced.

The three schemes, done for the city like almost all work in the Canongate, are remarkable for the free use of colour on rendered walls, the re-introduction of traditional features like street-arcades (compare surviving arcade at Gladstone's Land further up the Royal Mile in the Lawnmarket) and the successful incorporation of shop-fronts; the shops have steadily become more prosperous and less dependent on seasonal trade.

14.   *NEW LANARK, LANARKSHIRE*

A self-contained industrial village of tenement blocks and spinning mills on the river Clyde, New Lanark owes its foundation to the meeting (1783) and subsequent partnership of the Glasgow manufacturer David Dale and the engineer Richard Arkwright. In 1799 Dale sold the mills to his son-in-law Robert Owen who combined sound management with much pioneer work in welfare and education. The village store, for example, was run on co-operative lines and self expression was encouraged in the education of the young.

By 1962 the Gourock Ropework Company, who had owned New Lanark since 1881, decided that they could not afford to maintain and improve the houses and offered them for £250 to Lanark Town Council who refused the offer by a majority of one.

Consequently in 1963 the Adam Housing Society Ltd. initiated rehabilitation of the village through the New Lanark Association (Housing Association registered under the Industrial and Provident Societies Act, 1893, with charitable status).

From a total of about 180 sub-standard houses, 22 houses with 7 garages have so far been completed:

Pilot Scheme 1966-7: 16 houses in Caithness Row with Museum and 7 garages. £4.16s.3d. per square foot.

Second Contract 1967-8: 6 houses in Nursery Buildings. £5.4s.0d. per square foot owing to larger site-works.

Average cost (tendered price) £4,000 per house.

58 site visits have so far been made by the architect.

Completed project would provide 132 improved houses and 53 garages at estimated total cost of £502,000.

Assessment:

1. This is a good subject for conservation. New Lanark has remained virtually unchanged on its secluded site, and no external changes are being made in the reconstruction work. Window and door openings are re-used without addition or alteration. Relaxation orders were obtained without difficulty where houses come below current standards.

2. Restored houses had to be comparable in tenant-appeal with new housing built by Lanark Town Council. Many housing applicants have asked to be transferred to the waiting lists of the New Lanark Association, and this may be due to the popularity of the fully fitted kitchen unit specially designed for this project.

3. A master television system has been installed and all services undergrounded (compare Inveraray).

4. Early survey showed that the whole job could be done on a system of seven basic plan-types. This greatly simplifies advance planning for successive phases by all concerned.

5. The unfortunate post-script is that the mills are to be closed in March, 1968, and the unity of work and life in New Lanark will be jeopardised. Could New Lanark be given the same status and assistance as other "New Towns" in this region?

Architects: Ian G. Lindsay and Partners, Edinburgh.

In 1743 the old Royal Burgh, capital of Argyll and centre of the herring industry consisted of a few buildings scattered round a run-down fifteenth century keep. It was accessible only on horseback or by pack-horse.

The 3rd Duke of Argyll, advised by Roger Morris, used the town site for his new Gothic Castle and laid out a new town half a mile to the south on the edge of Loch Fyne. This was the time of the Jacobite rising of 1745 and communications were greatly improved by the construction of military roads.

The "Georgian Capital of Argyll" declined after the 1914-18 war and became increasingly difficult for Argyll Estates to maintain and modernize In 1957 the present Duke handed over the town to the Minister of Works at an agreed valuation so that the Ministry could undertake a conservation programme; this was jointly financed by the Scottish Development Department and the Historic Buildings Council for Scotland.

The initial contract was accepted in July 1958 (pilot project of 4 houses). The middle contract provided 29 more houses in an average time of eleven working days per house, thanks to maximum standardization and prefabrication. Even so, the problem of "decanting" tenants in the course of the work was acute; some families had to move five times.

The final contract was completed in June 1961 and a total of 64 houses was produced at an average cost of £1,634 (tendered price) the actual average being £2,049; contingencies due to dry rot and defective structure and services were impossible to assess at pre-contract stage with properties fully occupied. Total number of dwellings before restoration was also difficult to guess owing to number of shared services and sub-tenancies.

142 site visits were made by the architect (car mileage 25,200).

Assessment:

1. Some form of social survey would have been useful at the early planning stage but it remains doubtful if the change from near-slum conditions to new houses could have been anticipated. Tenant-reaction was unpredictable, bearing no relation to initial statement of needs, and based entirely on assessment of the planning of new kitchens.

2. Disappointments: No master television system was feasible and each chimney-head now supports several elaborate aerials. No financial allowance was made for outhouses, boundary walls, footpaths and open areas. There was general lack of co-operation in the improvement of street-lighting and the concealment of cables.
   N.B. Some agreed policy should be evolved between the various government departments and local authorities for acceptable aesthetic standards of service-supply within a Conservation Area. It should not be left to the persuasive qualities of the architect in charge of the commission.

Architects: Ian G. Lindsay and Partners, Edinburgh.

FIFE

The Sandhaven (above) and Tanhouse Brae (top right) at Culross, the National Trust for Scotland's largest and most costly group-project. Both here and at Falkland (below right) the Electricity Board has restored 'un-improvable' cottages as sub-stations.

FIFE

Contrasting interiors in restored houses in Culross;
bottom left is in the 'Study', open to visitors.
Architects for *NTS: Ian G. Lindsay and Partners.*

The Giles tenement block at the harbour, Pittenweem, *DURING* and *AFTER* restoration for re-sale under the *NTS* revolving fund scheme. The hard rendering was stripped, revealing windows which had been blocked, and structural weaknesses including the chimney-gable which was rebuilt in brick. Owner of neighbouring house agreed to overall colour-washing of exterior. Architects: *Wheeler and Sproson.*

The Trust owns 20 'little houses' in Cathedral and High Streets; most of these date from re-building of town after the Battle of Dunkeld, 1689.

Cathedral Street, Dunkeld, *BEFORE* and *AFTER* restoration (the house to right was almost exactly reproduced)

(Above), improved and restored houses in the symmetrical layout of Inveraray. Architects for *NTS* at Dunkeld and Scottish Development Department at Inveraray: *Ian G. Lindsay and Partners.*

Cathedral Street, Dunkeld, from the Cross, with Cathedral at west end. This project is now complete.

EDINBURGH'S ROYAL MILE
Lawnmarket and Canongate

Mylne's Court, Lawnmarket *DURING* (1967) restoration, by *Ian G. Lindsay and Partners* for Edinburgh University. Stair tower (seen also below right) retained; wall to be rebuilt.

(Below) Huntly House (City Museum) and the Canongate, with high-level lighting.

Mylne's Court, Lawnmarket, *BEFORE* (1957) restoration.

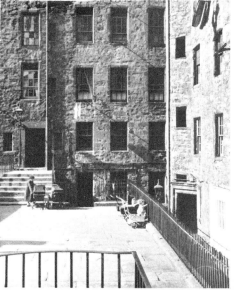

Chessel's Court looking from (above)
and towards (below) the new street
arcade. (see text). Architects,
Robert Hurd and Partners.

NEW NEIGHBOURS

The large scheme at Dysart for the Burgh of Kirkcaldy (*Wheeler and Sproson,* Architects) is a sequel to the same firm's pioneer work at Burntisland, also in Fife. (Above) is the link block between The Towers (17*c*) and new housing.

(Left), shows the deliberately suppressed roof line of the new hall attached to Lamb's House, Leith, (16*c*). Detail showing restored shutter-board windows in Lamb's House itself. (Architects: *Robert Hurd and Partners* who also restored the house as an old people's centre in 1962, for the National Trust for Scotland).

Edinburgh

The extension to the Standard Life Insurance office adjacent to George Street, with green glass and bronze-section curtain-walling (Architect: *Michael Laird,* in consultation with *Sir Robert Matthew*).

Continuing belief in the status-value of architecture has led to the maintenance of much of Glasgow's unrivalled Victorian heritage. The National Commercial Bank in Gordon Street (left) has been well cleaned and in Buchanan Street the frontages of the Royal Bank and Western Club have been retained despite internal re-building – the latter as part of a commercial redevelopment.

Of the two surviving churches by Alexander Thomson, that in St. Vincent Street has been fully restored (left) but the shell of the burnt-out Caledonia Road Church (see drawing on previous page) will only be retained as a 'motorway monument' (both by *Sir Frank Mears and Partners* for the City authorities).

The commercialised and down-at-heel Georgian terraces of Carlton Place were improved by overall painting.

The great Park Circus layout is now the subject of a more ambitious voluntary scheme.

OLD ABERDEEN

Wright's and Cooper's Place, Old Aberdeen, *AFTER* restoration, showing the growth of the new University development round the old town. (*Robert Hurd and Partners,* Architects).

(Above) Shorehead, Portsoy, *BEFORE* restoration.

(Left) Tenement houses at New Lanark awaiting restoration.

(Right), the Wallace Tower, Aberdeen, *BEFORE* it was taken down and re-erected at the expense of Marks and Spencers who re-developed the site. (*City Architect's Department*). It now stands near Old Aberdeen on something like its original open site.

St. George's Church, Charlotte Square, Edinburgh, (left) rescued from collapse and now being converted by *MOPBW* as document store and exhibition gallery.

**NEW
LEASE
OF
LIFE**

(Left) The Old Tolbooth, Stonehaven *BEFORE* restoration as Museum and tearoom by *T. H. Thoms,* Architect for the Town Council.

(Right) Dalry House, Edinburgh, *AFTER* restoration as old people's centre by *Robert Hurd and Partners,* Architects.

HADDINGTON (see text)

The broad picture of Britain's greatest classical-romantic city remains largely intact. Its future survival poses urgent problems not only of condition (especially the proper repair of decaying ornament) but of use; how to contain, and sometimes even reverse, the change-over to commercial or office purposes; and how to make the New Town (the collective name given to a dozen successive Georgian developments) in every possible way as desirable a place to live in as when it was built.

In the 1st New Town of 1767, Adam's Charlotte Square was the subject of a pre-war preservation order but earlier, less distinctive buildings which complement the symmetrical layout are still under pressure like this one demolished in 1967, the bi-centenary year.

GEORGIAN EDINBURGH

The 2nd New Town of 1802 is the most precariously balanced in type and quality of use; one side of the monumental entry to Gt. King Street is equivocally blank, without glazing-bars. By contrast the splendid sequence of the 1822 Moray Estate is relatively prosperous, in mixed use.

At the West End, mainly laid out in 1815 but executed later, the City has chosen the Melville Street area (where some business owners have already over-cleaned their frontages) for a pilot improvement scheme. The unspoilt shops and flats of nearby William Street offer an even greater opportunity for up-grading by rehabilitation. Another minor street of similar quality (Cumberland Street in the 2nd New Town) is being studied for a pilot project by the Drummond Housing Association.

J. Adburgham/Colin McWilliam

LANDSCAPE DESIGN IN CONSERVATION

Physical landscape features are important in determining the location and layout of towns and, together with climate, the siting and design of buildings. Landscape in the broadest sense is not sufficiently acknowledged as a creative factor in design today.

Attitudes to landscape have varied in the course of history, sometimes imposing a man-made pattern, even a pseudo-natural one, on the existing scene. The modern tendency towards wilfully ignoring natural patterns of ecology and seemliness extends into all aspects of urban design.

The kind influences of nature can be harnessed for human recreation in towns, often on a very small scale. Human comfort in walking or resting, skilled planting to create a small world apart, the use of water, the study of sun, wind and rain, all these can be considered in the creation of places where nature would be glad to take charge, and people would be glad to come.

The experienced landscape designer, with knowledge of all these factors, should be in attendance at all deliberations on urban planning, and all those responsible for planning should realize the importance of the subject.

David Lloyd/Colin McWilliam

SYLVAN SUBURBIA

The green suburb, from the early nineteenth to early twentieth centuries, has made a distinctive contribution to English architecture, despite the pressures of incongruous development, including high flats, and the tendency to internal deterioration. The Victorian Society has had a part in gaining due recognition for a hitherto despised, because unknown, type of development.

The idea of miniature country houses separated by trees and often associated with, or bordering, public parks had started with Nash's Regent's Park layout, though pairs of semi-detached houses were included in a 1793 plan for the Eyre Estate, north of the Park.

Birkenhead Park (Paxton, 1843-7) had its fringe of villas, now threatened by replacement and depressed by the possibility of a new road. The Glebe, Blackheath (1849) had been subject to a Compulsory Purchase Order but, following an Inquiry, it has been suggested as a conservation area. Bedford Park, Chiswick (Carr, 1876) has been similarly dealt with, but not before it has been eroded by incongruous development. It is especially important for details such as wooden fences to be retained and restored in this case. Orchards Way, Southampton (Collins, 1920s and '30s) is fortunately well maintained and not yet threatened.

The Victorian Society, in these and other instances, are keen that these suburban areas should be appreciated and properly provided for – not just lumped together with the rest of our vast and generally nondescript suburban environment.

Hanover Court, flats for old people in New Street, Plymouth, sponsored by the Hanover Housing Association. Architects: Ballantyne and Ballantyne. Photograph by Tom Molland.

IVING CONTINUITY IN CONSERVATION

The balanced urban communities which can still be found living in some small and stable historic towns have almost disappeared in the great majority of expanding and economically flourishing towns of this country. This is the reason — with the emphasis on balance — why I have ventured to offer a contribution. It may seem strange that I am to talk exclusively about new modern housing, under the general title "Conservation and Development". Nor have I any learned theories or research to give in support. Instead, I am offering the services of a working established organization which is ready to make a significant contribution to the continuity of historic towns.

I believe that close-knit urban communities set in our historical heritage have a permanent place in the ways of living in Britain; and that it is essential to include modern developments so as to conserve them. I am suggesting in the title that the introduction of compatible modern housing in or adjacent to conservation areas provides essential continuity and support for economic viability. Most of us feel that modern developments in general threaten to overwhelm historical considerations. I will try to demonstrate that there is one form of new development which could make an appropriate, positive and early contribution.

Housing Societies

Sir Keith Joseph, M.P., the then Minister, said at the time of introducing The Housing Act, 1964, that the Housing Corporation "will unlock new sources of house building initiative". He meant that the Housing Societies to be formed would represent a new and different force in housing development — if only on a minor scale. For the last three years these Housing Societies have emerged from professional, commercial, governmental and academic quarters and it should now be possible to look at the nature of this new initiative and measure its relevance to the problems of Historic Towns and Cities.

It is fair to say that Housing Societies represent a new form of co-operative housing in Britain mainly because there is present in all of them a know-how and expertise in matters of housing and property development. Before a Society is registered, the Corporation ensure that the Management Committee consists of people with a wide variety of practical experience. This is reflected in the calibre of Societies which include accountants, architects, bankers, builders, housing managers, property developers, building society executives, University dons, Members of Parliament, of county and local Councils, local businessmen and women. The general quality is high and the Corporation is satisfied that each Society has access to the professional expertise necessary to promote and manage the schemes for which it will be responsible.

In many Housing Societies an evident enthusiasm has been generated by the drawing together of the separate specialists involved in housing examination of intended developments. The creation of a successful team is a distinguishing mark of the expanding Housing Societies. These are now finding that as the movement grows, it offers opportunities to the participants to further in one way and another their own business economies. This is the one aspect of motivation in Housing Societies; the other is the real belief that they are doing something thoroughly worthwhile by placing their expertise at the service of the community at large. Thus, there is a combination of altruism and self-interest.

There are now 450 Cost Rent Societies promoting Housing Societies spread throughout England, Scotland and Wales. In the North of England there are 66 of these with heavier concentrations in Manchester, Liverpool and Leeds conurbations than elsewhere. But each Housing Society is expected to spread its activities over as wide as area as is commensurate with its supervision and management responsibilities.

A virtue of this widespread movement is that it can build for local people what local people want. Here one would expect an appreciation of local history and existing environment. Expert professional and large private housing developments at times seem to lack an awareness of locality. Local enthusiasm is difficult to sustain without the finance and expertise to achieve its desires. In the Housing Society movement we believe we have the best of both worlds. In the registered Housing Societies there is a formidable array of expert and local talent which is quite unique. Apart from the need for more Housing Societies in some less crowded parts of the country, the Minister's prediction that a new house building initiative would be unlocked, has been fulfilled.

3.

Finance and Scheme Progress
The Housing Corporation can draw on £100m. ready Government money to lend to Housing Societies representing one-third of the capital cost of all projects; the remaining two-thirds will be financed from private sources, notably Building Societies. Thus we are embarked on a £300m. programme. The attraction to a Building Society or other private investor is that the Corporation money is, if anything, the risk capital, lent at an earlier point in time, but ranking as second mortgage behind the two-thirds investment by the Building Society who lend at the current recommended rate for owner occupiers; the Corporation lending at ¼% more. The loan repayments are spread over forty years.

The progress made to date, in financial terms, shows that we are almost one-third of the way through the programme in the total of schemes approved. Schemes to the estimated value of *£92m.* have been approved: *£36m.* on the Cost Rent and *£56m.* on the co-ownership terms. These sums will provide a total of 21,400 dwellings.

It should be emphasized that this is a *current* programme. At the present time, Housing Societies are seeking suitable urban sites for their co-ownership schemes. If Planning or Local Authorities, Civic Societies or elsewhere wishes to suggest a site suitable for careful residential development, then it would be investigated forthwith.

4.

Nineteenth Century Zones of Large Towns
The North of England's share of this is 4,700 dwellings, out of which there are twenty schemes complete and being occupied. The first phase of the

programme during 1965/1966 was dominated by schemes of flats in the major urban areas. In most of these are zones of large nineteenth century houses which can no longer be used as single family houses. Unless such zones have succumbed to pressures for office or trading uses, these houses are in multi-occupation and rented to the private sector often at rents not dissimilar to those emerging from redevelopment schemes of new dwellings promoted on a non-profit basis by Housing Societies. At the same time, Housing Societies are producing infinitely more convenient dwellings and greatly increasing their number. The sites of these former spacious houses are frequently well treed, and can provide pleasant settings in positions giving easy access to the town at large.

There have been objections from some preservationist quarters to the introduction of schemes of flats in such zones. It is sometimes said that these intrude on the family housing status of the areas. But once the process of multi-occupation of aging housing sets in, incipient urban decay follows all too soon. The redevelopment of some sites for middle income occupation underpins standards and rateable values and encourages more circumspect use of historic buildings of merit that are to be retained. The insertion of higher density compact dwellings in appropriate places has other benefits affecting traffic generation and social balance.

Considerable central space is occupied in northern towns by old warehouses and factories which were necessarily sited close to railways and market outlets. Changes in distribution, commercial mergers and obsolescence of many of the buildings themselves are some of the factors leading to necessary redevelopment. All too often there is clear felling and the replacement with dead at dusk office blocks and shops. Here again, if the air is clean, and there is some history and nature in the environment, Housing Society schemes are possible.

There is the implication and possibility in the Housing Corporation's programme that certain private elements will return to full urban living in provincial towns; thus is dependent on the efforts and co-operation of several public authorities. By no means least is the fact that these residents will need and care about the listed buildings and conservation areas in such town centres.

Smaller towns and villages
Housing Societies are generally uninterested in participating in suburban developments remote from routine services. Sites are sought with easy access to a majority of daily needs. In many smaller towns which have experienced rapid housing expansion in recent years the outward sprawl has not been matched by refurbishing and infilling the historic core. In these circumstances, Housing Societies are more interested in sites closer to the interesting historic buildings than to the "black glass facia" of new shops.

In the use of common amenity ground and readiness to build terrace houses, society schemes are in a sense returning to the concept of the village green. In the re-appraisal of village functions proceeding at present, British people are reconfirming their rural predilections. But so often the rural village atmosphere to which they so earnestly commute is destroyed by the modern housing that is built for them.

With the steady decline of agricultural labour it is virtually impossible to conserve a historically valuable village as it is. New life is essential. Often the old cottages are hovels, however folksy and charming they may look. Provided there is evidence of demand, and a Housing Society can arrive in time, it can play its part in such circumstances.

6.

Summary

The current form of co-operative housing in this country under the Housing Act, 1964, has an immediate and adjoining relevance to conservation and change in historic towns.

Housing Societies are now established throughout the country and their broadly based management committees provide a wide variety of expertise and local knowledge.

In the unified development and ownership of schemes, the insistence on high standards and mandatory use of architects there is the promise that this private housing will enhance the neighbourhoods of conservation areas and historic buildings.

The major scope is in relation to Victorian and nineteenth century properties but care in design, elevation and external finishes of schemes will make them compatible with the neighbouring historical surroundings of older towns and villages.

History in J. Burckhardt's words is "the record of what one age finds worthy of note in another". Whilst we presume to set the record of historical buildings straight, we are surely even more anxious to ensure that our contemporary contribution will be recognized as worthy by succeeding generations. Many Housing Societies are keen to join such an endeavour.

RT SIX – CONSERVATION POLICIES IN EUROPE AND AMERICA

EGAL, FISCAL AND ECONOMIC REMEDIES N WESTERN EUROPE –

rom a paper first delivered by
ruce Watkin, Royal Fine Art Commission,
o an International Council on Monuments and
ites (ICOMOS) Symposium in March, 1967

HE FRENCH SYSTEM FOR CONSERVATION AND REVITALIZATION IN HISTORIC CENTRES

rancois Sorlin,
  Inspecteur Générale des Monuments Historiques,
  Ministère des Affaires Culturelles

HE CONSERVATION OF HISTORIC CITIES IN UROPE

Richard W. Hare BA(Arch) FRIBA
  Brandt Potter Hare Partnership

A MATTER OF DEGREE

Donald W. Insall ARIBA AMTPI SPDip
  Donald W. Insall and Associates

LEGAL, FISCAL AND ECONOMIC REMEDIES IN WESTERN EUROPE

1. LEGAL MEASURES

1.1   Though we have many different political systems and the degree of our respect for the rights or duties of individuals varies, we are all agreed that legislation is required to (i) prevent the thoughtless destruction of our cultural monuments and (ii) allow (in principle at least) the intervention of the state (or local authority) to ensure their maintenance and repair.

Listing of such monuments is the first essential. This has been carried out in all countries in Western Europe. In most it is coupled with a system by which the owners of the buildings listed must give notice of their intention to demolish or alter them, so that the relevant authorities can consider preventing the demolition or the alteration, or making an outright purchase of the building, or some compromise.

The lists vary considerably in their size and their force in law. In France there are about 30,000 buildings listed. In the United Kingdom the figure is over 100,000. In some countries the listing varies sharply from one region to the next, as in Western Germany where the Land of Nordrhein — Westphalen has listed over 15,000 and some other Laender have hardly begun. In fact, of all the countries in Western Europe, Denmark is the only one which has expressed itself satisfied that its listing is approximately complete.

While this listing usually prevents the demolition of historic buildings without notice, it rarely ensures their survival in good repair. In France and in Norway and Sweden, regular maintenance is required by law of all listed buildings, but it cannot be enforced in the United Kingdom or many other countries such as Switzerland. In the United Kingdom if we wish to ensure maintenance we have to acquire the building. Some form of compulsion to maintain a listed building would now seem to be universally desirable.

In France and Portugal the setting of individual listed buildings is also protected, automatically by the listing procedure. France also has special and complex legislation for the protection of rural and urban sites (under its law of 1930). Somewhat simpler, but still general, provision for the protection of sites is found in the Netherlands, and in Spain (under the law of 1933 and the town planning order of 1956), while in Western Germany, Italy and Sweden there are special laws for the protection of individual urban sites; the most important are those for the protection of Venice.

In other countries, particularly those of northern Europe such as Denmark and the United Kingdom, more reliance is put on the wide use of planning powers.

Both methods can be effective but, if only the protection of a site or the setting of a building is required, there is much to be said for the

Norway; Stave Church, Borgund.

use of the simpler provisions of (for example) English town planning law
rather than the complex procedures of the old French law on sites.

1.2

Positive Measures for Rehabilitation

All countries now have powers to acquire, by compulsion if necessary,
buildings or whole areas of towns in order to ensure the making of roads
or the improvement of housing conditions. Good use can sometimes be
made of these powers in historic centres. Most have powers to acquire
sites of archaeological and historic interest and many have given their
central or local governments power to acquire urban sites or old town
centres. In most cases, however, the powers are very restricted like those
for archaeological sites in Greece and Italy or are of only local application,
like the powers for the restoration of Santiago de Compostela in Northern
Spain. Or again they may have been provided without the financial help
required. As an instance, Sweden has recently given its local authorities
power to acquire old streets or historic quarters in order to preserve them.
Outside Stockholm few are likely to be sufficiently wealthy to do this
without state help.

Nevertheless a great deal has been done in countries with little direct
legislative aid but with generous government financial help, as in parts of
Western Germany (particularly those where the Laender are keen on this
work) and also in Portugal.

But the administrative and financial complexity involved in using the
combined, but unrelated, powers of public health, housing, highway and
historic building legislation for restoring historic towns has been too much
for most countries. Nearly all are, therefore, studying the complete
system of French legislation and are considering how they can apply
its provisions and intentions in their own special circumstances.

1.3

The "Malraux law"

The French law of 4 August, 1962, not only completes the French system
of protecting historic and artistic buildings and sites, but also because it
has provided Western Europe with its first practical experience of the
full co-operation of town planning, housing and historic monument
organizations in the rehabilitation of whole historic towns.

Briefly, this young act provides the legal means for the comprehensive
restoration of every "urban site" of historic interest in France. It makes
it possible, it does not make it easy or inexpensive.

1.4

Summary

In the field of negative protection most countries in Western Europe feel
they have sufficient legal provisions. But it is still felt to be insufficient
in Austria and Italy and to be deficient to some degree in West Germany,
Switzerland and the United Kingdom.

In the field of positive preservation most countries are studying the
application of the special French law of 1962 and trying to adapt its
provisions or principles (sometimes successfully) to their own circumstances. Belgium and Italy were among the first to prepare similar laws.

But of course no law is of much value if it does not have public understanding and respect. Nor is it of much value without finance to carry
out its positive provisions. Attitudes in Western Europe vary widely and
one expert said recently that we wanted less law and more money. There
is a great deal of truth in this.

Guadalupe (Caceres), Parador Nacional de Turismo.
(This and the photograph of Leon on p. 218 are by courtesy of the Spanish National Tourist Office).

2. FISCAL REMEDIES

It is difficult to be particular and probably useless to generalize on this subject. At the same time it is probably fair to say that almost every government in Western Europe contributes to the protection and preservation of historic buildings, whether in public or private ownership, both by direct grants and by hidden subsidies in the form of tax concessions. Contributions to private owners are, naturally, not often generous.

Income tax rebates are granted in Belgium, Denmark, France and Norway. Capital tax allowances are given in the Netherlands and exemption from inheritance duties in Italy (in respect of the "Ville Venete"), the Netherlands and the United Kingdom (in respect of properties bequeathed to the private but charitable "National Trust").

Low interest loans are granted in France, in respect of historic centres designated under the 1962 law, and in Greece and Italy for the restoration of other historic buildings.

Outright grants are given in Belgium (up to 60% from the State, 20% from the province and 10% from the commune for classified buildings), in France (up to 50% for the "classified" and up to 40% for the other listed buildings) and in the Netherlands (up to 60% from the State and up to 15% from the local government). Large individual grants based solely on need are made by the West German Government and by some of its Laender, by the Spanish Government and in the United Kingdom. Rather smaller grants are made in most Scandinavian countries; this seems to be a reflection of the fact that the larger buildings there are already in public ownership or are not such a burden to their owners as in many other countries.

Compensation for any loss of value due to listing is not common, but any such loss is usually recognized by lower valuation for tax purposes.

Many countries complain of the difficulties facing those trying to retain historic buildings caused by the rapid rise in the value or price of urban land. This is a big subject and deserves special study. I can only say here that it does not seem to be so acute in those countries with well-established and comprehensive planning systems.

3. ECONOMIC REMEDIES, INCLUDING TOURISM

It is rare for historic monuments or other cultural institutions to be self-supporting solely from the fees paid by visitors. In the United Kingdom there is only one, the great stone monument of Stonehenge where maintenance costs are very low and in this case a pure economist would be very scornful of the small return earned in relation to the capital value employed!

Generally the cost of maintaining and restoring historic buildings can only be met by outside help in the form of subsidies or gifts, or by finding a new user who can pay a fair rent or otherwise pay for its cost. Most of the important buildings in historic centres can only be kept by a combination of both sources of income.

No governments in Western Europe pretend that their historical monuments can be kept without financial sacrifices and their questions are directed to

Leon, another of the Chain of Government Sponsored Hotels (*paradores*) throughout Spain.

Verona, Piazza dei Signori

finding out how low the costs can be kept. At the same time they now realize that (i) they have a duty to make sure that their inhabitants are decently housed and well educated (which involves the expenditure of public money) and (ii) cultural assets are also tourist assets and bring indirect financial rewards.

In the restoration of historic towns, therefore, when allowance has been made for the use of housing funds, the improvement of living conditions, the increased rents obtainable for much of the improved property, the new life in the town and the increased cultural and tourist assets provided, a fair assessment may well show that the whole exercize is not only less costly (in purely financial terms) than the normal procedure which involves slow decay and destruction followed by new building on fresh land, but (on a wider balance sheet) even profitable.

Increased leisure and increased personal incomes have led to a rapid rise in the tourist industry of Western Europe in the last twenty years. It has brought a lost of money to historic towns and monuments. Some of this has been well used, for instance by the Spanish Government in the "paradores". But it has brought its problems too. Every country now complains of the demands made by motor traffic on its old towns. Many are also concerned at the wear and tear caused to their buildings by the increased number of visitors.

The tourist industry could, I think, contribute more to help historic towns and buildings which are, of course, one of its chief assets. In this connection it is instructive to compare the amount of the contributions made from central sources to the maintenance of historic towns and buildings in the various countries of Western Europe, with the huge income which many obtain from their foreign visitors. France, not unexpectedly, has the best record in this respect and there the ratio is about 2½ to 100. That of the Netherlands, Spain and the United Kingdom is about 1 to 100. In Italy, which has the most lucrative tourist industry in the world and must be the most dependent for it on its historical monuments, the ratio is less than one half.

I do not expect this indirect plea to the tourist industry, to contribute more, to be well received by that industry. It has its own difficulties. But I feel that it could well make a bigger and very sensible investment in one of its greatest assets and that some of its difficulties, such as those due to cut-throat competition, might be overcome by international agreement.

I have not referred to the diversion of resources from other needs to our own need. We all know of items of expenditure in our Governments' budgets which we should like to cut if we could only divert the resources to our own work. For myself I realize too well that to divert expenditure to, say, the burial of one kilometer of electricity line in order to save a site or view from disfigurement may prevent the electrification of five farms.

Increase in our real wealth is the only ultimate answer but even this brings special problems in Western Europe. Demands for increased production mean more concrete, more roads and more electricity. In many crowded parts of the west such demands cannot be met without damaging some part of our artistic heritage, urban or rural.

I am therefore glad to find such wide agreement throughout Western Europe generally that regional planning, on a very wide scale, is desirable to cope with such difficulties.

M. F. Sorlin

IE FRENCH SYSTEM FOR CONSERVATION AND REVITALIZATION
HISTORIC CENTRES

INFLUENCES

Recent legislation in France in the preservation and revitalization of
historic centres (towns, villages and historic areas of towns) results from
the growing belief in the protection of monuments. This in turn is
brought about by the new type of civilization in which we are caught up.

This civilization, the development of which has accelerated considerably
since the end of the Second World War, now puts as much dangerous
pressure on historic centres as on the most significant monuments.

In his notable paper to the 4th Council of Europe Symposium held in
the Hague in May, 1967, Professor Gazzola declared that though we still
believed that our towns owed their individuality to the mere presence of
ancient monuments which have resisted the attack of time and man himself, experience had taught us that even if these monuments remained
intact, our towns and villages would none the less lose with frightening
rapidity their particular character and historical value.

"We then discovered," the Professor went on, "that buildings which
fitted the traditional definition of a monument were no more than one
of the aspects of the significant character of an historic group, and that
other factors, which had been neglected, as secondary or minor, played
a part no less important than the architectural masterpieces."

For this reason, under the twofold influence of the former belief, and
the realization of new dangers, the idea arose that it was necessary to
preserve groups of historic buildings, and to find new uses for them.

OBJECTIVES

These two considerations formed the foundations of the French law of
4th August, 1962, in which the basic intention, according to André
Malraux, was to integrate the past with the future.

This intention must be achieved while bearing in mind that historic
centres must no longer be thought of as decaying or mummified areas
of the town but as living elements endowed with aesthetic, economic
and social functions according to their character.

The definition of these functions, which are part of regional and urban
planning, derives from the following principles:
(a) In most cases there is an advantage in assigning to the buildings of
which the historic areas are made up functions related to those for
which they were built: historical continuity may then be exploited without reconstruction involving capital expenditure. However, such a
solution is not always possible; it is only practicable in groups of buildings where the architectural structure permits a logical use of historic
premises.

Autun, silhouette of the town.

Bar le Duc.

(b) The new uses must necessarily contribute to the economic and social integration of the historic area of the city. It is increasingly clear that there can be no question of restoring a centre of this kind simply to make it into a living museum for the interest of tourists and art-lovers alone. Effective preservation cannot take place without revitalization, which implies that the historic core acquires some new role in the life of the city.

Currently towns, villages and historic areas of towns are usually inhabited by the poor, who have insufficient resources to keep up old buildings which in addition lack basic amenities. Consequently one is aware of a continuing movement of people to new developments in the suburbs, which causes decline and subsequent decay in areas containing old buildings.

This migration is a social imbalance which can only be counteracted by seeking new uses for these buildings: residential, where the living quarters have been modernized; small workshops for craftsmen; and commercial premises where little traffic is involved.

(c) Cultural and tourist possibilities need careful investigation as they are particularly suited to historic centres: educational establishments; museums and galleries; the hotel industry.

Based on these principles, the departments concerned with the preservation of the French cultural heritage drew up appropriate judicial, technical and financial provisions in the Act of the 4th August, 1962.

CRITERIA IN SELECTION

.1
To put the system into practice, there was first of all a methodical survey of historic centres likely to benefit from the new law's provisions. An inventory was consequently made of more than a thousand historic towns and villages. The choice of those in urgent need of some intervention was based on the following principles :

.2
Homogeneity
The historic area must be clearly defined by architectural or topographical landmarks, and it must be complete within itself. This "homogeneity" must result not only from the urban grouping in a literal sense (for example, fortified towns or hilltop settlements) but also from the continued existence of old roads, the scale of buildings, as well as the original massing.

It is often true that this homogeneity of historic towns is in inverse proportion to the development which has taken place in the surrounding region. In France more than two-thirds of integral historic towns are south of the Loire, in the region generally known as the "French Desert" because of its low level of economic activity.

.3
Historical, Archaeological and Architectural Interest
This interest lies less in the "monumental" character of particular buildings making up the group than in the overall quality. There are usually within these groups important buildings separated by buildings which, viewed in isolation, are not worth the description "monument", but which have group value from an historical point of view, or from an architectural or visual one.

.4
Agreement between the authorities and local public opinion
An important element of choice is involved here: even though in

principle the 1962 Act allows for historic centres to be "classified" on the decision of the Conseil d'Etat alone, the French Administration has adopted the principle of first of all obtaining the co-operation of local authorities and the support of public opinion.

As well as for political and psychological reasons, this preliminary co-operation is at the same time indispensable for economic reasons. As we shall see later, the French system involves financial participation by the State, by local groups, and by owners. This participation can only be voluntary, except in the case of eviction or compulsory purchase, which rarely occurs.

3.5

Economic and Social Possibilities
Revitalization presupposes that in the town under consideration there exist the necessary financial resources for inaugurating local participation, and a population ready to occupy the restored premises in the historic areas. This is why the French Administration acts with circumspection in inaugurating the new system, choosing the centres which fulfil the requirements mentioned before.

This policy means at the moment the exclusion of those villages where one cannot be sure of finding the necessary resources, and the effort essential is deployed on cities and the larger market towns. At this point in time, forty historic centres have been designated, with the co-operation of the local authorities. The main ones are in Paris (Marais district), Aix en Provence, Arles, Avignon, Bourges, Chartres, Colmar, Dijon, Lyon (Saint Jean, Saint Paul, Saint Georges districts), Le Mans, Pézenas, Rouen, Sarlat, Senlis, Troyes and Uzès.

If one excludes Pézenas, Sarlat, Senlis and Uzès, where the designation was based on exceptional historical and archaeological interest, the towns concerned are important ones where the revitalization experiment may be carried out with every possibility of success.

4. WAYS AND MEANS

4.1

In France historic centres designated in this way are called "secteurs sauvegardés" – literally "protected areas". Decisions on areas to be so protected, and on their limits, are taken by a national commission composed of architects, archaeologists, town planners, specialists in regional planning, and local authority representatives.

As soon as a town is specified as needing to be designated a protected area, on the basis of the principles outlined, negotiations are begun with the town concerned to encourage co-operation in the scheme. The people are consulted through a Public Inquiry system during which the observations and suggestions of the landlords are collated.

Once the limits of the "secteur" have been defined jointly by the Ministry of Cultural Affairs and the Ministry of Works, there is a period of two years during which the Administration draws up the details of the plan for conservation and enhancement of the designated area. During this delay, all work likely to modify the structure or the appearance of buildings included in the "secteur" is prohibited, unless carried out with the sanction of the Ministry of Cultural Affairs.

This measure is primarily to prevent the building being stripped of moveable and immoveable interesting features, such as carvings, iron-

Paris, Marais, Hôtel de Béthune-Sully.

Paris, Marais, Hôtel de Beauvais.

work, woodwork, paintings, etc. for sale to dealers and collectors. This practice was common before the law intervened. It is now effectively checked.

The working out in detail of the conservation plan and policy is the responsibility of one or more architect-planners selected jointly by the Ministers of Cultural Affairs and Works. They work in continuous collaboration with research organizations involving archaeologists, sociologists and economists. The plan comprises two complementary parts :
(a) an architectural directive
(b) a detailed town map.
Throughout the two years necessary for this to be done, the local authorities and the residents are consulted frequently, particularly in demographic, economic and social surveys carried out by the research teams. At the end of the two-year period, the plan is adopted on the decision of the two Ministers, which is taken after consultation with the national commission. It then becomes obligatory to carry out its recommendations for an unlimited period; growth and eventual changes within the designated area may now only take place in accordance with the dictates of the plan.

The technical departments of the Ministry of Cultural Affairs are responsible for the enforcing of the plan.

4.2

Technique – Architectural Directive
To finalize this directive a detailed investigation is carried out of the "secteur's" condition. This investigation comprises the following information:
— architectural interest of each of the buildings and state of preservation (buildings or parts of buildings to be restored or buildings ready for demolition; soundness of fabric);
— sketches of the elevation, taken from photographs so that the appearance of the whole grouping is obtained;
— an analytical index, building by building, showing the approximate construction date, materials used, subsequent alterations, open spaces, original gardens, and any particular features such as cellars, ramps, balustrades, woodwork, ironwork, interior décor, etc.

Once this information is collated, the draft directive shows :
— demolitions to be considered;
— structures to be built up;
— materials and fittings to be used;
— open spaces, and areas to be opened up;
— old features to be maintained;
— and the appearance of the street: shops, street signs and lighting.
This directive is accompanied by a timetable for its implementation, including :
— preserved buildings;
— buildings to be destroyed:
— key groupings;
— inside areas of planting;
— and mass and appearance of the adjacent buildings.
In drawing up the timetable, the greatest possible consideration is given to the reports on demographic and social aspects furnished by the

Avignon, reconstruction in character.

Paris, Place des Vosges, shop windows in arcade.

MINISTÈRE DES AFFAIRES CULTURELLES — MINISTÈRE DE L'ÉQUIPEMENT

VILLE DE CHARTRES
LOI DU 4 AOÛT 1962

PLAN DE SAUVEGARDE ET DE MISE EN VALEUR

NORD

research bodies, which clarify the nature of the present population, its resources, its static or migratory characteristics, and the functions likely to be assigned to the restored properties.

Technique — The Conservation Plan in Detail

The preparation of this plan must of necessity be based on the provisions of the development plan for the town and the region. The detailed plan for the area to be protected will be conceived in sympathy with this (access; road networks; sanitation improvements; utility networks; educational, industrial, commercial and residential buildings). Elsewhere within the plan are incorporated the recommendations of the architectural directive, establishing particularly the width of roads, building lines, massing and scale.

It is clear that from the technical point of view the conservation and enhancement plan is the king pin in the system. The possibility of revitalizing the designated area depends in fact on its conception and effective application. If the uses decided for the area are too much in its former tradition there is a risk of the situation as it was prior to designation remaining the same, or even getting worse. If, on the other hand, they appear too revolutionary, structural modifications may result which would destroy completely the old fabric, losing the character one is striving to preserve.

Particular attention is paid to problems of traffic and the parking of cars, which, for well-known reasons, form one of the principal instruments of potential destruction in historic towns: cracking of frail structures within buildings, and of paving, by the repeated passing of vehicles, especially heavy vehicles, increasing erosion of stone through the emission of harmful fumes, and the blocking of squares and streets, etc.

The greatest possible effort is made to create relief roads round the historic core, leaving the central streets to pedestrians: peripheral highways, car parks outside or underground, tunnels beneath towns or their historic areas. Since the law began to be put into practice, twenty conservation and enhancement plans have been approved, and work started.

Finance

This depends on the co-operation of public authorities, national and local, and on private landlords. There is a loans and subsidies system which may be used either by landlords acting alone or in syndicates, or by organizations set up on the initiative of the local authorities, generally taking the form of "Sociétés d'économie mixte".

In the former case — works carried out by landlords — the landlords can obtain state aid up to the equivalent of 80% of the total expenditure. This aid consists partly of mid- and long-term loans, for about 60% of the total, and 20% subsidy by the state. It is self-evident that work done privately must conform to the dictates of the conservation and enhancement plan, and be overseen by the technical departments of the Ministry of Cultural Affairs.

In the second case, which is the most usual — work done by groups — the scheme is carried out by a particular type of Society, which includes representatives from the town's officials, from local landlords' associations, from banks and from Chambers of Commerce. These Sociétés receive delegated powers from the Administration. They may acquire buildings for restoration or demolition, either by consent or by eviction.

In almost all cases "contracts of association" are drawn up with the landlords, which allow the Societies to act on behalf of the latter, throughout the work. Once the restoration is finished, including conservation of the building as a whole, and improvement of the environment, the landlords take possession of their property again, on the condition that they refund to the Société the agreed amount for the work done. If on the other hand the landlords refuse to agree contracts with the Societies, they can be evicted, with the Society becoming the landlord of the property. After the work has been carried out, the building is in this case resold without profit, the old landlord keeping the right of first refusal, or it is let to new occupants.

The rent obviously takes into account the increased value of the building due to the work having been carried out. There might have been a danger of tenants being evicted who, before the restoration of the building used to pay very insignificant rents, according to their means, because of the age and discomfort of the properties.

There are therefore two possible solutions: either the former occupants are rehoused outside the historic area, in the newly developed areas, where there is accommodation for reasonable rent; or they accept some increase in the original rent, the extra being taken care of by the Society in the form of a housing subsidy.

In any case, French legislation restricts the advantage of such an allowance to people of inadequate means or with family responsibilities. Single people or households without children but with a low income therefore have to be replaced by people with higher incomes.

That is, without any doubt, the most delicate social problem the new régime comes up against. The French administration is not in favour of enormous population movements, which are likely to stimulate discontent, and is currently trying to find judicial and financial means to reduce the magnitude of the problem.

5.   *EXPERIENCE SO FAR*

5.1   The forty conservation areas already designated in historic towns vary considerably in area, from 20 hectares (50 acres) to the 180 hectares (450 acres) of the Marais district of Paris. All these areas have one characteristic in common: they all have a remarkable homogeneity, and their historical, archaeological and aesthetic unity has not been seriously altered.

They have examples of all the types of old construction existing in France: medieval houses, mostly with timber-framing (Bourges, Chartres, Colmar, Treguier, Vannes), Renaissance houses (Pézenas, Sarlat, Lyon, Saumur, Chinon), seventeenth and eighteenth century buildings (Marais district in Paris, Aix en Provence, Avignon, Dijon, Richelieu, Senlis, Uzès). The continued existence of their unity and homogeneity is due to their being either groups away from the main roads, and so from economic development, or towns which have retained their function as commercial and residential centres, and where expansion has taken place in the suburbs, outside the boundaries.

The same is true of the areas of large cities (le Marais in Paris, and the Saint Jean district in Lyon) where important industrial activity has continued for two centuries. In this case, the buildings have generally been kept up by their owners, with roads and architectural structures scarcely modified, with the exception of a few thoughtless alterations and demolitions in the nineteenth century. Nevertheless, commercial premises at ground level present a façade problem which is solved by prohibiting partitions and reinstalling plate glass windows in the low arcades. Elsewhere, inappropriate additions in courtyards and gardens are equally numerous, but generally this problem is easily overcome in prohibiting them.

Progressive restoration and revitalization of these groups has now begun, with experimental work on sections which have been carefully chosen, and which are of relatively limited area: from 2½ acres to 20 at the most. These works are being carried out with the twofold intention of producing rapid spectacular results in the areas most susceptible in this respect, and to produce an example of general enhancement which from the point of view of the population in general will be worth emulating. A number of lessons may be learnt from these initial experiments.

The Cost of the Work
Contrary to the opinions of those not in favour of revitalization in historic centres, the cost of the operation is generally no higher than that of demolishing old buildings followed by rebuilding.

Thus, at Avignon, the average cost of revitalization works out at 1,600 francs (£114) per square metre, while new building of the same standard, in this town, comes out at 1,800 francs (£129) a square metre. In Lyon, the cost per square metre in houses restored in the Saint Jean district is 1,400 francs (£100) against an average of 2,000 francs (£143) on average for new buildings.

It must nevertheless be emphasized that in the early years of putting the system into practice, public authorities will be obliged to make costly investments since no great return can be recouped from the owners or landlords for four or five years.

The average outlay in investing in these experimental sections is actually of the order of 40 million francs (£3 m) over 2½ acres. When the system for the repayment of loans is working as intended, this outlay will fall to 8 million francs (£667,000) on 2½ acres, corresponding to the total of non-recoverable subsidies paid to landlords.

Nevertheless, these subsidies are scarcely higher than those offered to landlords of new houses. They come into the category of the French Government's policy of improving the environment, and are included in the statutory provision of the number of new or modernized homes which must be made available annually. This forecast is, for the period 1970–1975, 500,000 homes a year, of which 60,000 will be renovated old units.

Restoration and revitalization of historic areas is therefore part of an economic and social process which now takes into account the preservation of France's cultural heritage.

5.3   *Psychological and Political Reactions*

Despite the precautions taken, the first experiments in revitalization have gone forward in difficult circumstances. In Paris and Lyon, particularly, "Comités de Défense" have been formed among the inhabitants to oppose the temporary rehousing of people while the work is in progress.

These reactions grow calmer as more and more of the former occupants return to their modernized homes; in 80% of cases, they have agreed either to pay increased rents or, in the case of landlords, to pay their assessed amount to the "Société d'économie mixte",

The situation is more difficult in the small towns, where the people are poorer than in the large cities, and the communal budget is often very small. For this reason, the work at Uzès has not yet begun, as the town, which is already overcommitted financially, is not able to play any financial role in the creation of a sanitation network which is fundamental to the planned restoration.

Everything nevertheless leads one to feel that with the help of example, the psychological and political difficulties will gradually be overcome.

5.4   *Technical Difficulties*

These are essentially of two kinds:

(i) *Removal of accretions and improvement of sanitation*

Many historic centres are encumbered with structures like parasites which have to be demolished, to allow the old buildings to stand in their own right, and at the same time to improve the environment by the re-establishment or creation of courtyards and gardens.

This is particularly the case in the Marais district of Paris, where the aristocratic population left towards the middle of the eighteenth century to establish themselves in the Faubourg Saint Germain, leaving a crowd of artisans to instal themselves in the old "hotels". The courtyards and gardens were transformed into workshops and warehouses; the majestic rooms were divided by partitions to form either living accommodation or workrooms.

The conservation and enhancement plan allows for the demolition of all these structures and accretions, and the re-establishment of conditions prevailing in the Turgot plan. These operations are not technically complicated, but they cause a notable increase in the cost of the work, and are therefore a serious financial problem.

The problem of new uses for these restored hotels de ville is equally delicate; the size and shape of the reception rooms is no longer relevant to the needs of modern living, and the only possible solution for the revitalization of three hundred large residences in the Marais district is their use by embassies or large companies requiring prestige offices.

The problem is different in the small towns or areas of the average middle class, where it is primarily a matter of creating inside the buildings natural and artificial lighting to standards consistent with modern living.

It is the problem of the removal of accretions which will permit the amalgamation of adjacent buildings or those which are too narrow, enlarging the habitable rooms, and replanting the interior courtyards and gardens. The experiment is currently going on in several towns; it is made more difficult when, as is the case at Pézenas, for example, each interior courtyard contains architecturally significant loggias which there can be no question of disturbing.

(ii) *Integration of modern architecture with historic urban fabric*
The listing of historic centres does not necessarily mean the retention of all the buildings of which they are composed. Many of these buildings are now, having been neglected, in a state approaching ruin, and their restoration would amount to reconstruction. Also, during the nineteenth century and the early part of the twentieth, hideous buildings were often constructed in the style of the time, which conflict violently with the architectural environment, and which will have to be demolished.

Finally, there are often open spaces in historic areas where demolitions have been carried out for reasons of hygiene or public safety. On sites of buildings no longer existing, or which will have to go, one must devise architecturally appropriate replacements. The feeling is now unanimous that these sites should not be filled by modern imitations of ancient buildings which result in a lamentable appearance of artificiality, and the best solution seems to be to set standards for massing and detailing, so as not to create a scale unsympathetic to the harmony of the group.

Once these standards are fixed, however, should one impose upon the architect inflexible restrictions on openings, the rhythm of façades, and the type of materials? The current opinion seems to be that one should respect the creative freedom of the artist, provided that he takes into account the fundamental urban design principles fixed by the conservation and enhancement plans.

So at Avignon, in the designated "la Balance" area, there have recently been built, on a site empty due to demolition for thirty years, modern buildings where the pitch of the roofs and the massing blend with the total impression of the old town, but whose façades have been freely treated, in accordance with the architect's own inspiration; the material used is nevertheless the same as that of the surrounding buildings.

But it is not impossible that in certain other cases buildings of steel and glass could not fit into historic areas, with a deliberate effect of contrast. Schemes of this type are being studied at the moment.

This is, it must be recognized, the most serious technical and aesthetic problem posed by the co-existence of traditional and our contemporary architecture. This is also one of the main reasons why revitalization of historic centres must be both cautious and progressive; the study of the different experiments will enable suitable methods and policy to be established.

6. *FUTURE PROSPECTS*

Despite the difficulties encountered, these are encouraging. First of all, public opinion is taking a growing interest in the cultural heritage of French towns. The continuing and irreversible development of a leisured society creates in the individual a need for knowledge and culture which can in part be met by the success of efforts to conserve and revitalize historic areas.

Already this interest is evident in France in the conspicuous increase in the number of "secteurs sauvegardés"; in less than a year, more than fifty towns have asked the advantages available and the means to revitalization open to them since the passing of the Act of 4th August, 1962. This is an encouraging development if one remembers that the first experiments encountered mistrust, and consequent hostility from local authorities and from the people.

In 1968, about thirty new "secteurs sauvegardés" will be designated, in line with the intervention to have created about two hundred in the next ten years. The main obstacle to overcome is obviously the financial burden inevitable for the state in the designation of new "secteurs". For this reason private landlords are warmly encouraged to ask individually to benefit from the loans and subsidies which the law allows. The number of requests increases annually. In the town of Aix en Provence alone more than fifty files with this end in view were deposited in 1967.

It is, we believe, by more and more frequent recourse to state-aided private initiative that the problem of conservation and revitalization of historic areas will be solved.

Photographs by courtesy of M. Sorlin.

Richard Hare

THE CONSERVATION OF HISTORIC CITIES IN EUROPE

1.
European Attitudes

Whilst interest in the conservation of historic towns and cities has only arisen in this country during the last ten years, sparked off by the destruction of the central area of Worcester for commercial development and "traffic improvements", the need to repair the devastation of two world wars has created, in Europe, a considerable body of knowledge of the theoretical and practical aspects of conservation. Since the nineteenth century there has arisen a new awareness of the unique qualities of the environment of historic towns; and their economic importance as tourist attractions has long been recognized. A study of the European approach will therefore provide a valuable yardstick against which current thinking in this country can be assessed.

Even on a short tour, the visitor will be surprised at the large number of historic towns which remain apparently unspoiled. Closer inspection reveals, however, that many of these cities are almost complete reconstructions, following severe devastation. St. Malo and Nuremberg are examples of cities largely rebuilt in their traditional form. Following wartime bombing a third of Rothenburg has also been reconstructed. In many cities whole groups of medieval and renaissance buildings have been skilfully restored, the opportunity being taken to remove unsuitable later extensions and to bring the interiors up to modern standards of comfort and convenience.

Whilst these techniques of scholarly, painstaking restoration are uncommon in this country, being largely restricted to the repair of churches and important historic monuments, they have for many years been the accepted methods in Europe. In Britain, mere copying is regarded as being rather immoral, an admission of the failure of the architect to integrate modern design into historic settings.

If, however, the historic city is regarded as a complete work of art, then the renewal of one decaying building in its original form becomes as logical as replacing a missing stone in a diamond ring. It is this concept of the historic city as a complete work of art that provides the basic framework of conservation policy. Within this framework conservation and redevelopment can be seen as aspects of the same process. Development is essential to keep the historic city alive, to create the economic background for the pre-servation of the environment, but it must always respect the integrity of the historic city — the basic relationship of the city with its site, and the surrounding landscape; the skyline and silhouette; the scale and pattern of the buildings; the colour and texture of the building materials and especially the form and enclosure of the urban spaces.

Where conservation policies have been most successful, new sites out-

Innsbruck, the Sense of Enclosure.

side the old centres have been found for commercial and industrial buildings which are of unsuitable scale and form. These sites provide room for future expansion, adequate parking space and easy access to traffic routes. Traffic generated by these large buildings can be kept out of the narrow city streets. In spite of the removal of the commercial centres to new sites, the old centres remain alive and prosperous.

Even outside the historic centre, the siting of large new buildings must be carefully considered in relation to the form and skyline of the whole city.

It is noteworthy that many cities in Europe have escaped the insidious "traffic improvements" which have eroded the fabric of so many of our own cities, by the demolition of historic buildings to provide vision splays at road junctions, destroying the enclosure of the urban spaces. It is also clear, however, that urgent action is required to provide by-passes, adequate car parks and pedestrian precincts if the quality of environment is to be retained.

Where it is essential for a building of unusual size and scale to be constructed in a historic centre, then siting and design become of crucial importance. The construction of the new Festival Hall at Salzburg against the face of the encircling cliffs renders the high fly tower required for operatic productions almost invisible against the cliff face. On any other site the bulk and outline of the fly tower would have destroyed the delicate silhouette of the spires, towers and domes of the churches and palaces of the city.

A study of urban spaces in Salzburg, Innsbruck, Berne, Murat, Gegenbach and many other cities indicates that the architectural quality of the individual buildings framing the spaces is not of major importance. The whole feeling of the space – the sense of enclosure – results directly from the proportions of the spaces and the outline and silhouette and colour of the building groups. Individual buildings can be replaced without any loss of character provided that the form and colour of the whole group of buildings is respected. In particular, perspective views of the sites must be considered with the greatest care. Roofs, dormers, chimneys and turrets far behind the building facades add character to the quality of spaces.

Where, as in Berne, each city block is surrounded by a continuous series of arcades, providing covered access to the whole of the central shopping area, modern shop fronts can be constructed within the arcades without harming the character of the elevations.

2.
Fribourg
The town of Fribourg in Switzerland is sited (like Durham) on a peninsular at the bend of a river. The original town was established at the bottom of the gorge, at the junction with a tributary. The town has developed in clearly visible stages on to the top of the peninsular within the river bend.

The buildings are generally three or four storeys high with steeply pitched tiled roofs, the walls being finished with rendering or stone, apparently growing out of the rocky promontory. Only the tower

Fribourg.

Berne, typical arcades incorporated in a luxury hotel.

of the Cathedral and the turret of a church break the irregular
silhouette of the houses on the ridge. Close to the Cathedral, where
the spine road breaks through the buildings to span the gorge, a
major redevelopment is in progress.

Before 1959 the authorities of the city and canton of Fribourg
bought up this group of derelict properties by the bridgehead. A
design competition was held for the remodelling of the houses to
provide a new office building for the local authority. By some
mischance, the winner of the first prize proposed a complete
demolition of all the houses in order to replace them with a multi-
storey office building. At this point the Federal Department of the
Interior prohibited the demolition of the existing houses. The Local
Authorities then sold the site to the Pension Fund of the C.I.B.A.
Chemical Company, who are now renovating the houses with the
aid of a 50% grant from the Federal Authorities.

The Architects, Suter & Suter of Basle, were required to retain
the external appearance of the whole group, but ugly nineteenth
century additions were removed. At the end of the remodelling,
the whole group will be restored to its eighteenth century appearance,
incorporating a small hotel, and an arcade of small shops with flats
above. No off-street parking or unloading spaces were required, and
it is difficult to see how any could have been provided on such a
narrow restricted site between a main road and a deep gorge.
When completed, this development will restore life to this section of
the city, whilst retaining the character of a most important site.

This example has been described in some detail in order to illustrate
the care which is now taken to prevent unsuitable development, and
the positive steps which are adopted to ensure that the redevelopment
of each site is assessed in the light of its impact on the city as a
whole. One multi-storey block on such a key site would have devalued the environment of the whole city. Recent developments at
Norwich, Winchester and York all serve to illustrate our own failure
to consider the impact of tall blocks on the character of historic
cities.

3.
Freedom and Control
Whilst straightforward reproduction of existing buildings is the normal
method of renewal, there are many examples at Regensberg and Bad
Mergentheim, for instance, where modern buildings have been
integrated into old settings. The designs are of a restrained character.
The modern facade is set beneath a steeply pitched roof following
the outline of adjacent buildings, and is gridded to form small, well-
proportioned panels, bringing the openings into scale with the fenestra-
tion of the existing buildings.

The materials of the roofs and walls are carefully controlled for
texture and colour to harmonize with the colouring of the whole
area. The importance of carefully controlled colour in blending new
buildings into old settings cannot be overstressed. For instance, in the
ancient University City of Tübingen, colour schedules have been drawn
up for large areas of the historic centre, to which all property owners
must conform.

Rotterdam, the Old Town Hall gives stability to the modern environment.

At times, the forcing of modern buildings into traditional outlines becomes ridiculous. At Ulm, where the whole of the medieval Munsterplatz was destroyed, only sparing the Cathedral itself, the reconstructed shops are set beneath steeply pitched tile roofs, the facades being broken up into illogical shapes and patterns purely to give an illusion of the form of the old square. When whole areas have been destroyed in this manner then the architect must have freedom to create a completely new environment, unhampered by the past.

Munich, Frankfurt and Cologne all illustrate the vital contribution which historic buildings can still make, even when the whole of their original surroundings have been destroyed. If they are isolated and set apart, the old buildings look incongruous, dead. Seen as focal points in the new townscape, or forming sides of compact urban spaces, their silhouette, form, colour and texture can contrast effectively with the harder rigid forms of modern architecture, giving a fourth dimension to the city.

4.
The Regensberg Study
Regensberg, one of the most perfectly presented medieval cities in Europe, provides the opportunity for a study in depth of current techniques of conservation in Germany. Founded, like York, as a Roman Camp at an important river crossing, Regensberg has been fortunate in escaping nineteenth century pressures for redevelopment and destruction in the wars, which have ravaged Europe in the last two thousand years. Over the centuries, however, the ancient buildings have become overcrowded and insanitary, the internal courtyards and gardens have been built over, and living conditions have become unacceptable.

Economic support has been given by the creation of a new University Town on the South side of the railway outside the city walls. Of the 30,000 inhabitants of the 8,000 dwellings in this ancient city, 15,000 will need to be transferred elsewhere. A Pilot Study for the conservation of the old city has been carried out by a Seminar of architects and planners, financed by the Federation of German Industry.

Among its recommendations, this Study Group proposes :
(i) A new ring road should be provided well beyond the city walls, rendering unnecessary the Traffic Engineer's proposals for forming a motorway along the South bank of the Danube, destroying a large number of ancient houses and warehouses, and cutting off the city from the river as effectively as the Embankment has destroyed London's links with the Thames.
(ii) Traffic entering the old city would terminate in multi-storey car parks within the walls.
(iii) The whole city centre would be largely reserved for pedestrians, with service road loops to each group of buildings.
(iv) In order to remove unsuitable commercial and business uses from the old city, a new commercial centre should be constructed on a deck above the railway station, with adequate car parking and restaurant and shopping facilities.

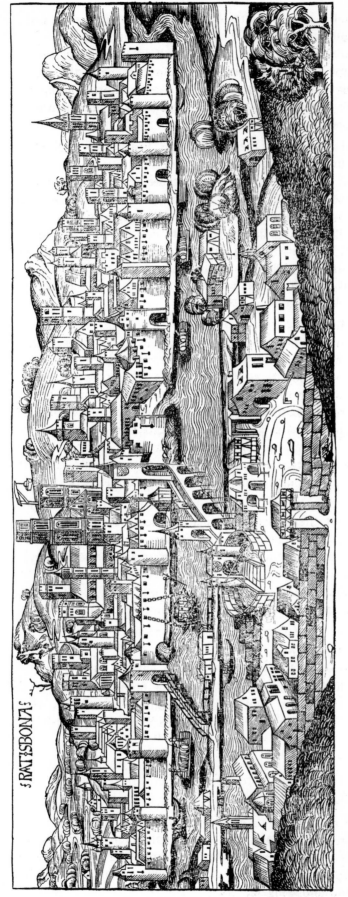

Regensberg 1493.

Midway between the old city and the University, at at the hub of the communications network of road and rail, the creation of this new centre is planned to reduce pressures for development within the old city. These recommendations can be paralleled in the plans for many historic towns in this country, but this report is unique in the detailed studies which have been made for the conservation of the building groups in the old city.

Following careful analyses of the archaeology, history, architectural character and condition of each property, alternative proposals have been put forward for the clearing of unsuitable additions, the conversion and improvement of the remaining houses for new uses, and for the construction, within the blocks, of new buildings, students' hostels, restaurants, clinics, etc. which would ensure that there is life in the city at all times of the day and night. New walkways will be threaded through the courtyards within these existing blocks. Models have been prepared to establish the most suitable building forms to occupy the internal courts.

At the present time the conservation of the first blocks is in progress. The Landesamt für Denkmalpflege are now engaged on the preparation of surveys of some 1,500 houses in order to prepare detailed plans for the conservation of additional blocks. The study group's proposals have been placed on exhibition in the city in order to foster public interest and discussion, before final decisions are taken.

If we are to benefit from European experience it is clear that considerable research is required into the successes or failures of conservation policies. A superficial study such as this can only draw attention to the remarkable state of preservation of so many towns an and cities — failure to tackle the mounting traffic problems which threaten to tear out the hearts of so many cities is counterbalanced by the apparent success achieved in the conservation of the scale and character of the urban spaces and building groups, and the preservation of the image of the city as a whole.

If the museum techniques adopted in the conservation of individual buildings sometimes produce rather dull and lifeless results, at least the integrity of the environment has been respected.

5.

A Possible Conservation Centre

The European approach requires the architect to have greater historical and archaeological knowledge, greater humility in design, greater respect for the past. If we are to encourage these skills, the formation in this country of a centre in conservation studies becomes imperative.

Here all the professions linked in the conservation teams would exchange information and initiate research. Here, linked with a University, students would be educated in the philosophies and techniques of conservation.

In an age of rapid change, refresher courses for practising architects and planners would enable them to keep up to date. Through the organization of regular conferences, current conservation techniques could be explained and analyzed.

Rathkeale, Limerick. Repainting goes a long way towards preservation. (Government help in Eire).

Ghent, a carefully cherished environment.

By linking the activities of the many trusts, preservation societies and amenity groups in the country, an informed public opinion would be stimulated, so that the needs of conservation could receive their proper priority in national planning.

Just as the architects and planners will require training in the special techniques of conservation, it is also vital to ensure that the traditional building skills required for the preservation of historic buildings are now allowed to die out.

In order to provide a nucleus of skilled craftsmen, it might be necessary to set up a network of regional centres, possibly based on enlarged and modernized cathedral workshops, where the crafts of mason, plumber, carpenter, plasterer can be kept alive long after they have disappeared from current building practice. By centralizing the demand for building materials, quarries could be re-opened, and stockpiles of salvaged materials built up.

In all these matters, the centre in conservation studies could provide the moving spirit, through which the preservation of our historic towns and cities would be assured.

France, Brantôme.

Donald Insall

"A MATTER OF DEGREE" – CONSERVING HISTORIC TOWNS IN THE U.S.A.

1. It has been said that "more monuments are destroyed by over-restoration than by neglect." This may be so in the case of buildings, but in very few cases does it apply to whole historic towns. A philosophical question in all conservation projects is in fact that of degree. What can we learn of this from the rapidly developing conservation movement on the other side of the Atlantic?

    Three key towns in the American conservation scene are Philadelphia, Annapolis and Williamsburg:-

2. *Philadelphia*

    The City exemplifies a highly developed conservation programme by skilled town-planners, led by Edmund Bacon. The emphasis is upon urban renewal - especially in decaying areas. The old "row" houses have been restored or rebuilt, or in many cases replaced by new houses designed to be in architectural sympathy but by no means all "pastiche." The advantage of accelerating land values has been captured by the new taller blocks within the islands so contained.

    The work of the National Parks Commission shows on the other hand something of the approach of the landscape gardener. The principle areas of national and historic interest are being cleared and laid out on a grand scale, but sometimes with more regard for a single historical period - and sometimes with curious results. Perhaps this kind of "weeding" expresses the philosophy of the gardener: its results are attractive, but in a different way.

3. *Annapolis*

    At Annapolis, the approaches to the City, strewn and tangled with overhead wires, contrast violently with its extremely fine and beautifully maintained older houses. The interiors of some of these are magnificent, and furnished with supreme taste. Here, as at Providence in Rhode Island, most of the work is being accomplished by private incentive, often utilizing the "rotating fund" principle. Technical expertise is high - as in one case noted where, to emphasize the thinness of the white glazing bars, the window puttying has been neatly painted black - a good example of very careful detailing.

4. *Williamsburg*

    Colonial Williamsburg (illustrated on p. 6) is a unique historical exhibit of supreme educational quality - though it could be a dangerous example if wrongly copied.
    Through traffic has been diverted by an underpass and cars are excluded from the historic area in high season. A free bus service runs between the principal monuments, and bicycles can be hired. A splendidly equipped headquarters gives lectures and film shows, and from its laboratories a programme of careful archaeological "digs" is in hand. Items like colonial

door furniture are faithfully reproduced and widely sold. The "stocks" have been rebuilt and employees wear correct period costume. The whole project is very much a restoration to one date. The degree is extreme, but illustrates the remarkable tenacity and thoroughness which, given the money, the task of restoration can be tackled and accomplished.

Which degree is right? The question has a Pilate-like ring. Right and wrong are rarely black and white. In this country, we follow the tradition of respect for identity - in fact may this not even be closer to democracy? It would be interesting to debate this further with American friends.

PART SEVEN – FOUR ASPECTS OF
                    CONSERVATION POLICY

policy

THE S.P.A.B. AND THE H.B.C.

The Rt. Hon. the Earl of Euston
   *Chairman of the Society for the
   Protection of Ancient Buildings*

PROGRESS AND FUTURE POLICY

From an address to the delegates of the Historic
Towns and Cities Conference by Lord Kennet
   *Joint Parliamentary Secretary, Ministry of
   Housing and Local Government*

THE HISTORIC TOWN AND TOURISM

A contribution from the British Travel
Association

HISTORIC BUILDINGS LAW

Compiled with the assistance of Cambridgeshire
and the Isle of Ely County Planning Department,
the Ministry of Housing and Local Government
and the Scottish Development Department

'HE S.P.A.B. AND THE H.B.C.

The Society for the Protection of Ancient Buildings

On the 10th March, 1877, William Morris, enraged by the threatened scraping and scouring of Tewkesbury Abbey, wrote these words in a letter to the Athenaeum :

> "What I wish for is that an Association should be set on foot to keep a watch on old monuments to protest against all "restoration" that means more than keeping out wind and weather, and by all means, literary and other, to awaken the feeling that our ancient builgings are not mere toys but sacred monuments of the nation's growth and hope."

As a result of this letter, the Society for the Protection of Ancient Buildings was founded on the 22nd March, 1877.

From its very aggressive beginning, the Society has travelled far. It was founded to prevent Victorian "restoration" and subsequent ruination of churches, too many of which had already been destroyed, and from this beginning, developed into a technical and advisory body, willing and, by reason of the constitution of its Committee, competent to give proper advice upon the methods to employ in dealing with historic buildings. To quote from the original manifesto — "how best to protect buildings ...... and otherwise to resist all tampering with either the fabric or the ornament of the building as it stands". These were the fundamentals of the manifesto compiled by our founder, and in spite of additional knowledge gained from the experience of ninety-one years this manifesto still holds its place and still governs in principle our actions today.

William Morris cannot possibly have envisaged the result of his action in founding the society. On the other hand he would have been relieved to find so many people engaged on the project of preservation and determined to find ways of circumventing the excessive pressures and problems of today. There is no doubt that if he had not had the imagination, initiative and driving force to bring about the S.P.A.B., many people would not be thinking as they do today. The guiding principles of the society to a great extent have become the accepted tenets of conservative repair although people are bound to differ on points of detail.

While the society's main work must be to place its accumulated experience and technical knowledge at the disposal of those who need it, the further ramifications of its work cover many fields:

(i) the investigation of cases of buildings suffering from neglect, or threatened by damaging treatment or destruction;

(ii) the preparation of surveys and reports on cities, towns and villages, streets and individual buildings;

(iii) the keeping of records of past repair work and case histories, which are available for study;

(iv) the holding of annual courses on the repair of old buildings; and

251

Norwich, Elm Hill. Photograph A. A. Wood.

(v) the administration of the Lethaby and Banister-Fletcher Scholarship which enables architectural students to study old buildings, their treatment and repair.

Since 1951 the S.P.A.B. has produced lists of houses threatened with demolition which are made available to those looking for houses to repair and inhabit. For this an index is maintained. In this way the society has been able to save both notable buildings and smaller buildings of all types and styles, and it has become an acknowledged and important part of the society's work to provide this service, not only for the public, but for county and local authorities who often have the problem of the "difficult" or "white elephant" house.

When the S.P.A.B. first began, it was dealing with the preservation of individual buildings, and very rarely with towns as a whole. The first reference to anything of this nature appeared in the Report of 1927 under the heading "Old Towns", when the society was pressing for the establishment of Ancient Monuments Committees with whom Traffic and Housing Committees should confer before road widening and demolition proposals were determined. In Norwich, such a Committee was set up, and through its efforts, among other satisfactory results, the reconditioning of Elm Hill, one of the loveliest streets in the country, was begun in 1926 by the City Engineer in consultation with an architect member of the S.P.A.B.

The post-war years brought an added responsibility in this direction. County and local authorities called upon the S.P.A.B. to prepare surveys of ancient buildings in certain cities and towns, for example, Bury, St. Albans, Gloucester and Kings Lynn. These were to prepare the way for future planning schemes or proposals for reconditioning or conversion of individual houses of interest. In recent years many humbler buildings have been threatened, at first by over-zealous and wholesale slum clearance, then almost immediately by widespread demolition for street widening. It can hardly be denied that buildings in this country have probably suffered more between the wars through these last two causes than through all the other causes put together.

* * * * * * * *

2.

The Historic Buildings Council
From its beginning the S.P.A.B. has played a great part in formulating legislation governing preservation, and possibly one of the most far-reaching is the Historic Buildings and Ancient Monuments Act. This has provided in many hundreds of cases the essential grant which has enabled an owner to continue the upkeep of his house. This brings me to the second part of my talk, the work of the Historic Buildings Councils of the Ministry of Housing.

In the Society's view, the Historic Buildings and Ancient Monuments Act is one of the most successful Acts in existence, and certainly successive Ministers have interpreted it in an imaginative and helpful manner, not only dealing with great houses, but with small houses of outstanding interest; bridges; barns; garden ornaments; chattels and windmills; and groups of buildings.

Since 1953, £5½ million has been spent on 1,154 different buildings.

In 1967, £453,000 was spent on 107 buildings including an increase of grants on 46 buildings. This included two grants for chattels and four for garden buildings.

Within the compass of these grants come the block grants, which, under the title of "town schemes" is the system of joint action with local authorities to secure the comprehensive repair of areas and groups of buildings of outstanding value in town centres. Like the S.P.A.B., the Historic Buildings Council has viewed with growing anxiety the wide problem of what is to be the eventual future of historic centres as places of use and amenity. The Council's last report referred to "proceeding from the preservation of single buildings to groups and from groups to areas where preservation as a restrictive and "negative" operation becomes ineffective unless closely allied to creative and "positive" planning action, especially in regard to the control of traffic". The result of the reports of the consultants appointed to study these problems in the historic towns of Bath, Chester, Chichester and York should be most relevant. However, certain facts are obvious, principally that financial assistance will always be required and that the "town schemes" which we operate in conjunction with local authorities can do no more than scratch the surface of the problem. The terms of reference of the Historic Buildings and Ancient Monuments Act, 1953, confine the Council to dealing with those groups of buildings which are of outstanding historic or architectural interest. It would be defeatist to seek to preserve only the most important of the historic towns. Ways must also be found of preserving the character of towns, large and small, which illustrate in the diversity of their architecture and planning the history and the building methods of the regions in which they lie.

One method would be to extend the scope of the Act. There are at least nine town schemes in operation, but the number of historic towns of outstanding interest is considerable, while many more, although less important, are clearly of national interest. The S.P.A.B. strongly advocates therefore, that additional funds should be placed at the disposal of the H.B.C. to enable them to give far greater aid in helping to secure the preservation of historic towns and cities.

PROGRESS AND FUTURE POLICY

1.

Progress

A good deal has been done to reduce the rate at which we have been losing our architectural and townscape heritage, and to increase the sensitivity
and practicality of the planning and new building which affects it. There
has been the transfer of the Historic Buildings Council from the Minister
of Works to the Minister of Housing: a simple administrative change, but
made because it brought the power to give money and the power to control
planning and preservation under the same roof. Then there was the Civic
Amenities Act which, although it is the private initiative of the President
of the Civic Trust, to whom in this capacity the whole country owes a
great debt of gratitude, was partly drafted by the Government. And the
Government found Parliamentary time for it and backed it in every way
possible. Conservation areas have now been declared by local authorities
under it and, in accordance with the circular we sent out to them when the
Bill was passed, I am going to review progress and, if necessary, take a more
forward line in helping the process forward.

I understand there has been some discussion about whether it is better to
designate your conservation area and then decide what to do about it, or
first to decide what to do about it and then designate. Let me repeat what
I said at the Guildhall meeting of the Civic Trust in Autumn 1967. I think
local authorities should designate first and think later. I say this because
the very fact that you have a shaded area on a publicly known map is
already a measure of conservation.

Then there are the four town studies, one of the many ideas which sprang
from a conference held in Cambridge by Richard Crossman when he was
Minister of Housing.

2.

Four Town Studies

Then there are the four town studies, one of the many ideas which sprang
from a conference held in Cambridge by Richard Crossman when he was
Minister of Housing. I am confident that they are going to be extremely
useful not only to the Councils of York, Chichester, Bath and Chester,
but also to those of other old cities who will easily be able to translate
much of their findings into their own terms.

3.

Town and Country Planning Bill

Lastly, there is the Town and Country Planning Bill and there are two
provisions in this which I want to point out especially to you. The first
is that people no longer have merely to state their intention of demolishing or altering a listed building and then sit back to see if anyone objects,
but they have explicitly to ask permission to do so. In effect, this amounts
to an automatic B.P.O. on all listed buildings, and marks a considerable
step forward in the firmness and clarity of our arrangements for preservation.

Second, is the new proposal about the compensation payable to the owner of a listed building when it is acquired by a local authority. In the past it has been possible, and I think you can all remember cases, for the owner of a listed building deliberately to allow it to decay. The local authority have had the remedy of compulsory purchase, but this could only be exercized if they were prepared to pay the full development value which, in the case of an old building standing in a busy commercial area, could be very high. It could, of course, be so high as to deter the local authority from making a B.P.O. in the first place, for fear that the owner would claim that it rendered the building incapable of reasonably beneficial use, and the authority to buy it from him - again at full development value. The Bill will change this so that when a local authority claims and, if need be, sustains its claim in Court, that the owner has deliberately allowed the listed building to decay for the purpose of obtaining consent to demolish it, the local authority can purchase it without paying any development value in the compensation. When this comes into force local authorities will be able to refuse consent to demolish buildings without the fear of being strung along by a developer thereafter deliberately allowing them to decay. Taking this with the power to carry out works under an enforcement notice, I believe that we should see a considerable increase in local authority achievement in preservation.

4.
Town Schemes
In 1954 a town scheme was started in Bath, in 1956 in King's Lynn, in 1962 in Harwich and Faversham, in 1965 in Winchester, in 1966 in York and Bradford on Avon, and in 1967 in Cheltenham. This is a quickening pace. Plans for new schemes are well advanced in Abingdon, Berwick, Bewdley, Salisbury and Stamford. And beyond those, others are coming along.

5.
Listed Buildings
Progress on the statutory list itself of buildings of historic and architectural interest, which is the necessary foundation stone of the whole edifice, has been very satisfying. In 1965, there were 315 local authority areas without statutory lists. At the end of 1967 there were 48 and by the end of 1968 the job will be virtually complete. The re-surveying of the first areas to be surveyed, some of them more than twenty years ago, is continuing. The process of adding buildings built up to 1914 to the statutory lists is now well under way, and the first twelve lists are now complete, and statutory.

So far, as you know, 1914 has been the terminal date, but I have been looking at this with the Advisory Committee on Listing, and we have come to the conclusion that there is no sufficient reason why this should be so. It would be difficult to extend the statutory list right up to buildings built this year: difficult because the investigators would have to be dashing round anywhere an interesting building is built, and because estimates of merit vary a great deal with recent buildings. It would also, perhaps, not be very well worthwhile, since few interesting buildings are demolished within a decade or two of their erection. So we have decided that the terminal date should be brought forward from 1914 to 1939, and the Advisory Committee, under Lord Holford, is at present working on a list of some fifty buildings, built between those two dates, which could be added to the statutory list.

6.
Extension of the Historic Buildings Bureau
There are already, as you will probably know, two bodies finding uses

for historic buildings which are threatened with demolition or decay. The first is our old friend the Society for the Protection of Ancient Buildings, who maintain a very useful index. Details from the index are circulated to members and are published in the press from time to time. The society greatly contribute to preserving old buildings, and I am sure will continue to do so. But there must be many historic buildings which are in danger because they cannot be found a use or purchaser, and which may not come to the notice of the S.P.A.B. It seems to us that there is scope for more than one body to co-operate in this task of bringing buyers and sellers together. I propose, therefore, to help the work already being done by the S.P.A.B. by extending the work of the other body which works in this field – the Historic Buildings Bureau. The S.P.A.B. and the Bureau will collaborate.

The Bureau, originally staffed by the Ministry of Public Building and Works, has been in existence for some time as an adjunct to the Historic Buildings Council, and it has helped the Council to find uses for buildings which the Council consider to be of outstanding interest and for which a use cannot be found through normal commercial channels. It has provided a useful service, but its scope has been limited to buildings which are eligible for grant from the Council, and these form a very small proportion of the total.

The Bureau will, in future, cover any buildings on the statutory lists, whether or not eligible for H.B.C. grant. It will be operated by my Ministry under the direction of one of our Senior Estate Officers, Mr. T. W. R. Bridson.

We have no intention or desire to usurp the function of estate agents. We have consulted the two professional institutions most concerned; the Royal Institution of Chartered Surveyors and the Chartered Auctioneers and Estate Agents Institute – and they fully agree with what we propose.

The owner of the building in question, or his agent, must have consented to accept the Bureau's services. This does not mean that the initiative must always come from the owner. It may be that he had applied for consent to demolish and that the local authority do not want to permit demolition, and that a difference develops as to whether a viable use for the building can be found. The local authority could then suggest that the Bureau should be called in. But the Bureau will only act if the owner agrees.

The Bureau will only accept buildings that have been in the hands of an estate agent for at least two months. And lastly, the owner must have notified his agent that he has asked for the Bureau's assistance.

When the Bureau accepts a building on its books it will circulate particulars to bodies that may be interested in acquiring it, including the estate agents' professional institutions, the local authority in whose area the building is, amenity societies, the National Trust, local authorities, and the larger industrial or commercial firms with an interest in the neighbourhood. The Bureau will also issue press notices in outstanding cases, so that the building gets general publicity.

The Bureau will not only circulate details of buildings, it will also do the same for prospective purchasers. It will be open to anyone to approach the Bureau with his requirements, and the Bureau will first try to match them with buildings on the books. If it cannot, it will circulate the buyer's requirements to appropriate bodies.

Once the Bureau succeeds in putting a buyer and a seller in touch, it will retire from the scene. It will then be up to the parties to negotiate, through their agents, in the usual way, and the Bureau will have no say in the price, and will give no guarantee about the condition of the building or the cost of repairs. There will be no charge for the service.

7.
Finance

I come now to the great question of finance. We must take into account the economic storms which are raging not only in this country but in the entire world. The Government, during the early part of 1968, took the measures which are to enable us to weather these storms. The hatches are battened down, everything useless has been cut, and many useful things have been postponed. But in a round of cuts and postponements, a prudent Government must keep a special eye open for wasting assets. If there is something which of its nature decays and loses value and which of its nature can have its life prolonged by moderate expenditure so that for a longer period than would have been the case without that expenditure it can generate a social or economically desirable return, a Government must be careful to see that this expenditure remains at a proper level, or even increases. Such is pre-eminently the case with our historic buildings. We cannot postpone the money we spend on their preservation because they will fall down if we do, and once they have fallen down they cannot reasonably be re-produced, and historic buildings and towns are tangible economic assets.

8.
Tourism

Consider the tourist trade. Why do people come to this country? They do not come for the sunshine or for the good food, or for the famous wines, or to ski. About £245 m. came in across the exchanges in 1967 with foreign tourists. As long ago as 1961 the city of Bath, population 82,000, estimated that its revenue from tourism, that is, both British tourists and foreign ones, was £3 m. I do not know, indeed it would probably be impossible to find out, in what proportion those things which are delightful or unique in our country attract other people to it for their holidays. But it is obvious that high on the list come our old cities and towns and our country houses. For these reasons the Government decided that not only shall Central Government expenditure on preservation not be cut, but that it shall be increased and in two ways.

9.
Revival of Dormant Powers

One is by the revived use of certain provisions in the 1953 Historic Buildings and Ancient Monuments Act. This Act empowers the Minister of Housing to acquire, repair, let and sell buildings of outstanding architectural or historic interest. It also empowers him to finance similar operations on the part of local authorities from the Land Fund, which was established under an earlier Act. For reasons best known to themselves the Government of the day, having introduced these provisions, made very little use of the former power, and none at all of the latter. The present Government intends to revive these long-dormant powers, and this will constitute a new addition to the various procedures and resources at our disposal.

We intend to use both these powers. First the appropriate Minister (that is, the Minister of Housing in England and the Secretaries of State in Scotland and Wales) will acquire the occasional really outstanding building or chattel, repair it if it needs to be repaired, and then if he thinks fit, hand it over to a body like the National Trust or, perhaps, to a local authority, to keep. The Government will also use Land Fund money in certain cases to help local authorities acquire listed buildings of historic and architectural interest. Mark the distinction. These can be any listed buildings, and need not be of outstanding interest, as those which the Minister himself can acquire must be. Naturally we shall seek to dovetail this as closely as possible with existing and further town schemes so that grants shall be handled in close relations with the H.B.C. repair grants, for the overall preservation and revival of a given area of an old town. The way this can be done must depend on experience and on circumstance. The consultants' reports on the four towns will throw light on how to begin. As soon as they are published, and as soon as they have been considered and collated by my Preservation Policy Group, I shall approach the authorities of those four towns and perhaps a few others, especially those where there is already successful experience of a town scheme, in order to discuss all this.

10.
Grant increases
We all know how small the Historic Building Council repair grants themselves are. They have been running for the last four years under a ceiling of £450,000 a year. During those years the cost of building has risen and I rather think that the cost of repairing historic buildings may have risen faster than general building costs. Because of these rises in cost, and because of the wasting asset aspect which I mentioned earlier, the Government has decided to raise that ceiling to £550,000 a year.

These two measures reflect an acknowledgement of the fact that however bad the economic weather, our existing social, cultural and economic assets must not be allowed to decay. Even so, of course, even with these increased levels of expenditure, everything in the preservation garden will still be far from rosy. We have an immense task ahead of us still if we are finally to staunch the loss of fine old buildings, and I look forward to the day when our present tribulations are over and the expenditure can be raised again.

But money is not all, although Governments are often tempted to think it is almost all, because it is one of the very few absolutely quantifiable variables in human society. You can always be certain how much grant you are putting out.

11.
New Development
I wish you could be equally certain who was a good architect and who a good planner because, if you could, you could then submit by statute all relevant matters to his judgment. But you cannot, so Central and local government must rely on employing the very best men they can find, and seeking the advice of others as appropriate. All this applies very much to the question of the control of new development in conservation areas. The best of such development at the moment is very, very good, and the worst not only defies description but positively defies perception. There are certain un-things put up in our Squares and High Streets where, if it were not for the

traffic, the only thing to do would be to shut one's eyes until one had passed by. It is not fair to ask the people of this country to put up with such a risk.

But consider the best. I am thinking of Brighton Square in the Lanes, of Lasdun's flats at St. James's Place in London, or, on the institutional scale, of the Cripps Building at St. John's College, Cambridge. If only we could be sure that all redevelopment in conservation areas was to be as good as that, I for one should sleep quieter at night. I am not sure what we can do to move things along in that direction but I am sure that something must be done. Future legislation should, after consultation with the professional bodies concerned and local authority organizations, allow the Minister to make regulations concerning the advice which local authorities ought to take before exercising their function of control in respect of new development in conservation areas. At a time when the general trend is towards the devolution of authority from the Centre to local councils in planning matters, this may seem to be going against the stream. But I am convinced that the worst new building in our old towns is so bad and that it is so urgent to bring the worst up to the present average level, and the average to the best, that these consultations must take place, and that, if it is at all possible, a system must be worked out.

12.

Historic Buildings Council

Lastly, I want to come back again for a moment to the Historic Buildings Council. And let me take this opportunity of praising them for the work they do. It is a remarkable body, one of those regular, industrious, highly expert, unpaid bodies on which so much of what is sensible about this country depends. Many of its members have been doing this work now for fifteen years, and its Chairman, Lord Hailes, for five years. I would like to speak personally about this, because I feel personally. Much of the life of a Parliamentary Secretary is boring, uncomfortable and arduous. But when, once a month, I see the large pink folder of the Historic Buildings Council recommendations, I know that I am going to have a pleasant hour looking through, and virtually invariably approving, some orderly, well thought out and civilized material.

The Civic Amenities Act gives the Minister of Housing, for the first time, the power to make not only grants for the repair of fine old buildings, but also loans. The loans have to come within the same ceiling, now raised to £550,000, but the point about this is, as it is with all loans, that they can be handled so as to constitute a revolving fund. When the loan money begins to come in, it can be used again, so that further loans will be able to be made, above the £550,000 ceiling, by the amount of the loan repayments. These loans are now about to be started up. The council will be working out the best way of using this power, and I have no doubt that one of the main fields will be town schemes again. But I have a feeling that there may also be a role for these loans among the great country houses. I am most anxious that the country houses, to which more visitors go every year, should become more and more self-supporting. Of course, there are dangers here: one must not stimulate so many visitors that the stairs wear out and the floors fall in, that the grass is destroyed and the vistas ruined by the erection of shelters to keep the rain off the queues. But up to that limit I am anxious that as many people as possible be attracted to these houses; that they pay for admission and thus contribute to their maintenance. These houses are our past. The social functions

London, St. James's Place, flats by Denys Lasdun and Partners in scale with St. James's Place (see over).

The same building facing Green Park.

which gave them their form are now, by our will, extinct. But another
social function — that of aesthetic enjoyment and historical interest — is
falling increasingly to their lot. I think we should look forward to the day
when the eligibility of a given great house to a Government loan for
repair might be linked with this prospect of being turned into a paying
concern. This takes great skill, but that skill is already available in the
hands of certain organizations, prominent among which is the British
Travel Association. And I hope that an increasing number of owners of
great houses will, as already many of them do, take advantage of the
advice they can give. We must devise a principle of partnership in this
between public and private enterprise. The private owner could combine
his private property (his house and park), his private initiative, and his
own sense of tradition and what is appropriate, with public skill from the
British Travel Association (which is a governmental organization) and
public money in the form of an Historic Buildings Council repair loan,
in order to get the best social and economic use out of the asset which
is his by law, but belongs to all of us by sentiment.

Bradford on Avon.

The Circus, Bath, begun 1754 by John Wood.

HISTORIC TOWNS AND TOURISM

Britain's international tourist trade is dependent upon our unique attractions - on culture, history and pageantry. These enable Britain to compete successfully in the growing international tourist market. All Britain's historic towns have a stake in international trade - over £350 million was spent by 4 million overseas visitors in 1967, (including the fares paid to British carriers). This amount is equal to 6% of our physical exports. The total is expected to exceed £500 million in the early 1970s.

Historic towns attract British holidaymakers and visitors in increasing numbers. Spending on travel and all forms of leisure probably exceeds £2,500 million per year.

Against the background of this massive economic activity the historic towns must look closely at the impact of tourism on the local economy. Research has not yet looked more than curiously at the effect of visitor spending - it could prove the potential importance of tourism to both large and small historic centres. Tourist spending on day visits amounts in many centres to ten shillings per head per visit. A detailed study on a historic town could quantify the actual value, although this is multiplied as visitor spending passes through the local economy.

With the present interest in history and archaeology, and the overseas tourist appeal, the creation of conservation areas and the preservation of historic buildings virtually results in the growth of a tourist attraction. Much of the investment in preservation can be returned through tourist spending - but there must be a corresponding investment in tourist facilities if the potential economic value of tourism to the local economy is to be fully realized.

The development of a tourist attraction must imply a considerable increase in the numbers of visitors. These can affect the atmosphere of towns for short periods of the year. The economic advantages, however, generally outweigh the social disadvantages, the resident population enjoying a far higher standard of facilities and amenities.

The planning decision rests with the local authority who must weigh the potential economic advantages of tourist development. Once this decision has been made it must be followed through and a continuous programme of tourist development carried out. Acceptance of the premise that a historic town is a tourist attraction implies a conscious policy throughout planning and a responsibility on the part of the authority to see that tourism is considered at every stage of development.

Bristol. While we may be unaware of our Victorian buildings American visitors come to see them.

Medieval and Georgian houses in the main street of Tewkesbury.

In the formation and execution of a conservation policy or in designating conservation areas, the following Acts, Circulars and Memoranda are relevant in Great Britain :

1. *THE PLANNING ACT AND ASSOCIATED LEGISLATION AND CIRCULARS*

1.1　*Town and Country Planning Act 1962*
(as amended by Civic Amenities Act 1967)
Covers the prevention of buildings of special architectural or historic interest being demolished or altered in such a way as seriously to affect their special value.

Excludes ecclesiastical buildings in use (nut not parsonages, etc.); buildings already preserved under A. M. Acts; buildings listed by M.o.W.; buildings on Crown land, unless agreed by appropriate authority.

Relevant Ministry: Ministry of Housing and Local Government (Scottish Development Department).

1.2　*Civic Amenities Act 1967*
Covers historic buildings and areas (conservation areas) and also tree preservation and planting and disposal of abandoned vehicles and other refuse.

1.3　*M.H.L.G. Circular 53/67 (S.D.D. Circular 56)*
Covers policy under Civic Amenities Act, 1967, including grants and loans for repairs and maintenance of historic buildings whether listed or not, and powers to grant-aid local preservation societies.

1.4　*Memorandum on Conservation Areas (Appendix to Circular 53/67) (S.D.D. Memo 57/67)*
Covers types of conservation area, action after designation, and the need for good public relations.

1.5　*M.H.L.G. Circular 51/63 (S.D.D. Circular 2/64)*
Covers publicity for certain developments.

1.6　*Town and Country Planning General Development Order 1963 (T. & C.P. General Development (Scotland) Order 1950)*
Covers Article 5 directions.

2. *THE ANCIENT MONUMENTS ACTS AND THOSE ASSOCIATED WITH REPAIR GRANTS*

2.1　*Ancient Monuments (Consolidation and Amendment) Act, 1913*
Covers ancient buildings, structures or earthworks.

Excludes ecclesiastical buildings in use; houses, unless occupied by caretaker only.

Relevant Ministry: Ministry of Public Building and Works (except Sec.18)

2.2　*Ancient Monuments Act, 1931*
Covers ancient buildings, structures or earthworks, including the

surrounding amenities of the Monuments.

Relevant Ministry: Ministry of Public Building and Works.

2.3   *Historic Buildings & Ancient Monuments Act, 1953*
Covers buildings of outstanding interest, and Ancient Monuments
(see items excluded under 1913 Act)

Relevant Ministry: Ministry of Housing and Local Government.

2.4   *Local Authorities (Historic Buildings) Act, 1962*
Covers contributions by L.As towards repairs and maintenance of
buildings of historic or architectural interest, and the upkeep of their
gardens. (Powers extended to Scotland by sect. 5 of Civic Amenities
Act, 1967. See S.D.D. Circular No. 56/1967).

3. THE HOUSING ACTS

3.1   *Housing Act, 1936 (Housing (Scot.) Act, 1966, sect. 177)*
Covers the desirability of preserving existing works of architectural or
historic interest.

3.2   *Housing Act, 1957*

3.3   *Housing (Financial Provisions) Act, 1958*
(Housing (Financial Provisions) (Scotland) Act, 1968)
Covers Grants by L.A. for improvement to older houses.

Relevant Ministry: M.H.L.G. (S.D.D.)

4. THE NATIONAL TRUST ACTS
(see National Trust for Scotland Order Confirmation Acts, 1935, etc.)

4.1   *National Trust Act, 1907*
Covers preservation of places of Historic Interest or natural beauty.

4.2   *National Trust Act, 1937*

4.3   *National Trust Act, 1939*
Relevant Ministry: Ministry of Public Building and Works, as certifying
authority only.

5. OTHER LEGISLATION

5.1   *Local Government Act, 1948*
Covers contribution to non-statutory bodies.
(The powers in sect. 339 of the Local Govt. (Scotland) Act, 1947, are
available).

5.2   *Public Health Act, 1936*
(See the Building (Scotland) Act, 1959, for the Scottish provisions)

5.3   *Public Health Act, 1961*

5.4   *General Rate Act, 1967 (see Local Govt. (Scotland) Act, 1966,
sect. 25(3))*

5.5   Note also the White Paper. *Old Houses into New Homes.*

Montacute, a National Trust property.

The Customs House, King's Lynn, designed by Henry Bell, 1683.

THE CONFERENCE ADMINISTRATION

President
THE RT HON THE EARL OF HAREWOOD

Chairman of Conference Advisory Committee
PATRICK NUTTGENS PhD MA ARIBA
Director, Institute of Advanced Architectural Studies

Joint Secretaries
MICHAEL BURBIDGE; MICHAEL HARRIS; PAMELA WARD

Hon Treasurers
GORDON THORPE ACIS AACCA; DAVID HATLIFF AACCA

Conference Council (* *indicates member of Advisory Committee*)

* Ancient Monuments Society
IVOR BULMER THOMAS MA
Secretary

Association of County Councils in Scotland
CLLR WALTER CAMERON
Lanarkshire

* Association of Municipal Corporations
CLLR S. E. BREARLEY JP MTPI
City of York

City and Borough Architects Society
S. A. G. COOKE ARIBA
Borough Architect, London Borough of Camden

Civic Trust
LESLIE LANE PPTPI FRICS
Director

Civic Trust for the North East
NEVILLE WHITTAKER MA BArch
Director

Civic Trust for the North West
GRAHAM ASHWORTH MCD BArch ARIBA AMTPI
Director

Civic Trust for Wales
PROFESSOR DEWI-PRYS THOMAS BArch ARIBA AMTPI
Welsh School of Architecture

* Convention of Royal Burghs
J. GIBSON KERR CBE WS
Agent and Clerk

* Council for British Archaeology
MAURICE BARLEY MA FSA FRHistS
University of Nottingham

County Architects Society
E. TABERNER ARIBA
County Architect, Cheshire

* County Councils Association
J. M. GORST MTPI MIMunE
County Planning Officer, W. Suffolk
ALD T. H. MALIA
Northumberland

* County Planning Officers Society
L. N. FRASER MEng MTPI AMICE
County Planning Officer, Yorks West Riding

* County Planning Officers Society for Scotland
T. T. HEWITSON DipArch ARIBA AMTPI
Town Planning Officer, Edinburgh

District Councils Association for Scotland
COL J. W. A. LOWIS
President

Georgian Group
COL R. A. ALEC-SMITH TD DL JP
Hon Secretary, Georgian Society for East Yorkshire

Incorporated Association of Architects and Surveyors
F. MYLES-WHITE ARIBA FIAS

* Institution of Municipal Engineers
R. S. BELLHOUSE CEng MIMunE MTPI DipTP
City Engineer and Planning Officer, York

* Institute of Landscape Architects
JOCELYN ADBURGHAM FILA MTPI LRIBA

National Housing and Town Planning Council
F. J. BERRY DPA(Lond)
General Secretary

National Trust
JOHN CORNFORTH

* National Trust for Scotland
THE HON MRS. E. F. O. GASCOIGNE

* Royal Incorporation of Architects in Scotland
R. W. K. C. ROGERSON BArch(Glas) FRIBA FRIAS FSAScot

* Royal Institute of British Architects
KENNETH BROWNE AADip ARIBA

* Royal Institution of Chartered Surveyors
J. B. W. ROBINS BA

* Royal Society of Arts
A. LLEWELLYN SMITH MBA MA FSA FRIBA

* Rural District Councils Association
S. W. Harvey MIMunE MIPHE AInstSP
Engineer and Surveyor, Chemlsford RDC

Saltire Society
GORDON STEELE

270

Scottish Civic Trust MAURICE LINDSAY
Scottish Counties of Cities Association CLLR ROBERT A. RAFFAN
Aberdeen
Scottish Georgian Society COLIN McWILLIAM
Hon Secretary
Scottish National Housing and Town Planning Council ROBERT F. POLLOCK
Hon Secretary
* Society for the Protection of Ancient Buildings THE RT HON THE EARL OF EUSTON
Chairman
* Town and Country Planning Association ARTHUR BLENKINSOP MP; DEREK SENIOR
* Town Planning Institute DONALD W. INSALL ARIBA AMTPI SPDip
* Urban District Councils Association L. E. SMITH
Clerk, Skipton UDC
* Victorian Society DAVID LLOYD BA AMTPI
York Civic Trust JOHN SHANNON JP

R. W. BRUNSKILL MA PhD ARIBA
University of Manchester School of Architecture
PROFESSOR COLIN BUCHANAN CBE
Imperial College of Science and Technology
ANTONY DALE BLitt FSA
Chief Investigator of Historic Buildings, MoHLG
PROFESSOR NIKOLAUS PEVSNER CBE
Birkbeck College, University of London
W. KONRAD SMIGIELSKI IngArch MTPI
Planning Officer, City of Leicester

Government departments approving the conference MINISTRY OF HOUSING AND LOCAL GOVERNMENT
and providing advice and assistance SCOTTISH DEVELOPMENT DEPARTMENT
WELSH OFFICE
MINISTRY OF TRANSPORT

Contributions from the following towards the cost of the Conference are acknowledged:

Marks and Spencer Limited
Sir Harold Samuel
F. W. Woolworth and Co. Ltd.
Capital and Counties Property Co. Ltd.
Boots Pure Drug Co. Ltd.
Applied Suppliers Ltd.
John Smith's Tadcaster Brewery Co. Ltd.
Granada Television Ltd.
Shepherd Building Group Ltd.
Casson, Conder and Partners
Lewis Solomon, Kaye and Partners
Architects Design Group
Owen Luder Partnership
Building Design Partnership
Clifford Culpin and Partners
Fry Drew and Partners
Gerald Eve and Co.
Ove Arup and Partners
The Haslemere Group of Companies
Louis de Soissons Peacock Hodges Robertson and Fraser
Hugh Wilson and Lewis Womersley

The Joseph Rowntree Memorial Trust in York made the initial grants for research, as a result of which the form of the Conference was prepared, government approval received and the organization set up.